POLITICS
AND
PRIVILEGE

POLITICS AND PRIVILEGE

HOW THE STATUS WARS SUSTAIN INEQUALITY

RORY McVEIGH,
WILLIAM CARBONARO,
CHANG LIU,
AND KENADI SILCOX

Columbia University Press   *New York*

Columbia University Press
Publishers Since 1893

New York   Chichester, West Sussex

Library of Congress Cataloging-in-Publication Data
Names: McVeigh, Rory author | Liu, Chang, author |
Silcox, Kenadi, author | Carbonaro, William, author
Title: Politics and Privilege : How the Status Wars Sustain Inequality /
Rory McVeigh, Chang Liu, Kenadi Silcox, and William Carbonaro.
Description: New York : Columbia University Press, [2026] |
Includes bibliographical references and index.
Identifiers: LCCN 2025013405 | ISBN 9780231217200 hardback |
ISBN 9780231217217 trade paperback | ISBN 9780231561617 ebook
Subjects: LCSH: Income distribution—United States—
History—21st century—United States | Power (Social sciences)—
United States—History—21st century—United States |
Social status—History—21st century—United States |
Conservatism—History—21st century—United States |
Political participation—History—21st century—United States |
United States—Politics and government—2017–2021
Classification: LCC HC110.I5 M376 2026 | DDC 339.220973—
dc23/eng/20250616

Cover design: Julia Kushnirsky
Cover image: Shutterstock

GPSR Authorized Representative: Easy Access System Europe,
Mustamäe tee 50, 10621 Tallinn, Estonia,
gpsr.requests@easproject.com

CONTENTS

1 It's the Economy, Stupid! Or Not? 1

2 Status Contestation and Politics Theory 24

3 Broad Support for Worker Unity 40

4 Race, Gender, and Status Preservation 54

5 LGBTQ, Immigration, Religion, and Status Preservation 81

6 Status Contestation and Political Polarization 111

7 Heated Status Boundaries 137

8 Looking to the Future: Crisis or New Coalition? 188

Methodological Appendix 203
Notes 225
Index 253

POLITICS
AND
PRIVILEGE

1

IT'S THE ECONOMY, STUPID!

Or Not?

I n 1992, the political strategist James Carville coined the phrase "It's the economy, stupid." It was his way of reminding presidential candidate Bill Clinton of what voters really care about, especially when they are enduring an economic downturn. Not only was the phrase catchy, it was good advice. The overall strength of the economy is a powerful predictor of electoral outcomes, with incumbents rewarded by voters when times are good and punished when times are bad.[1] Often overlooked, however, is that the phrase and the strategy disregard economic inequality as a factor that might motivate political action. They instead promote a view that we are all in the same boat—a boat that sinks during recessions and rises during economic expansion.[2] Yet even when the overall economy is strong, income and wealth inequality in the United States are staggeringly high, and elected officials do little to solve the problem.[3] In recent decades, a number of social movements and some progressive politicians have advocated powerfully for action to reduce economic inequality.[4] However, to date they have been unable to build coalitions strong enough to achieve significant change.

Americans seem to have a split personality when it comes to their views on economic inequality. Gallup polling, for example, consistently shows that just over 60 percent of those sampled think that income should be more evenly distributed in the United States, and about 30 percent say that the distribution is fair.[5] Nevertheless, a national poll conducted in 2023 by the American Communities Project/Ipsos shows that 68 percent of respondents believe that "hard work and grit" is the most important determinant of success in the United States.[6] What's more, the number of Americans who name inequality ("the gap between the rich and poor") as the most significant problem facing the United States consistently falls below 2 percent in Gallup polling.[7]

So why is the American political process so unresponsive when it comes to income and wealth inequality? If the vast majority of wealth is concentrated in the hands of a small percentage of the people, what prevents the majority of Americans from rising up together to demand change? Karl Marx and Friedrich Engels famously called for such a coalition in *The Communist Manifesto*, penned in 1848: "The proletarians have nothing to lose but their chains. They have a world to win. *Working Men of All Countries, Unite.*"[8] We do not intend to make a case for or against capitalism or Marx's critique of capitalism. However, we do aim to shed new light on the question of worker unity. Marx viewed capitalism as inherently unstable because it rests on a sharp conflict of interest between wealthy property owners and those who own only their capacity to work. While typically not invoking Marx, populist appeals to address the gap between the "haves" and the "have-nots" have often resonated with Americans at different historical moments.[9] We see this in recent support for Occupy Wall Street, for Bernie Sanders's scathing critique of concentration of wealth in the hands of the top 1 percent, and even in Donald Trump's brand of conservative populism that appeals to white working-class grievances.[10]

Notably, Trump's populist rhetoric departed substantially from his actual policies during his first term in office. However, promises to revive the manufacturing economy and placing blame on foreigners for the workers' plight lands well with many white Americans who are not thriving in today's global economy.[11]

Despite its resonance with many Americans, populism, as a movement, repeatedly fails to forge a united coalition strong enough to bring about enduring progressive change. American workers are not united, much less poised, to overthrow capitalism. Data provided by the Federal Reserve Bank of St. Louis indicate that in 2019 the top 10 percent of families owned 76 percent of the nation's wealth. Even more striking, the bottom 50 percent of families held only 1 percent of the nation's wealth.[12] More than half of Americans live precariously each day, either living in poverty or at risk to falling into poverty if confronted with an unexpected major expense. Many of these same people nevertheless align themselves with a political party—the Republican Party—that is most committed to preserving the wealth of those at the top.[13]

Scholars since Marx have viewed political democracy as the key to benefiting from the efficiencies of competitive capitalism while also ensuring that the wealth generated by the system is broadly distributed. If workers are unhappy with their economic circumstances, after all, they can organize and they can vote for political candidates who promote worker-friendly public policy.[14] Labor unions, in fact, have played an important role in many countries, leveraging organization and strength in numbers to get a seat at the bargaining table and to develop and advocate for policies that promote a higher standard of living for all citizens.[15] The United States, on the other hand, is "exceptional" in terms of levels of inequality and failure to address inequality within democratic political institutions.[16]

Notably, theories of politics and electoral behavior rest on an assumption that social class *should* matter in American politics. The question of whether and how much social class influences American voters has been central to most studies of voting behavior.[17] Renowned scholars such as Seymour Martin Lipset and Walter Korpi argued that the class struggle anticipated by Marx actually plays out within democratic political institutions in the United States, with poor and working-class voters gravitating toward the Democratic Party and prosperous voters favoring the Republican Party.[18] Cross-pressures, according to this line of thought, temper this "civilized" form of class struggle. In other words, voters are not solely concerned with class-based interests and choose their political representatives based on a range of preferences that they hold for policies related to collective identities and cultural values as well as social class. Until recently, scholars credited these kinds of cross-pressures with promoting political stability and moderation since voters can find something to like about both major parties in the United States.[19] Today, however, arguments about moderation and stability in American politics seem quaint and outdated.[20] Democrats and Republicans are far apart in their politics, and the lack of common ground ultimately contributed to a violent insurrection attempt on January 6, 2021, incited by the losing presidential candidate and incumbent president Donald Trump (see figure 1.1). After losing the election (and even before), Trump repeatedly made false claims about a stolen election, and he schemed to stay in power in ways that were illegal, violent, and in some instances farcical, as his lawyers and henchmen concocted "legal theories" that ran roughshod over the spirit and the letter of legal democratic procedures. The insurrection attempt cannot be pinned, exclusively, on one aspiring dictator, however. As culpable as Trump was in events leading to the January 6 debacle,

FIGURE 1.1 Crowd gathering before the assault on the nation's Capitol building, January 6, 2021. Joe Biggs, a member of the Proud Boys (plaid shirt in the front and center of the photo) was later convicted of seditious conspiracy. Getty Images.

we should not forget that he initiated a coup with unwavering support from Republican lawmakers, and he remained popular with a sizable chunk of ordinary Americans even as evidence of his incompetence and misdeeds continued to mount. Indeed, American voters reelected Trump to the presidency in November 2024 even though he had been indicted on four felonies, was found by the court to be liable for sexual abuse, and had been decimated by his opponent, Vice President Kamala Harris, in a debate in which Trump displayed his increasingly extreme rhetoric. For example, a clearly frustrated Trump chose to use the occasion to spread an unfounded rumor that Haitian immigrants in Springfield, Ohio, were "eating the dogs! The people that came in, they are eating the cats!"[21]

POLITICS AND STATUS HIERARCHIES

In this book, we will show that conflict over status privileges (rather than social class, cultural values, or identity politics) are currently driving the political process in the United States. Status is a word that is bandied about in casual conversations. While its intended meaning can vary in everyday usage, people typically think of it in terms of perceived value that cannot be reduced to dollars and cents, often reflecting lifestyles that people maintain. Max Weber, whose writings played a central role in shaping the discipline of sociology, famously distinguished among class, power, and status as distinct but interrelated bases for inequality in society.[22] For our purposes, we borrow a definition from the sociologist Cecilia Ridgeway. Status, as she describes it, "is a comparative social ranking of people, groups, or objects in terms of the social esteem, honor, and respect accorded to them."[23] In the Jim Crow South, for example, a Black man might have been economically prosperous but was nevertheless denied esteem or respect from white members of the community because of the color of his skin.

Social scientists commonly focus on competition over material resources when examining intergroup conflict, but many others seek to identify the role of status, particularly in terms of how members of a dominant group respond to a perceived threat to their status. Going back many decades, scholars have focused on how the size of a subordinated group—with a particular focus on Black Americans—poses both a material and status threat to members of a dominant or privileged group.[24] More recently, some scholars have used experiments to assess how white Americans respond when exposed to information about demographic transitions that will place the white population in the numerical minority in the not-too-distant future.[25] Indeed, much of our understanding of how status operates in society is based on social psychological studies that focus on micro-level interactions between people, often using small group experiments to see how status differences linked to group memberships or identities affect individual decision-making processes.[26] We view this work as important because it identifies ways in which status differences hold important consequences for individuals in a broad array of settings. However, in our work, we focus instead on how status hierarchies form as structures that maintain group inequalities at the societal level and how these status hierarchies intersect with politics to inhibit formation of progressive coalitions.

We find Ridgeway's ideas about status particularly useful for thinking about the intersection of status and politics. As she expresses it, "As a micro motive for behavior, status is as significant as money and power. At a *macro* level, status stabilizes resource and power inequality by transforming it into cultural status beliefs about group differences regarding who is 'better' (esteemed and competent)."[27] While recognizing the importance of social psychological approaches to status, Ridgeway offers a structural theory—"the cultural schema theory of status." As she describes it, "Status hierarchies and rankings are a cultural invention that people have developed to manage a fundamental tension in the human condition. Whether they like it or not, people are repeatedly in situations in which they are cooperatively interdependent with others to achieve what they need and want to survive and prosper. But this shared need to coordinate on a cooperative goal effort creates a nested set of competitive tensions."[28]

From this perspective, status hierarchies, once formed, provide strong incentives for beneficiaries of the hierarchies to defend their positions.[29] As we will discuss in greater depth in the chapters ahead, the payoff that comes from being at the top of a status hierarchy is not merely symbolic. The symbolic value of status is accompanied by a broad range of special treatments that are largely taken for granted by the beneficiaries. These circumstances, in turn, can prompt anger and resistance from status beneficiaries in response to an attempt to simply level the playing field by demanding equal treatment for all people.

Ridgeway's cultural schema theory of status aligns well with contemporary understandings of how racial inequality is formed and sustained. Eduardo Bonilla-Silva published a seminal article in 1997 that laid the groundwork in sociology for a structural and relational understanding of racism.[30] Importantly, the theory does not focus on labor market conflict but instead argues that we should think of race in terms of how it can structure social life—much in the same way that many scholars have analyzed social class in structural terms. Race can operate independently of social class and typically intersects with class, gender, and other salient attributes that affect peoples' lives.[31]

Bonilla-Silva argued that race is structural in the sense that racial categories are constructed and used to assign people to different positions in society. People draw on deeply embedded cultural schemas (similar to Ridgeway's conceptualization) and come to think of people with different racial identities as being well suited for some positions but not others. Although fewer people in the contemporary era openly express racial or ethnic animosity or admit to holding biases, the consolidation (or overlap) of racial identities and social positions continues to structure the way in which people understand racial and ethnic differences and the way in which they respond to those differences. The alignment of racial identity and social position allows racism to continue to operate but "without racists."

"Racism without racists" is a phrase that Bonilla-Silva used in later work to emphasize how racism is so deeply rooted in the organizational structure of society that it remains powerful without the need for overt expressions of bigotry that were once common in American society.[32] Structural racism obscures individual agency, allowing members of a dominant group to feel like they are "color-blind" even while they are acting in ways that sustain inequality.

But how, exactly, are race and gender categories used to "assign" people to different positions in society? The sociologist Victor Ray's recent theorizing helps to ground structural theories of race and gender by identifying organizations—such as workplaces and schools—as sites where people match identities and positions in observable and consequential ways.[33] Ray's focus on organizational settings also makes it easier to think about varying degrees to which organizations are "racialized" or "gendered." A highly racialized workplace, for example, has a strong correlation between racial identities and positions in ways that provide white people in the organization with greater access to valued resources and power. In other settings, however, we might find that people with different racial identities are evenly dispersed across social positions in ways that suggest that race is not structuring rewards or social relations in that setting. Analyzing this *variation* opens promising paths for uncovering the most important causes of racialization within organizations but also within society. Attention to variation is critical because in American society some people are highly motivated to preserve status advantages; some are highly motivated to acquire status equality; and many fall somewhere in between. This variation, as we will show, helps us make sense of political behavior in the United States.

We emphasize that different sources of status can motivate political behavior.[34] These can include the esteem and consequent societal privileges gained by virtue of one's racial identity, gender, sexual orientation, gender identity, citizenship, or religious identity. Key to this focus on status hierarchies is the idea that categories having to do with race, gender, sexual orientation, and other identities are not objectively "real" but are instead socially constructed. In other words, categories such as African American, woman, or immigrant do not represent fixed attributes or an inherent objective reality. People instead create categories and give them meaning over time as they attempt to organize and make sense of the world in which they live.[35] Differential power in society often drives this process, as the most powerful people draw and enforce exclusionary boundaries around categories to protect the advantages they may hold.[36] Status hierarchies thus form as people draw on stereotypes and other cultural schemas, allowing them to use categorical distinctions to relegate people to different positions in society, with these differential assignments having important implications for gaining access to resources, rights, privileges, and social esteem.[37] Actions that channel people into roles deemed culturally appropriate for women or for men, for example, create a structure of inequality if these actions are common within a society or within institutions or organizations. When status hierarchies form, beneficiaries typically come to assume that privileges and esteem that they enjoy by virtue of their position within the status hierarchy are natural and deserved.[38] Efforts to challenge status hierarchies must overcome resistance from those who have a stake in the status quo and who equate what is traditional with what is correct, moral, or natural.

HOW DO YOU STUDY SOMETHING WHEN PEOPLE DENY ITS EXISTENCE?

The general questions we ask at this perilous historical moment require fresh ideas and innovative methods of study. Why is economic inequality so extreme and so durable in the United States? Why can't the problem be addressed in the political arena, and why is democracy itself in jeopardy? To address these questions, we began by imagining what kind of social change organization might be attractive to a wide swath of Americans who feel as if the elite are prospering at the expense of the majority. We designed a web page for this imagined organization so that we could see how real people respond to it. Will they agree with the stated goals? Would they consider supporting or joining such an organization? While assessing these reactions, we can manipulate key aspects of the web page to see if those manipulations affect the way that people feel about the organization. This research strategy, as we will show, provides us with a way to directly test our arguments about status hierarchies and their role in structuring American politics. We aim to show how status contestation has implications not only for addressing income and wealth inequality but also for solving pressing problems related to the environment, reproductive freedom, gun violence, and other hotly contested issues.

To isolate the effect of status preservation goals in our study, we must confront two important obstacles. First, as noted, many Americans may not be aware of the extent to which their desire to maintain status advantages over others affects their political behavior. They may also believe that the status advantages that they enjoy are normal and deserved based on perceived group differences in skills and behaviors.[39] When that is the case, asking people straightforward questions about whether a desire to preserve status privileges motivates their political behavior would be a waste of time. A second issue has to do with "social desirability bias." This means that people tend to respond to a researcher or to a survey in ways that they think would meet the approval of the researcher—putting their best foot forward and concealing any prejudices that they may hold. This occurs both consciously and subconsciously.[40]

These issues can be addressed with an experimental research design—a method that is surprisingly underutilized in sociological studies of politics and collective action. We find that an experiment can be particularly useful in identifying barriers to alliance formation in politics. Contrary to Marx's expectations, the "proletariat"—or those who own only their capacity to labor—never became a numerical majority in modern democratic societies that could simply overthrow capitalism with their votes.[41] To secure political victories and subsequent benefits for workers they would first need to unite among themselves. However, to form a majority, they would also need to form alliances with a significant number of people who may not be in the working class but are also not part of the economic elite. Forming such alliances has proven to be difficult since both partners in an alliance typically expect to gain something from the arrangement and are reluctant to make concessions to partners if those concessions entail sacrifice or compromise without reward.[42]

Our experiment, therefore, aims to identify conditions that can overcome these barriers. As is true of most experiments, ours deploys a bit of deception to identify subconscious political preferences and account for the tendency in many people to present themselves most favorably to researchers. Earlier, we mentioned our imagined progressive organization and its web page. Here, we say more about how it figures into our actual research. We designed six versions of a web page for a fictitious organization: One America for Working People. Each version is identical except for one section under the heading "Fighting for a Better Future." We manipulate the content in that section across the six versions to see if people's views of the organization are different depending on which version of the web page they received. You can see the full image of the web page in figure 1.2.[43] In the experiment, we use this version as a "control," or as a basis of comparison.

Our fictitious organization doesn't pull any punches in terms of its critique of wealthy corporations and political corruption. The mission statement makes it clear that One America for Working People is not calling for modest reform but instead a fundamental reordering of economic and political power. The web page also emphasizes the need to unite in the face of efforts to keep working people divided. The content under the heading "Fighting for a Better Future" is where the action is in terms of the power of our experiment. This version of the web page (the control) only addresses "economic equality" under that subheading. The text makes three main points. One emphasizes the large earnings gap between CEOs and workers. The second highlights politicians' reliance on campaign contributions from the wealthy. Finally, there is a call to action that states that only a united population can hold politicians and corporate executives accountable.

This version of the web page advocates unity in resisting forces generating economic inequality in the United States. Everyone is welcome and encouraged to join— but there is no mention of how the organization might address other forms of inequality in society. This may be an attractive path for those who only experience economic disadvantage, but it raises questions about why people who receive unjust treatment in other respects might join

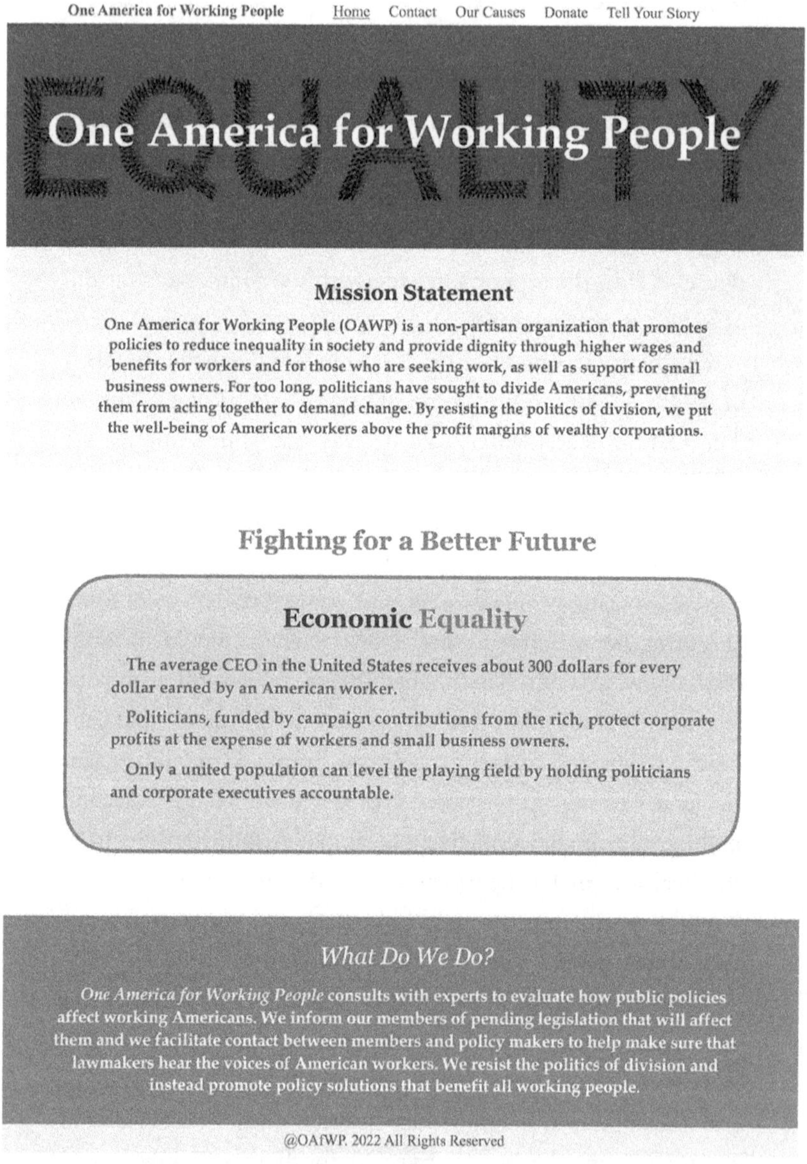

One America for Working People
Home
Contact
Our Causes
Donate
Tell Your Story
EQUALITY
One America for Working People
Mission Statement
One America for Working People (OAWP) is a non-partisan organization that promotes policies to reduce inequality in society and provide dignity through higher wages and benefits for workers and for those who are seeking work, as well as support for small business owners. For too long, politicians have sought to divide Americans, preventing them from acting together to demand change. By resisting the politics of division, we put the well-being of American workers above the profit margins of wealthy corporations.
Fighting for a Better Future
Economic Equality
The average CEO in the United States receives about 300 dollars for every dollar earned by an American worker.
Politicians, funded by campaign contributions from the rich, protect corporate profits at the expense of workers and small business owners.
Only a united population can level the playing field by holding politicians and corporate executives accountable.
What Do We Do?
One America for Working People consults with experts to evaluate how public policies affect working Americans. We inform our members of pending legislation that will affect them and we facilitate contact between members and policy makers to help make sure that lawmakers hear the voices of American workers. We resist the politics of division and instead promote policy solutions that benefit all working people.
@OAfWP. 2022 All Rights Reserved

FIGURE 1.2 Web page for experiment assessing responses to progressive alliance (the control treatment)

such an alliance if the organization focuses only on economic inequality. Presumably, the organization would be stronger if it could, in fact, attract a diverse coalition that could more effectively resist the kinds of divide and conquer maneuvers that it condemns on the web page. To attract that broad support, however, it would need to broaden its appeal in a process that the sociologist David Snow and his colleagues refer to as "frame extension."[44] This involves efforts to portray (or frame) the organization's goals in a way that links together two or more objectives, emphasizing the compatibility of those objectives in a way that expands the potential appeal of the organization.

The other five versions of the web page essentially ask potential supporters to "put up or shut up" when it comes to resisting efforts to divide American workers. These versions present alliance formation as a two-way street—they deploy the frame extension tactics described. In these versions, the organization explicitly expresses commitment to combatting other specific forms of inequality so that workers can form a united front to promote economic equality for all. The content of each web page is identical to the "control" version except for our experimental manipulation in the "Fighting for a Better Future" section. In that section, we insert a short paragraph next to the paragraph about economic inequality. Figure 1.3 provides an image of the web page that has an added paragraph about racial equality. Note that the content and format of the paragraph align closely with the paragraph on economic equality. It first establishes a problem—that racial discrimination and violence motivated by racism are enduring features of American society. Corresponding with the paragraph on economic equality, it specifies that the political and economic elite use race to divide American workers. Finally, the organization commits to combatting racism so that workers can unite to promote equality for all. The web page

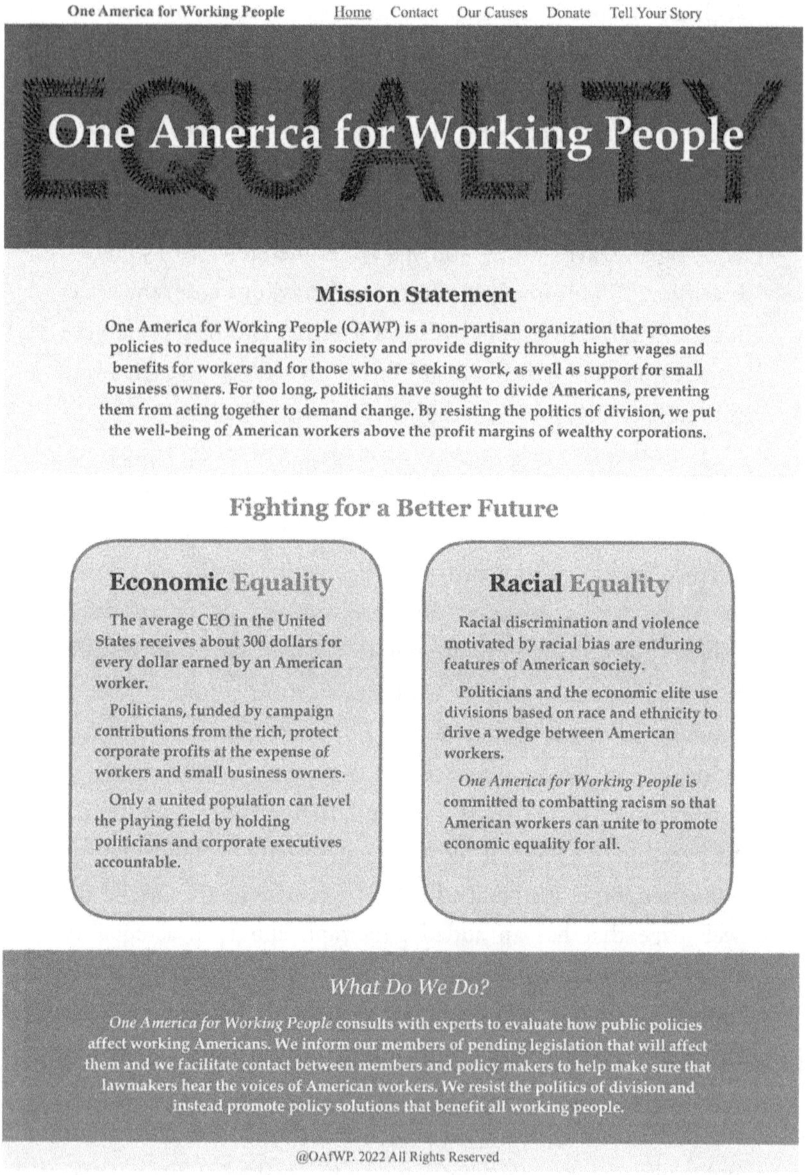
One America for Working People
Home
Contact
Our Causes
Donate
Tell Your Story
EQUALITY
One America for Working People
Mission Statement
One America for Working People (OAWP) is a non-partisan organization that promotes policies to reduce inequality in society and provide dignity through higher wages and benefits for workers and for those who are seeking work, as well as support for small business owners. For too long, politicians have sought to divide Americans, preventing them from acting together to demand change. By resisting the politics of division, we put the well-being of American workers above the profit margins of wealthy corporations.
Fighting for a Better Future
Economic Equality
The average CEO in the United States receives about 300 dollars for every dollar earned by an American worker.
Politicians, funded by campaign contributions from the rich, protect corporate profits at the expense of workers and small business owners.
Only a united population can level the playing field by holding politicians and corporate executives accountable.
Racial Equality
Racial discrimination and violence motivated by racial bias are enduring features of American society.
Politicians and the economic elite use divisions based on race and ethnicity to drive a wedge between American workers.
One America for Working People is committed to combatting racism so that American workers can unite to promote economic equality for all.
What Do We Do?
One America for Working People consults with experts to evaluate how public policies affect working Americans. We inform our members of pending legislation that will affect them and we facilitate contact between members and policy makers to help make sure that lawmakers hear the voices of American workers. We resist the politics of division and instead promote policy solutions that benefit all working people.
@OAfWP. 2022 All Rights Reserved

FIGURE 1.3 Web page for experiment assessing responses to progressive alliance (racial equality treatment)

is making a case for the idea that fighting for economic equality and combatting racism are compatible goals, rather than a
forced choice between peoples' economic interests and their
views on cultural or social policy issues. Because the web pages
are identical except for the insertion of the paragraph on racial
equality, we can compare responses to these two web pages to see
if the single difference in the pages makes people more, or less,
supportive of the organization. If they show less support, that
indicates a preference for leaving racial inequities intact, or at
least it indicates that people tend to be unwilling to support the
organization if it involves a reciprocal form of alliance. Because
the added content only refers to discrimination and violence—
rather than any specific policy goals—we can assess the extent to
which simply affording people equal status (freedom from discrimination and violence) affects support for the organization.

As we will describe in greater depth in chapter 4, status
derived from Americans' racial identities is extremely important
in shaping politics in the United States and inhibiting formation
of a diverse progressive coalition. However, we will also make the
case that race is one of several status hierarchies shaping American politics. The lead author of this study (McVeigh) and the
sociologist Kevin Estep used the term "multidimensional privilege hierarchies" in their analysis of the rise of Trumpism, noting
the way that Trump appealed to a broad range of voters who
were concerned about losing status privilege based on a number of identities, including gender, sexual orientation and gender
identity, citizenship, and religion.[45] To assess how these other
status hierarchies shape political decision-making, we include
additional versions of the web page in our experiment. As was
true of the version presented in figure 1.3, they are identical to the
control page except for an additional paragraph inserted into the
section "Fighting for a Better Future." The third version, rather

than including a paragraph about racial equality, has a similarly structured paragraph speaking to gender equality. It first asserts that discrimination and violence motivated by gender bias are enduring features of American society. It proposes that economic and political elites use divisions based on gender to divide American workers, and it states that the organization is committed to combatting sexism so that all American workers can unite to promote economic equality for all.

We follow the same format to create versions of the web page that indicate that the organization fights for LGBTQ equality, immigrant equality, and religious equality. For the latter, the web page refers to discrimination and violence directed toward non-Christian religious groups. We include the "non-Christian" phrasing so that study participants will not think of this in terms of contemporary conservative arguments about religious liberty that attempt to justify discrimination against LGBTQ people.[46] By developing these additional web pages, we will be able to assess the relative importance that each status hierarchy plays in affecting peoples' support for, or opposition to, the overall organization.

We created six identical surveys and inserted one of the web pages described into each one (each survey includes only one of the web pages). We informed all our participants that we are interested in studying civic life and are interested in obtaining their feedback on the design and content of a web page of a new civic organization. We first ask several questions about their perceptions of the organization. A couple of questions about the appearance of the web page disguise the fact that we are primarily interested in their reactions to the statements and goals of the organization. The respondents do not know that there are other versions of the web page that we are not showing them. We ask respondents about the extent to which they agree or disagree with various statements on the web page (the mission statement and the content under "Fighting for a Better Future"). We also ask about their willingness to volunteer time to the organization and their willingness to oppose it. We ask about their perceptions of the organization's ideology (ranging from very conservative to very liberal) and the extent to which they think the organization will be successful. After the questions about the organization, we ask about their opinions on a broad range of policy issues, and we collect information about the respondents (age, gender, income, racial identity, political ideology, education levels, political affiliations, religiosity, marital status, and other attributes).

The Magic of Experiments

An experimental design is a powerful way to identify cause and effect relationships, and the reason it works is surprisingly intuitive. In our experiment, we contracted with Ipsos Inc. to obtain a large sample of participants to fill out different versions of our survey. Ipsos specializes in developing samples for market research, social science research, and political polling. Our analyses included just under 2,600 people who completed the survey (from April 8 to May 9, 2022), which they accessed online. Ipsos uses quota sampling so that the overall sample resembles the United States population on demographic features such as racial distribution, age, and education. Because they did not use strict probability sampling, the results of our analyses cannot be generalized to the US population. With an experiment, however, our goal is to instead identify cause and effect relations *within the sample* rather than estimate population parameters beyond the sample.[47]

The true "magic" of the experiment comes from random assignment to our treatment groups. We assigned each participant to only one of our six groups, and each participant had an equal chance of assignment to any one of those groups. Because of the large sample, and the random assignment to groups, we can be confident that the composition of each group is very similar, even though the individuals making up the groups are all unique. For example, the percentage of people who identify as being Republican should be very similar in all six groups, and that is something that we can verify because we asked a question about political party identity.[48] Indeed, across our six groups the percentage indicating they are Republicans falls within a narrow range (from 28.1 percent to 30.8 percent), which is a difference well within the bounds of what we would expect to find simply due to chance. Even better, with random assignment, the groups should also be similar when it comes to attributes that we have no way of measuring or chose not to measure (such as the average shoe size in the group). Why is this important? Because the groups are similar in every respect (even when considering things that we did not measure), different average responses to our questions across the groups are attributable to the one thing that was different about what members of each group experienced—our experimental manipulations. In other words, we can determine whether those who received a version of the website in which the organization commits to combatting racism, sexism, homophobia, xenophobia, or religious bigotry tend to express less support for the organization when compared to those who evaluated a version of the web page that only mentions economic equality. We can also see if the responses to our experimental manipulations differ depending on attributes of the respondents, such as their political party affiliation.

Throughout the book, we will discuss why different status hierarchies shape political decision-making and we will draw on our experimental findings to assess our arguments. We will also use the data to show how status contestation is at the heart of polarization of party politics. Status preservation goals not only inhibit alliance formation among those who would otherwise support a progressive economic agenda but also push people who identify with the Democrats and with the Republicans into opposite corners in a way that stalls legislative progress on pressing policy issues. We will present the findings from our analyses in a user-friendly way that allows for easy interpretation. There are methodologically complex issues that must be addressed, but we will discuss those issues in a methodological appendix at the end of the book to assure the statistically inclined readers that our results our trustworthy without bogging down the main text with technical details. Our overall story is not simply about numbers, charts, and graphs, however. Throughout the book, we will consider the historical formation of different status hierarchies and their relationship with party politics, and you will hear from people responding to questions we ask them about what they were thinking when considering support or opposition to One America for Working People.

LOOKING AHEAD

In the next chapter, we lay the groundwork for our analyses by presenting what we refer to as our "status contestation and politics theory." We developed the theory because it is important for us to explain *why* and *how* we expect that status hierarchies shape American politics and to compare our approach to other ways of thinking about political behavior. We are committed to presenting our ideas and analyses in ways that allow all readers to follow what we are doing with interest. We make a case for paying attention to how the benefits people derive from status advantages can be so important to them that it is often their primary consideration in politics and shapes the way in which they understand and act on a broad range of political issues. Yet simultaneously, many Americans are increasingly aware of how they are being harmed by status hierarchies and are motivated to challenge status inequalities. After presenting the theory, in chapter 3 we examine how much support there is among those who participated in our study for the general goal of reducing income and wealth inequality. We do this by considering their responses to a question about their views of the mission statement on the web page for One America for Working People. Recall that the mission statement does not mention any status hierarchies and instead focuses on the need for all people to come together to fight to reduce economic inequality. We find that support for these general goals is remarkably high and that support for the mission statement is strong across various subgroups in our sample. For example, even those who identify as conservative tend to support the mission statement of the organization.

In chapter 4, we give particular attention to how status battles pertaining to race and gender affect prospects for a progressive economic alliance. Racial and gender hierarchies were firmly established long before the nation's founding. We discuss how this plays out in American politics and how changes in race relations and gender dynamics have led many Americans to prioritize defense of white male privilege over class-based interests. Chapter 5 takes on the incorporation of nativism, homophobia, and religious bigotry into party politics. In both chapters 4 and 5, we emphasize that groups disadvantaged by status hierarchies do not passively accept a subordinate position. Within the Republican Party, we see beneficiaries of multiple status hierarchies trying to hold the line against an increasingly multicultural society at a time when traditional sources of privilege face intensified challenges.

In chapter 6, we consider the implications of status defense for political polarization that characterizes contemporary politics. We find that policy preferences among self-declared Democrats and Republicans, and among those who do not identify with one of the two major parties, have more overlap than might be expected. Political polarization becomes highly visible, however, when we consider how status interests shape policy preferences in ways that promote consistency across issues in terms of favoring liberal or conservative positions. Polarization, in turn, stands in the way of solving important social problems, as well as addressing economic inequality.

Although our experiment takes us a long way toward understanding forces driving contemporary politics in the United States, the experimental findings cannot tell the entire story. From the experiment, we can observe how people respond to the opportunities to support a progressive and diverse political alliance and how that affects their policy preferences. Yet we feel it is important to pay attention to how people explain their own responses to One America for Working People. In chapter 7, we provide research subjects with an opportunity to explain their reactions to our fictitious organization, paying particular attention to how they feel about the framing that casts fighting for economic equality and status-based equality as necessarily interconnected.

In the final chapter, we take stock of what we have learned and draw attention to the ways that our work provides us with fresh perspective on an old problem: inequality. We conclude the book by drawing out lessons for the future—a future that appears more dire with each passing day. Perhaps surprisingly, we find that our analysis offers a glimmer of hope for a more harmonious and equitable world.

2

STATUS CONTESTATION AND POLITICS THEORY

When social scientists develop theories, they aim to sort out the messiness of social life by identifying patterns in human behavior, social interaction, and various events or outcomes of interest. They work not only to reveal such patterns but also to provide a logically sound explanation for why they exist. Like natural scientists, social scientists are trying to understand the *causes* of things that are worthy of our attention. In our study, we are interested in discovering and explaining what prevents Americans from acting together to form effective coalitions that aim to reduce inequality. These coalitions could potentially form within party politics or outside of traditional political institutions deploying social movement activism (or both). We presume that people's willingness to fight for equality varies across individuals and knowable factors *cause* them to be willing or unwilling to act. While our focus is on identifying barriers, answers to our core questions also help us to understand how people can overcome those barriers, acting collectively to reduce inequality.

A common approach to developing theory involves organizing social life by placing people into what we perceive to be meaningful categories and thinking logically about why people within those categories might think or act in a particular way.[1] When it comes to voting, for example, the political sociologist Seymour Martin Lipset thought in terms of identifying the social bases of politics.[2] Based on particular attributes of individuals (such as social class, religious identity, education level, gender, and racial identity), we should be able to predict their political behavior. The key idea behind this approach is that people with shared attributes should have had similar experiences in life and therefore should have similar political interests. For example, we might consider the extent to which evangelical Protestants in the United States, because of their common religious socialization, should be more likely than other Americans to support political candidates who promote socially conservative policies.[3] Because people hold multiple identities and possess multiple potentially relevant attributes, it is necessary to consider a full range of characteristics that might influence their political behavior.[4]

These types of patterns are certainly worth noting. However, there are important limitations to this general approach. First, the presumptions social scientists make about what attributes or categories are meaningful largely determine the range of conclusions we can draw. Many important causes of social behavior escape our attention—much depends on our capacity to identify what is worth considering, and that capacity can be influenced by our own biases or preconceptions. Second, typically there are substantial differences within the categories we presume to be meaningful. Many evangelicals, for example, are quite progressive and work for progressive causes. Should we simply ignore those who do not meet our expectations, taking satisfaction in knowing that "on average" our expectations are confirmed? Third, there is a tendency to treat people as if their ideas, preferences, and actions develop in isolation, and we neglect the extent to which relationships between people, rather than thought processes within people, produce understandings of the world, understandings of ourselves, and courses of action that we might take.[5]

For these reasons, we opt for a different approach in this study. Rather than focusing on individual attributes as predictors of willingness to engage in progressive coalitions, we instead focus primarily on a process—status contestation—and consider the extent to which this process shapes political behavior in the United States. We take it as a given that not all people prioritize status interests in political life, but we seek to identify those who do and to assess the extent to which status contestation is central to maintaining divisions that preserve inequality.

STATUS AND PREFERENTIAL TREATMENT

More than six decades ago, Joseph Gusfield developed the status politics theory in his study of the temperance movement in the United States. Gusfield was a prolific scholar whose academic career began in the 1950s and stretched well into the next millennium. Perhaps he is best known for his classic 1963 book, *Symbolic Crusade: Status Politics and the American Temperance Movement*.[6] Regarding temperance, he argued that activists and supporters mainly pursued symbolic victories. He asserted that temperance activism was rooted in the downwardly mobile old middle class (e.g., small-scale manufacturers, shop owners, and farmers). As economic transitions began to leave them behind, that group's members sought solace by shifting attention to status and lifestyle, seeking to gain positive recognition of their values, as reflected in sobriety and piety. In other words, temperance activists wanted to feel superior about their way of life and to be acknowledged for it. In Gusfield's view, that positive recognition was worth fighting for.

We do not doubt that symbolic victories, as described by Gusfield, can be highly gratifying. We also do not doubt the sincerity of those who might engage in such a "symbolic crusade." Indeed, some scholars have characterized "moral reform movements" as emerging from conflicts over morality or cultural values, with participants and adherents primarily motivated by desires to preserve a way of life and to defend values developed through lifelong socialization processes.[7] We see such arguments as incomplete, however, as they fail to consider the hierarchical nature of relationships between combatants. When people engage in conflict over values and issues pertaining to LGBTQ people, for example, it is grossly misleading to ignore the ways in which opponents of LGBTQ rights are arguing from a position of privilege—a position where they are not victims of disrespect, disdain, and violence in heteronormative and cisnormative societies.

Nicola Beisel has argued that scholars such as Gusfield and those who have studied moral reform movements have relied on an exaggerated view of the distinction that Max Weber made between class and status. In her analysis of the antivice movement of the late 1890s, which was led by the infamous Anthony Comstock, Beisel emphasized how status preservation held important consequences not just in terms of social esteem earned by abstaining from vice but also in securing favored treatment that comes with social esteem.[8] Many of Comstock's supporters feared that if their children succumbed to the temptations of vice, it would bring disgrace upon their families, cutting them off from social ties that were vital to maintaining their position within the class structure.

Along these lines, we argue that status motivates political behavior primarily because people tend to place high value on preferential treatment that they receive resulting from their position at the top of status hierarchies. To account for a broad range of status benefits, we developed what we call the *status contestation and politics theory*. The model, depicted in figure 2.1, indicates that the strength or weakness of support for more egalitarian policies is ultimately rooted in battles over status. The nature of status contestation can either reduce or enhance consensus around progressive politics as it operates through two key mechanisms displayed in the model. First, conflict between those who wish to preserve status hierarchies and those who aim to overturn status hierarchies affects the level of support or opposition to progressive political alliances (such as our One America for Working People). Second, status contestation affects the degree of polarization that exists in party politics. The levels of polarization and support or opposition to progressive alliances, in turn, determine whether a broad consensus can emerge to pressure lawmakers to enact policies to reduce inequality in society.

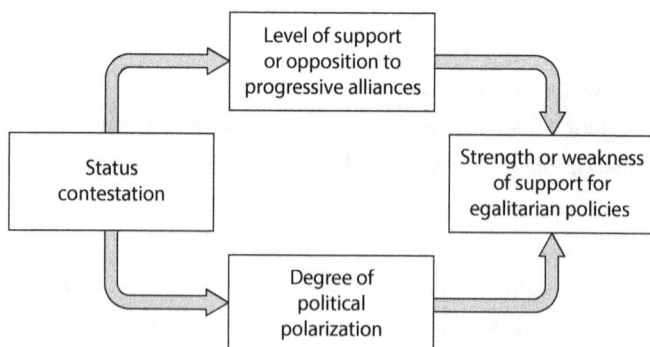

FIGURE 2.1 Status contestation and politics theory

In short, our model stipulates that movement toward a more egalitarian society depends on who wins the battles to maintain or overturn status hierarchies. Conservative victories—or even stalemates—favor the status quo.

Contestation Over Progressive Alliances

As depicted in figure 2.1, differential treatment based on one's position in a status hierarchy provides strong incentive to engage in collective action. Differential treatment becomes recognizable as a shared experience—one that can trigger a collective defensive response when taken-for-granted preferential treatment slips away. Denial of privileged treatment can also trigger emotions, such as anger or a sense of injustice, that help sustain opposition.[9]

In recent decades, scholars have come to appreciate the power that status positioning plays in shaping people's life trajectories and overall well-being. This focus was, in part, a reaction to an important book published in the late 1970s by William Julius Wilson, *The Declining Significance of Race*.[10] Wilson's book offered an overview of three periods of American history; each was associated with different sources of racial conflict and racial inequality. Throughout much of US history, he argued, racial conflict and racial inequality emerged from economic circumstances. Slavery structured race relations in brutal fashion in the antebellum period. In the years following the Civil War, while the United States experienced a pronounced shift from an agrarian to an industrial economy, much of the conflict and perpetuation of inequality resulted from white workers resisting competition in the labor market from Black Americans and immigrants.[11] Wilson noted, however, that by the 1970s—for the first time—social class position at birth had become a strong predictor of one's ultimate position (as an adult) in the class structure for Black Americans as well as for white Americans. Throughout most of American history, race so powerfully structured life chances for Black individuals and families that it overpowered the well-known advantages that come from being born into prosperous families.[12] Black workers' inclusion in industrial unions, as well as high labor demand during the booming post–World War II economy—including tremendous expansion in government jobs—contributed to the development of a sizable Black middle class. A subsequent shift toward a global, high-tech economy, Wilson argued, created a situation where those (regardless of racial identity) who held college degrees were well positioned to succeed, while those lacking higher education would suffer from a decline in available jobs that could provide a living wage, benefits, and dignity. Initially, economic restructuring disproportionately harmed Black inner-city residents because manufacturing jobs abandoned the central cities, shutting off what had been a path to upward mobility for Black families.

The provocative title of Wilson's book, as well as what many viewed as an overly optimistic depiction of prospects for middle-class Black Americans in the modern era, motivated important new research among scholars who aimed to show that Black Americans and other people of color continue to face significant barriers in American society. Douglas Massey and Nancy Denton arrived early on the scene, making a strong case for the ongoing importance of residential segregation in restricting opportunities for Black Americans.[13] Mary Patillo's work highlighted ways in which segregation and ongoing poverty hold implications for middle-class as well as poor and working-class Black families, calling attention to the way that middle-class Black families tend to live in close proximity to poverty-stricken and crime-ridden neighborhoods.[14] Perhaps most importantly for our purposes, as we described earlier, Eduardo Bonilla-Silva was prominent among scholars who focused on systemic racism, drawing attention to how racism should be viewed in structural terms, rather than as an attitude or a bias that mainly resides in the heads of individuals.

Once we recognize the structural aspects of racism, sexism, or other socially constructed categories that are ordered hierarchically, it becomes clear that the importance of status in maintaining inequality tends to be underestimated. This is true if we consider the past as well as the present. In the antebellum South, for example, most wealth generated by exploitation of enslaved people was held by a relatively small proportion of the white population who owned large plantations. This staggering inequality among white Southerners could not have endured during or after the Civil War if most white Southerners did not highly value the many privileges accorded to whiteness that were psychic but also tangible—linked to the extreme preferential treatment that was accorded to white people and denied to Black people.[15] In the contemporary era, a racial status hierarchy harms Black people and other people of color in the labor market but also in myriad ways in which preferential treatment or "white privilege" structures social relations in the United States.[16] For example, we see the consequences of status hierarchies as they play out in law enforcement and police violence, in classrooms where race shapes perceptions of students' abilities and their conduct, and in everyday commerce where Black people and other people of color often attract unwarranted suspicion when they are simply buying groceries or shopping for clothes. White Americans subjected to similar treatment would immediately feel a strong sense of injustice, but because white skin does not attract these types of scrutiny, the privileges that result from racial hierarchies may either go unnoticed or seem natural to the beneficiaries.[17]

Scholars have long noted the ways that status based on gender is accompanied by differential treatment that powerfully
shapes social relations in ways that extend far beyond economic
inequality. The academic literature covering gender inequality is
too extensive for us to summarize here, but just a few examples
bring the point home. Scholars have documented the ways in
which women are expected to take on primary responsibilities
for child-rearing, cooking, and cleaning. Women's viewpoints
are often dismissed or discounted based on stereotypes char-
acterizing women as emotional, irrational, and less capable of
carrying out tasks presumed to be better suited for men.[18] As
we will show in later chapters, status hierarchies based on sexual
orientation and gender identity, citizenship, and religion also
come with differential treatment that is consequential for beneficiaries as well as victims. Differential treatment linked to status
hierarchies, we argue, can be so consequential that we should not
be surprised that status contestation plays a central role in political contestation. Beneficiaries are motivated to ward off threats
to their privileges while nonbeneficiaries have a strong incentive
to demand a level playing field.

Consolidation of Policy Preferences

Our theoretical model also indicates that status contestation
contributes to policy preference consolidation (political polarization). Indeed, as we will argue, status contestation contributes
strongly to the polarization that currently afflicts party politics
in the United States. Before we address polarization directly,
however, we must consider how the American political system,
in many ways, guards against threats to the economically privileged. This can lead voters to prioritize status goals when they

engage in the political process because the avenues for rectifying economic inequality are blocked.

When engaged in activism—perhaps supporting an organization such as One America for Working People—it is possible for people to align their political preferences with the specific goals forwarded by the social movement organization. Its members make decisions about possible alliance formations. It is important to consider that when people instead participate only in party politics they are, in fact, choosing to engage in multiple alliances. For example, regardless of one's views on abortion, if a person supports the Republican Party for any reason, they are allying with abortion opponents. Similarly, if someone supports the Democratic Party for any reason, that puts them in alliance with proponents of LGBTQ equality. When deciding which political party or candidate to support, voters must enter alliances with candidates and voters representing a broad range of issues. We argue that status preservation plays a central role in determining which set of alliances people choose.

We do not claim that voters are uninterested in pursuing economic gains when participating in party politics. In general, we argue that political analysts underestimate the extent to which Americans value their status interests and overestimate the extent to which they feel that their political representatives can or will bring about significant change in their economic standing. Notably, the framers of the American political system intentionally sought to inhibit collective efforts to reduce economic inequality. We see this clearly in *The Federalist Papers*—a series of essays written by Alexander Hamilton, James Madison, and John Jay that made a case for implementing the United States Constitution. In Federalist Paper No. 10, Madison wrote at length about how the Constitution would control the problem of "factions," by which he was referring to conflicting interests that emerge from people's different stations in life. Madison saw intergroup conflict as natural and, not unlike Karl Marx, saw the divide between the propertied and nonpropertied as a fundamental and inevitable source of conflict. As he expressed it, "So strong is this propensity of mankind to fall into mutual animosities, that where no substantial occasion presents itself, the most frivolous and fanciful distinctions have been sufficient to kindle their unfriendly passions and excite their most violent conflicts. But the most common and durable source of factions has been the various and unequal distributions of property. Those who hold and those who are without property have ever formed distinct interests in society."[19]

Contrary to Marx, Madison sought to devise a political system that would protect property owners and limit opportunities for political mobilization of those without property. He reasoned that it is impossible or inadvisable to eliminate the causes of factions (for example, confiscating property thereby eliminating inequality) and we should therefore seek to contain the potential conflict. Madison offered a republican form of government as the solution. Elected representatives must serve a constituency large enough to ensure that their districts contain people with diverse interests. If a representative must be attentive to competing and intersecting interests of constituents, it serves as a check against dominance of a numerical majority united on one side of a single faction. In other words, the republican form of government forces voters to moderate their economic demands and choose representatives who will forward some but not all of their preferences. In a pure democracy, on the other hand, people would vote directly for their preferred position on each policy under consideration.

Several other features of the political system reinforce the conservative nature of republican government in the United

States. Small, sparsely populated states such as Wyoming and Montana elect the same number of senators as heavily populated ones such as California, Illinois, and New York. Similarly, reliance on the Electoral College in presidential elections—with each state granted a fixed number of electors based on population size—gives more weight to Republican states than Democratic states. The margin of victory in the state of California, for example, is not relevant in determining the number of electoral votes awarded by the state. Just in the current century, American voters elected two Republican presidents even though those candidates received fewer popular votes in the nation than their opponents did (George W. Bush in 2000 and Donald Trump in 2016). What is more, the threat of a filibuster in the Senate makes it virtually impossible, in a divided nation, to pass legislation that moves the ball too far in one direction or another. Conservative state legislatures in many states have artfully gerrymandered congressional districts in ways that diminish representation of Black and Brown voters, poor voters, as well as progressive voters in urban locations.[20] The US Supreme Court, with six conservative justices—three appointed by Donald Trump—has largely abandoned its responsibility to protect the franchise for Black and Brown voters and other voters of color, and conservative legislators, particularly at the state level, have passed legislation making it more difficult for people with fewer resources to vote. Campaign contributions from wealthy donors have long tipped the scale in favor of legislators who favor conservative economic policies. In 2010, the Supreme Court exacerbated the problem with its ruling in *Citizens United v. Federal Election Commission*. The court ruled that large corporations and wealthy individuals are free to contribute unlimited sums of money to political action committees of their preferred candidate, as long as they do not directly coordinate their activities with candidates.

This is not to say that the government offers no economic advantages for those without wealth. Importantly, social security and Medicare guard against poverty for the aged, and a precarious safety net provides subsistence for poor Americans but fails to lift them out of poverty.[21] Participation in political institutions, however, is clearly more effective for those who want to preserve wealth than for those who want to redistribute it.[22] With all of these advantages, wealthy Americans have successfully pushed the narrative that all Americans benefit equally from economic growth and the success of large corporations translates into broadly shared prosperity.[23] Given limited prospects for reducing economic inequality by participating in electoral politics, it is not surprising that workers might instead prioritize political action that preserves or advances their varied status interests.

POLARIZED POLITICS

Building support for a progressive coalition can be particularly daunting when politicians holding office and the people they represent are highly polarized. As Delia Baldassarri and Peter Bearman point out, political polarization can result when people seek to reduce cognitive dissonance in their lives.[24] In other words, many people find it uncomfortable to balance friendships, acquaintances, ideas, and values when their friends and acquaintances do not share their core political positions or when their positions appear to be in conflict. Under ordinary circumstances, people can simply avoid discussing political issues when disagreements might disrupt friendship ties. At times, however, particular issues may receive so much media attention or so much attention from politicians that it becomes untenable for people to sweep their own political views under the rug. Responses to the COVID-19 pandemic, for example, became highly politicized, leading many Americans to reconsider friendship ties based on mask protocol, vaccine requirements, and social distancing practices.[25]

Scholars have taken note of political polarization in the United States, giving particular attention to what they refer to as "affective polarization."[26] The term refers to the increasing tendency for Americans in one of the two major political parties to feel closer to those who share their political affiliation while at the same time feeling animosity toward those in the opposing party. One key feature of contemporary polarization includes nationalization of elections, wherein voters have become much more likely to vote for candidates of the same party in both local and national elections. This process has involved issue sorting, in which political party identity now aligns closely with racial, ethnic, and cultural identities as well as ideological divisions across a range of issues. Researchers emphasize the extent to which voters receive cues from politicians that help them match political party identity with positions taken on different policies.[27] These kinds of cues are often necessary for voters who may not immediately recognize how they might be affected by a particular policy agenda. For example, in a recent study, the lead author of this book (McVeigh), along with William Carbonaro and Emmanuel Cannady, found that a sample of white men did not react negatively to policy agendas that threatened their advantages unless they were made aware that the agenda was being promoted by either a "Black alliance" or a "women's alliance." Other scholars have shown that much of the animosity that American voters feel toward members of opposing political parties can be traced to negative feelings they have toward group compositions of those opposing parties.[28]

Affective polarization is highly relevant to our argument, and we agree that shared group interests have been incorporated into party politics in ways that have created stark distance between

Democrats and Republicans, accompanied by high levels of animosity that limit coalition formation across parties. We argue, however, that prior scholarship has not appreciated the extent to which status hierarchies drive this polarization process. We aim to show that it is not simply feelings of closeness or hostility toward out-group members concentrated in other parties that leads to polarization. We instead argue that the political parties have taken positions on protecting or overturning various status hierarchies. As we have argued, the stakes are high not solely because of the symbolic rewards that come with social esteem but because of the differential treatment that people receive depending on their position within those hierarchies. For some voters, preserving their place within status hierarchies is so consequential that they will not ally with voters who seek to overturn those hierarchies even if it may improve their economic circumstances. For others, overturning status hierarchies is so important that they have little interest in mobilizing against economic inequality if doing so leaves status hierarchies intact. We examine these claims with our unique data in the coming chapters. In chapter 3, we assess how much support One America for Working People garners when our study participants only consider the organization's mission statement, which calls for worker unity to address economic inequality.

CONCLUSION

To sum up, our status contestation and politics theory is based on a key assumption that scholars and political pundits have substantially underestimated and, in some cases, misunderstood the role that status contestation plays in shaping political behavior in the United States. We see status in structural terms, with a number of salient status hierarchies generating not only different levels of esteem to those situated at the top of the status hierarchy but also differential treatment that can be highly consequential for status beneficiaries as well as for those who are excluded from enjoying the benefits. A desire to either preserve status hierarchies or overturn them imposes constraints on political alliances that people might otherwise enter. Status conflict also strongly contributes to political polarization that stymies consensus needed to pressure political officeholders to enact progressive legislation.

Importantly, our theory charts a new course for scholars who study political processes. We break sharply from those who dismissively write about "identity politics" as political action that undermines concern for the collective good.[29] We instead focus on historical construction of status hierarchies, their ongoing relevance in contemporary life, and the way that they have come to structure party politics in the United States.

3

BROAD SUPPORT FOR
WORKER UNITY

"American exceptionalism" is a term often invoked by conservative as well as by progressive Americans. Conservatives typically speak of exceptionalism in cultural terms but do not completely disassociate it from the nation's wealth and military might. The core idea is that God has uniquely blessed the United States. Prosperity is evidence of God's favor, and Americans therefore have a responsibility to display a particular set of values for the rest of the world to emulate.[1] Progressives, on the other hand, are more likely to point to the nation's exceptional status as a wealthy nation characterized by extreme inequality—a nation that lags behind other wealthy nations in terms of quality-of-life conditions such as educational achievement, child poverty, gun violence, human rights violations (including mass incarceration), and public health.[2] Relatedly, scholars have argued that America is exceptional in terms of a lack of class consciousness among its people. Some have tried to trace this phenomenon to the country's unique history—presumed to have produced a culture that valorizes rugged individualism and a frontier spirit.[3] Others have pointed to a winner-take-all two-party political system that undermines worker solidarity and representation stemming from barriers to electing candidates from parties that are not primarily focused on workers' interests.[4] The nation's ethnic and religious divisions also inhibit class consciousness.[5] Relatively unfettered power has allowed economic and political elites to control political narratives, putting forth the view that business strength and economic growth benefit all Americans through job creation.[6] Those who need a job to survive—and have a limited safety net beneath them—are particularly vulnerable to these appeals. As the political scientist John Gaventa has shown in his brilliant study of Appalachian coal mining, economic dependence leaves people highly vulnerable to ideological manipulation from those who hold power over them.[7]

In many wealthy democratic nations, labor unions have played an important role in raising class consciousness and successfully promoting policies that provide economic security for citizens. However, labor unions have been in decline in the United States for about half a century. This resulted from conservative attacks on organized labor as well as changes in the economy that have altered the organizing landscape.[8] Twenty-eight states, mostly in the south and mountain west, have "right-to-work" laws that prohibit requiring union membership as a condition of employment. Supporters of these laws have argued that unions and the resulting high cost of labor deter businesses from moving into their communities and providing badly needed jobs.[9] However, lack of union power results in lower wages and limited job security and, even so, these conditions have done little to attract or retain jobs in communities. In the contemporary global economy, corporations have not hesitated to seek out even cheaper labor overseas and to replace workers with machines.[10] Newman and Skocpol point out that union decline has disrupted what were once strong links among rank-and-file union members, their communities, and the Democratic Party.[11] In light of discussions about the relative lack of class consciousness in the United States, in this chapter we take a look at how participants in our study responded to the mission statement of One America For Working People—an organization that aims to generate class-conscious coalitions to combat inequality. To get started, we examine the attributes of the participants in our study.

Who Are the Participants?

Our sample, while large, diverse, and national in scope, is not based on strict probability sampling, so we are careful not to generalize our findings to all Americans. As we discussed in chapter 1, we instead focus primarily on an experimental design that allows us to identify cause and effect relationships *within* our sample. The size and diversity of the sample, however, facilitates our efforts to determine whether different types of people respond in different ways to our experimental manipulations. Because we are interested in how status preservation structures American politics, we can see if Republicans and Democrats respond differently to the altered versions of the web page.

In table 3.1, we summarize the attributes of those who participated in our study. We break the numbers down by education level (college degree or not). We make this distinction because a college degree is a key determinant of whether individuals can prosper in today's global economy or whether they are in circumstances that are more precarious because of declines in the number of well-paying jobs for those without advanced education. Scholars and political pundits have noted the extent to which many white Americans without a college degree have moved to the Republican Party and were particularly supportive of Donald Trump's presidential campaigns.[12] We also note

TABLE 3.1 DESCRIPTIVE STATISTICS FOR STUDY PARTICIPANTS

Variable	Attribute	With college degree (%)	Without college degree (%)	Total sample (%)	Number of cases
Ideology	Very liberal	10.87	7.33	8.97	233
	Liberal	16.27	10.85	13.36	347
	Slightly liberal	11.87	7.33	9.43	245
	Moderate	27.63	29.74	28.76	747
	Slightly conservative	8.46	9.63	9.09	236
	Conservative	14.52	14.51	14.52	377
	Very conservative	8.80	13.65	11.40	296
	Don't know	1.58	6.97	4.47	116
Party	Republican	26.30	32.42	29.59	764
	Democrat	43.55	33.86	38.34	990
	Independent	24.46	22.91	23.63	610
	Other	5.70	10.81	8.44	218
Married	Yes	55.98	46.94	51.14	1,326
	No	44.02	53.06	48.86	1,267
Children in home	Yes	25.71	23.60	24.58	633
	No	74.29	76.40	75.42	1,942
Gender	Woman	55.32	64.75	60.38	1,565
	Man	44.43	34.96	39.35	1,020
	Other	0.25	0.29	.27	7

(continued)

TABLE 3.1 (*continued*)

Variable	Attribute	With college degree (%)	Without college degree (%)	Total sample (%)	Number of cases
Race/ethnicity	White non-Hispanic	75.60	69.76	72.47	1,882
	Black/African American	6.64	11.35	8.63	224
	Hispanic/Latino(a)	6.97	10.34	9.32	242
	Asian American	5.81	2.01	3.77	98
	Other	4.98	6.54	5.81	151
Importance of religion	Very	33.22	38.77	36.20	940
	Somewhat	27.49	27.78	27.65	718
	Not very	16.86	13.28	14.94	388
	Not at all	22.43	20.17	551	551
Household income	0–29,999	12.49	34.46	24.28	620
	30,000–54,999	21.40	31.58	26.86	696
	55,000–89,999	26.64	20.94	23.58	611
	90,000 or more	39.47	13.02	25.28	655
Social class	Lower	4.57	17.73	11.63	302
	Working	26.27	49.68	38.83	1,008
	Middle	64.34	31.44	46.69	1,212
	Upper	4.82	1.15	2.85	74
Mean age		54.32	53.75	54.02	2,571

distinctions by education because the social change organization featured in our experiment explicitly makes its pitch to working-class people.

The data presented in table 3.1 depict some stark differences between college graduates and those without a four-year college degree. Notably, the college graduates are more likely to identify as liberal and vote for the Democratic Party. They are more likely to be married and have children in the home, reflecting the resources that facilitate family formation in contemporary America.[13] Women are overrepresented among those who don't hold a four-year degree but also somewhat overrepresented among those who do hold a degree (reflecting overrepresentation of women in the sample as a whole). The data also show the educational advantages of white respondents. The two education groups are quite similar in terms of the importance placed on religion, with those without a degree being somewhat more likely to indicate they are very religious. College graduates enjoy a sizable advantage, however, when it comes to household income and, as expected, they are more likely to identify as middle class.

Popularity of Mission Statement

Considering the complex array of factors undermining class consciousness in the United States, we might expect that Americans would show little enthusiasm for our fictitious organization. After all, it calls attention to glaring inequality in the United States and aims to unite working people to challenge the power structure holding them down. These are not moderate goals. The organization has a strong populist flavor to it—it pits the majority of Americans against the economic and political elite. However, the web page does not offer any nationalist or ethnonationalist rhetoric found in contemporary right-wing populist movements in the United States and throughout the world.[14] It also specifies that "the people" it represents are working people and small business owners (as opposed to a more undifferentiated claim on behalf of the masses). The framing on the web page—even the control page—emphasizes inclusion, rather than exclusion. Importantly, the writing under the heading "What Do We Do?" focuses on public policy and the organization's goal of providing supporters with information needed to fight effectively within the political system. Although the organization displays elements of populism as a "discursive strategy"—a ploy that is common in American politics—the organization more closely resembles a progressive organization oriented toward forming coalitions to support policy that would reduce inequality.[15]

Organizations typically use a mission statement (placed at the top of the web page shown to our study participants and reproduced in figure 3.1) to provide a clear and concise description of

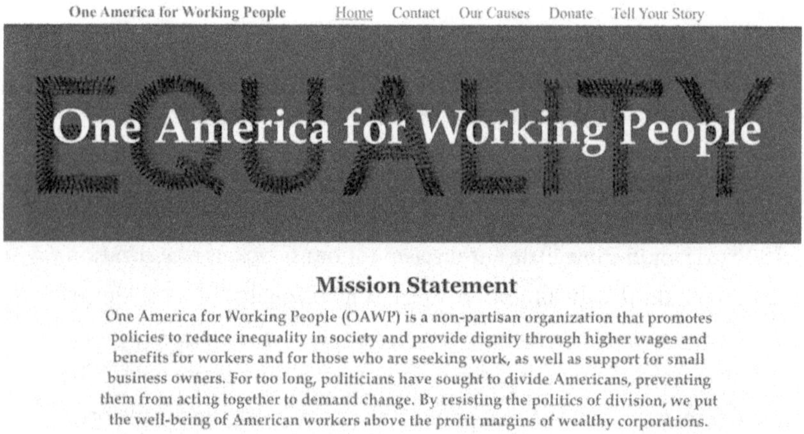

One America for Working People   Home   Contact   Our Causes   Donate   Tell Your Story

One America for Working People

Mission Statement

One America for Working People (OAWP) is a non-partisan organization that promotes policies to reduce inequality in society and provide dignity through higher wages and benefits for workers and for those who are seeking work, as well as support for small business owners. For too long, politicians have sought to divide Americans, preventing them from acting together to demand change. By resisting the politics of division, we put the well-being of American workers above the profit margins of wealthy corporations.

FIGURE 3.1 Mission statement for One American for Working People

the organization and its purpose. In our study, the mission state-ment is identical across all six versions of the web page. Notably, the mission statement focuses exclusively on addressing economic inequality. Although it does speak to the importance of resisting efforts to divide workers, it clearly states that the organization's primary mission is to reduce economic inequality to provide dignity for all workers through higher wages and benefits. The mission statement also indicates that the organization represents small business owners, as well as workers, and is nonpartisan.

Perhaps surprisingly, our data indicate that the organization's primary goals, as articulated in the mission statement, are quite popular. Contrary to elite framing indicating that success of big business generates jobs and a high standard of living for all, study participants show substantial support for a different vision that is highly critical of corporate America and the role of wealth in the political process. In fact, well over a third of respondents (37.3 per-cent) strongly support the mission statement while another 32.2 percent indicate that they "somewhat support" it. Another 21.5 percent say that they are "neutral" and only 9.1 percent oppose the mission statement (either "somewhat" or "strongly"). Ameri-cans in our sample are dissatisfied with current levels of inequal-ity, and relatively few have fully bought into the idea that what is good for large corporations is good for everyone.

It is possible that support for One America is coming from one or two large groups and that the organization, while popu-lar, is not broadly popular. This idea, after all, is consistent with narratives about political polarization in the United States. Here, our diverse sample comes in handy. We can see whether support for the organization is concentrated among a few groups, such as respondents affiliated with the Democratic Party or among those who self-identify as liberal, or whether the mission statement resonates with a broader segment of the people in the sample.

Broad Support for a Progressive Agenda

A closer look at our data indicates that support for One America's mission statement is not limited to subsets of the sample. In figure 3.2, for example, we consider a comparison between those who have a four-year college degree and those who do not. Notably, the mission statement is popular with both groups. In fact, among those with a college degree, 37 percent indicate they are strongly supportive, and another 34 percent are somewhat supportive. Those without a college degree are strikingly similar, with 37 percent being strongly supportive and 30 percent somewhat supportive. For both groups, a minority of respondents do not indicate support, and most of those participants characterize themselves as "neutral" rather than opposed to the mission statement.

Scholars have noted how the racial divide in American politics has led many white Americans, regardless of class, to favor

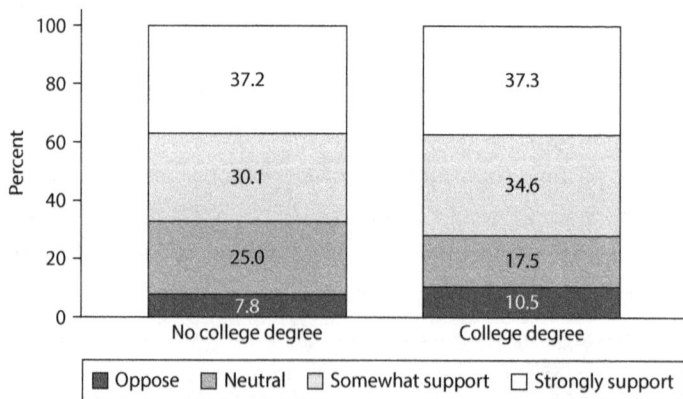

FIGURE 3.2 Support for mission statement by college degree attainment

conservative policies, including economic policies.[16] Democratic political candidates in so-called "swing states" or swing districts with predominantly white populations have sought to win elections by distancing themselves from progressive Democrats in more "blue" regions of the country. Yet as figure 3.3 reveals, the appeal of the progressive mission statement of One America for Working People cuts across racial and ethnic boundaries. In fact, an overwhelming majority of white respondents (67.9 percent) indicate at least some level of support for the mission statement. Approval from Black respondents is higher, with 56.2 percent strongly supporting the mission statement and another 24.6 percent indicating that they are somewhat supportive. The support shown by Latino(a) and Asian American respondents, as well as

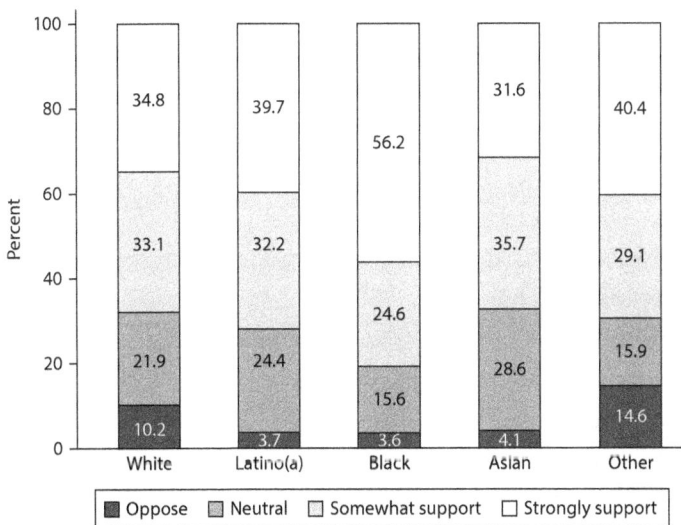

FIGURE 3.3 Support for mission statement by racial/ethnic identity

those who fall into the "other" racial category, is similar to that shown by white respondents, with substantial majorities indicating that they are strongly or somewhat supportive. Despite the polarization that exists in American politics, it is plainly evident that Americans, regardless of their racial and ethnic identities, are not happy about income and wealth inequality. We see strong support across racial boundaries for the progressive economic agenda articulated in the mission statement.

Given the progressive agenda of One America for Working People, we might expect that support for the mission statement would vary sharply based on political party identity. As we noted, scholars studying recent political polarization have called attention to the ways in which voters have been more effectively "sorted" across parties in ways that have promoted more internal cohesion and consistency within parties.[17] Data presented in figure 3.4 do show that self-identified Democrats are especially enthusiastic about the mission statement. Just over half of Democrats (51.7 percent) indicate strong approval and another 30.7 percent say that they somewhat approve. Perhaps what is most striking, however, is that the mission statement receives majority approval from Independents, "others," and even among Republicans. Once again, we see a promising path to a progressive economic coalition that, in this case, even transcends political party affiliation.

We have been referring to the organization's mission statement as liberal or progressive because it calls attention to inequality in wealth and income in the United States and advocates uniting people behind an agenda to reduce inequality. This is distinct from conservative arguments about limiting government intervention in the economy and instead relying on free market capitalism to distribute economic rewards. Yet we should

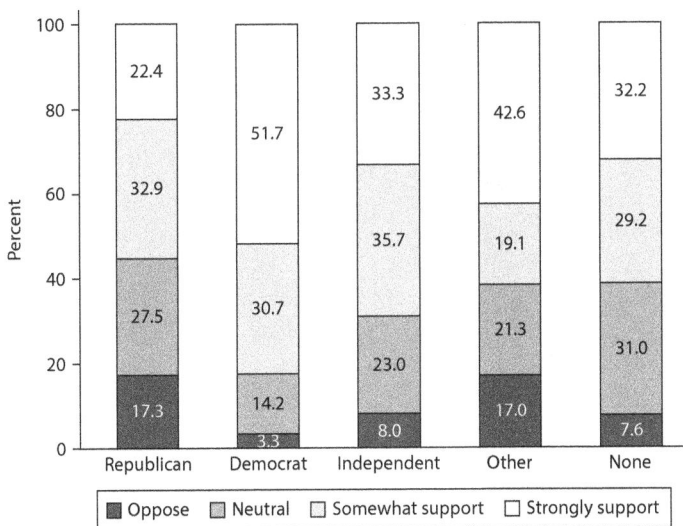

FIGURE 3.4 Support for mission statement by party identity

not jump to the conclusion that the average American, or our study participants, would embrace or reject the mission statement according to our (rather than their) understandings of what it means to be progressive or conservative. As figure 3.5 shows, people in our study who identify as liberal are, in fact, more likely to support the mission statement. Indeed, only a small percentage of them indicate that they are neutral, much less unsupportive. Yet again, we want to call attention to the broad support we find for the mission of One America for Working People. Among those who self-identify as moderate, almost 70 percent are at least somewhat supportive. Strikingly, more than half of self-identified conservatives support the mission statement and almost one-fourth of them "strongly support" it.

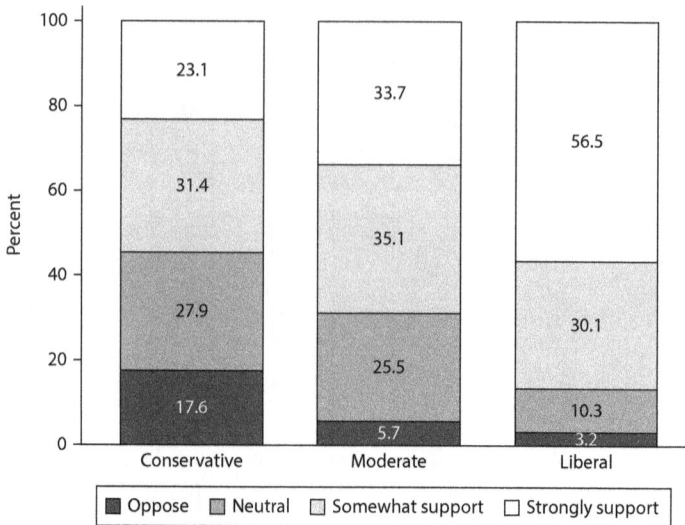

FIGURE 3.5 Support for mission statement by ideology

Note: "Liberal" includes those who identify as very liberal, liberal, and slightly liberal. "Conservative" includes those who identify as strongly conservative, conservative, and slightly conservative.

A POPULAR AGENDA:
SO WHAT IS THE PROBLEM?

Data from the Organization for Economic Co-operation and Development (OECD) indicate that in 2019 more than 20 percent of American children lived in poverty. The United States ranks last among OECD nations on this measure. Child poverty in Denmark, by comparison, stands at 2.9 percent. Child poverty in the United States is substantially higher than it is in Canada and even exceeds the child poverty rate in Mexico, its neighbor to the south.[18] America is truly exceptional. Although it may be true that class consciousness is lower in the United States than in many other countries, and that citizens are less motivated to take progressive action, our data indicate that a sizable majority of Americans in our sample are not satisfied with current levels of inequality and support a progressive agenda for change. Although it is common in the American political arena to see progressive candidates, policies, and organizations denigrated and labeled unflatteringly as socialist and un-American, we find that the support for change among our participants is not only prevalent but also widespread. Indeed, even many of those who think of themselves as "very conservative" or who identify with the Republican Party express support for an agenda that reflects the rhetoric of progressive firebrands like the Vermont senator Bernie Sanders, the Massachusetts senator Elizabeth Warren, or the New York Congressperson Alexandria Ocasio-Cortez.

It is notable that the mission statement strongly implies that the organization is calling for a diverse coalition and not exclusively seeking to mobilize white working-class people. Yet white people in our study showed quite a bit of enthusiasm for forming such a coalition. One might conclude, therefore, that the racial divide and other divides in American society are not insurmountable. We caution, however, against moving too quickly to that conclusion. Our argument in the preceding chapters emphasizes the way in which status preservation goals structure politics in the United States. There is nothing in the mission statement that calls for members of dominant groups to forfeit status benefits. The message is that everyone is welcome to join an effort to combat class inequality. In the next chapter, we begin to examine how views of the organization differ when status inequalities are included in the mix. We give particular attention to how Republicans, Democrats, and Independents respond differently to the inclusion of status goals in the organization's broader agenda.

4

RACE, GENDER,
AND STATUS PRESERVATION

We now turn our attention to confronting our status contestation and politics theory with data. One key element of the theory is that support for a progressive alliance to reduce inequality should depend on how people feel about status boundaries. Do they feel that status advantages that they value are under threat, and do they want to preserve them? Or do they instead feel that they or others in society are harmed by status hierarchies and the hierarchies should be dismantled? In this chapter, we focus on how status hierarchies related to race and gender structure support or opposition to One America for Working People.

When analyzing political behavior, it is important to keep in mind that most people in the United States spend relatively little time thinking about politics. They are more likely to be focused on earning a living, taking care of their families, or enjoying some well-deserved leisure time. They receive political information from a variety of sources and often in a haphazard fashion.[1] Repeal of the fairness doctrine in the late 1980s, and development of the Internet and social media, have powerfully affected the ways in which people receive news. The fairness doctrine stipulated that an entity with a broadcast license issued by the government must provide a public service by engaging in controversial topics of public interest while also providing a balanced treatment of the issues—presenting competing viewpoints or perspectives. Contemporary media critics often speak glowingly about the good old days when the entire nation turned to Walter Cronkite, anchor of the *CBS Evening News* (or the evening news broadcast by NBC or ABC), to get a neutral and trustworthy report on the issues of the day. During Ronald Reagan's second term as president, the Federal Communications Commission (FCC) chair Mark Fowler led a successful effort to repeal the doctrine, arguing that it violated the First Amendment of the Constitution.[2] Conservative broadcasters such as Rush Limbaugh and Glenn Beck were poised to take advantage of the new opening, launching talk-radio shows that attracted huge audiences. Notably, this new breed of conservative commentators tended to have backgrounds in the entertainment industry rather than in journalism.[3]

Repeal of the fairness doctrine intersected with changing communication technologies, including the growth of cable news networks, the Internet, and social media, in ways that balkanized the delivery and reception of news. Today, people can easily connect with a news source any time—day or night—and they can select news outlets that entertain them and those that spin the news in ways that reinforce their ideological leanings. Fox News consistently dominates the cable news ratings wars, relying on a strategy that has little to do with informing the public and much to do with ginning up partisan anger that drives their ratings.[4] A recent Pew poll indicates that in 2021, approximately half of adults surveyed said that they get news from social media "often" (19 percent) or "sometimes" (29 percent).[5] As we have learned in recent years, social media puts a world of information at people's fingertips but also serves as a powerful tool for spread of disinformation.

The volume and variety of political news that is available can create the impression that political behavior is easily swayed by fast-moving news cycles and the latest crisis, scandal, or conspiracy theory that spreads like a virus through modern communication networks. In our analyses, however, we offer a different perspective. We assume that political noise that bombards us daily is important, but perhaps it is less important than the structures in place that shape the way we process information and the way that we see ourselves in relation to political actors, parties, and platforms. To understand that process, however, it is necessary to first consider the historical construction of status boundaries, how they were incorporated into party politics, and ways in which these boundaries continue to influence contemporary understandings of rights and privileges in American society.

RACE AND STATUS HIERARCHIES

Throughout the nation's history, Americans have engaged, often violently, with questions about who belongs and who has a right to share in the American dream. Spikes in immigration have repeatedly met popular resistance. In the 1850s, the Know Nothing Party, also known as the Native American Party or the American Party, emerged as the political wing of a broader, staunchly anti-Catholic nativist movement. In the 1890s, the American Protective Association (APA) carried the anti-Catholic, anti-immigrant banner. The APA was in many ways a forerunner for the second rise of the Ku Klux Klan in the 1920s (see figure 4.1), which attracted millions of members and grew particularly strong in several Midwestern and western states.[6] Klansmen at the time promoted white supremacy but more directly targeted the rise of immigration from central and southern European nations, which

FIGURE 4.1 Klansmen march in Washington, DC. August 8, 1925.
Bettmann Archive/Getty Images.

brought millions of Catholics and (in smaller raw numbers) Jews to the United States. In response to the broad anti-immigrant sentiment, Congress passed severely restrictive immigration legislation in 1924 that was designed to sharply curtail immigration from countries whose emigrants had not already established a substantial footprint in the country prior to 1890.[7]

Immigration waves of the late 1800s and early 1900s played a key role in the formation of a distinctly American brand of sociology at the beginning of the twentieth century. Scholars at the University of Chicago grappled with core questions about how societies and communities can incorporate immigrant populations. Early Chicago sociologists did not focus on the rise of reactionary social and political movements but were interested instead in urbanization and the incorporation of, and the assimilation of, immigrants into cities and neighborhoods.[8] Perhaps most notably, Robert Park and his colleague Ernest Burgess posited that through increased contact between groups, immigrant populations could ultimately assimilate into dominant society, losing much of their cultural heritage and their "foreignness" in the process.[9] Park's predictions about white ethnic assimilation have largely played out. Although members of white ethnic groups may continue to identify with some aspects of their ancestral national heritage, distinctions based on a German American, Italian American, or Irish American identity play little role in determining one's life trajectory in the United Sates.[10]

Importantly, Aldon Morris reminds us that Park expressed skepticism about whether Black Americans *could* fully assimilate into American society. While viewed at the time as a progressive thinker, Park's ideas were firmly grounded in the racism of the era. Park held to prevailing beliefs about eugenics, or inherent genetic differences among racial groups in intelligence and talents.[11] Morris makes a powerful case for looking beyond the Chicago School to locate the roots of American sociology, turning instead to the work of W. E. B. Du Bois. After earning a bachelor's degree at Fisk University, Du Bois became the first Black American to earn a PhD from Harvard. Despite his academic credentials, sociologists have long overlooked the importance of his work. Yet in his professorship at Atlanta University, Du Bois was a prolific scholar whose writings on race relations and the Black experience anticipated in many ways race scholarship of the twenty-first century. Du Bois viewed race largely as a social construction, as opposed to perceiving fixed genetically determined categories, and he highlighted the ways in which inequality is shaped by power differentials rather than by cultural deficiencies.[12]

Du Bois's view of race and racial inequality is strikingly modern. Historically, white people have used advantages in power and resources to secure a privileged position at the top of a socially constructed racial hierarchy.[13] This process cuts across institutional domains in ways that make status the driving force of racial inequality in multiple aspects of social life. Construction and maintenance of a racial hierarchy is a process of granting esteem and privilege based on skin color or ethnic origin. It reinforces beliefs in white supremacy and the deservedness of privilege granted to white people but denied to Black people and other people of color.[14] For our purposes, this understanding of race aligns well with historical intersections of race and politics.

From the nation's founding, there have been concerted efforts to suppress political participation of nonwhite Americans using status, in the form of white supremacist ideology, to justify the exclusion.[15] Perhaps there is no clearer example than the "compromise" granted in adoption of the United States Constitution that stipulated that enslaved Black people would be counted as three-fifths of a person when calculating apportionment of Congressional seats. In other words, the Constitution firmly established that Black people did not count as much as white people. The system of slavery itself rested on a belief that white people are entitled to control over the bodies of Black people. When slavery was abolished, Southern states enacted Jim Crow laws explicitly designed to use race to grant privileges to white people that were denied to Black Southerners. Jim Crow laws and accompanying norms were all-encompassing, forcing enactment of white supremacy displays in everyday social interactions. White Southerners could not only monopolize jobs, land, and the franchise but also compel compliance with a humiliating set of social practices designed to reinforce racial status boundaries, granting myriad special privileges to white people.[16] This entailed not only segregated public and private facilities but also expectations that Black people would show deference to white people whenever their paths crossed. The threat of brutal violence provided the foundation for maintaining the racial order. Indeed, thousands of lynchings and other forms of racial terrorism served as constant reminders of the danger of challenging white privilege.[17]

Enforcement of racial boundaries has not been confined to Southern states. White Americans have practiced what Charles Tilly refers to as "opportunity hoarding," using racial categories to exclude nonwhite people from gaining fair access to valuable resources such as jobs, housing, schools, labor union membership, political patronage networks, social clubs, and other private facilities.[18] These forms of exclusion maintain status boundaries, in which people use skin color and racial identity to establish rules and norms about who is entitled to a vast array of societal privileges and who is not.[19]

The nation's history of racism is not just a story of Black and white people. The Chinese Exclusion Act of 1882 was unusual in that it specified a single national origin for exclusion during a time of intense anti-Chinese rhetoric and violence in the United States. Not long after, Congress also barred Japanese immigration using a special provision of broader anti-immigrant legislation passed in 1924.[20] Sources of hostility directed toward Chinese and Japanese immigrants at the time were complex, and they were intertwined with economic and political factors. However, this complexity does not negate the fact that arguments for exclusion centered on claims that Chinese and Japanese immigrants could not assimilate into American society because of inherent traits that made them inferior to the native white population— claims that characterized them as being uniquely deviant and possessing undesirable attributes. Catherine Lee describes the process in terms of "race-making," drawing on cultural stereotypes in the process of setting Chinese and Japanese people apart in ways that constructed imagined inherent racial traits that would permanently distinguish them from a white "race" deemed to be superior.[21] This has resulted in individualized and collective atrocities, such as the use of Japanese ancestry to confiscate property and forcibly place American citizens into internment camps during World War II—an injustice that was not imposed on German or Italian Americans (see figure 4.2).[22]

Anti-Asian stereotypes endure and have even spiked in recent years, in several instances spurred on by racist statements from Donald Trump during his first term as president. Origins of the COVID-19 pandemic in Wuhan, China, also motivated hate crimes directed against Asian Americans of varied national ancestries, as the pandemic's origins provided fodder for white

FIGURE 4.2 Japanese Americans confined to an internment camp in Santa Anita, California, during World War II. The site is now the home of a horse racing track. Getty Images.

supremacist rhetoric and the othering of Asian Americans. Indeed, a poll conducted by the Pew Research Center in April 2022 indicated that 72 percent of Asian Americans worry about being victimized by hate crime and 36 percent have made changes in their daily routines to minimize the risk.[23] At the same time, Americans of central Asian or Middle Eastern ancestry remain targets of discrimination, stereotypes, and violence spurred on by right-wing politicians and news outlets mining anti-Muslim terrorist tropes.[24] War between Israel and Hamas in Gaza has led to a sharp increase in hate crimes directed toward Americans of Arab descent as well as Jewish Americans.[25]

We cannot begin to understand present-day bigotry directed toward Latinos and American Indian populations in the United States without acknowledging early processes of racialization and dehumanization. The United States extracted massive tracts of land and resources through genocidal policies driven by unquestioned presumptions of white supremacy, buttressed by a belief that white Americans could claim land at any price—including the slaughter of people who possessed the desired land—because they were uniquely blessed by a Christian God. This violence includes white settlers' indifference to the fact they exposed Indigenous people to diseases like smallpox and measles, to which they had no immunity, leading to death of upwards of 70 percent of their population.[26] Hundreds of years later, some may acknowledge this sordid history, but few consider the need for any form of reparations. The legacy of racial violence, land confiscation, and social control measures directed toward Indigenous people on the continent has left American Indians today disproportionally facing poverty, spatial confinement, and stereotypes used to ignore or even rationalize American genocide.[27] Relatedly, many Americans today miss the irony as they enthusiastically embrace plans to build barriers on the southern border to deny entrance to immigrants from Mexico and other Latin American nations into land that was taken by force from Mexico.[28] At the same time, Latino people who have lived in the United States for many generations face discrimination and are often viewed by white Americans as foreign or not fully American.[29]

Several social scientific theories aim to account for racial conflict and inequality in the United States. Some, for example, identify intergroup contact as a key factor in understanding harmonious or conflictual relations.[30] Scholars commonly assess perceptions of threat or competition, noting how people mobilize in defense of, or in pursuit of, valued resources based on solidarity rooted in shared ethnic identity.[31] Yet intergroup inequality is often maintained without overt conflict.[32] Importantly, as emphasized by group position theory, underlying all forms of interracial conflict and inequality is an assessment of a status hierarchy.[33] Ethnic competition for resources, for example, only makes sense if members of at least one group feel that their racial or ethnic identity entitles them to resources and privileges denied to members of another group.[34]

Although expressions of overt racism have declined over time in the United States and scholars and laypeople have largely abandoned eugenics in their understanding of race and inequality, contemporary scholarship reveals how racism is built into the structure of society in ways that facilitate racist practices while offering cover for beneficiaries of unequal treatment. Differential treatment of racialized groups by police, treatment that leads to mass incarceration and, all too often, police-initiated violence and killings represent a visible tip of the iceberg when it comes to differential treatment stemming from racial status hierarchies. White people in the United States, for example, are largely free from racial discrimination, stereotypes, race-based hate crimes, general suspicion, scrutiny, and disrespect experienced daily by Black, Brown, and other Americans of color. Status privileges, we argue, are central to political behavior in the United States because when faced with a choice, many beneficiaries of white privilege both consciously and subconsciously prioritize preservation of status benefits over improvements in their class position, while using the lens of status preservation to interpret a broad array of public policies and cultural practices.[35]

The alignment of racial status hierarchies and political parties has varied over time. In the American South, for example, the Democratic Party was the party of white supremacy throughout much of the nation's history. In the Jim Crow era, Black voters were not permitted to join the Democratic Party in the South, and poll taxes, rigged literacy tests, and violence and terror were used to deny the franchise to Black Southerners.[36] The civil rights struggle of the 1960s did much to realign party alliances. When the national Democratic Party, in response to pressure from the civil rights movement, backed the Civil Rights Act of 1964 and the Voting Rights Act of 1965, Republican politicians began courting disgruntled white voters.[37] While the change did not take place overnight, over time party positions have become increasingly clear at least in terms of which party—the Democratic Party—is more committed to dismantling the racial status hierarchy while the Republican Party appeals to voters by reinforcing the hierarchy.[38]

GENDER AND STATUS HIERARCHIES

Status hierarchies are most durable when status inequality has a taken-for-granted quality. If people generally see differences in esteem as natural and appropriate, status boundaries are difficult to dislodge and may simply go unchallenged. Status hierarchies gain extraordinary stability if they are deemed to be ordained by

God, deeply embedded in sacred texts and religious teaching.[39] However, religious texts and teaching are malleable. Indeed, in the United States the Christian faith has played a central role in mobilization of the American civil rights movement but also of the Ku Klux Klan.[40] Likewise, proponents and opponents of traditional gender roles have grounded their arguments in different interpretations of biblical passages.[41] However, in the United States the concept of complementarianism is deeply rooted in conservative Christian teaching. The core idea is that men and women are equally valued in the eyes of God, but they have different roles to play, with men acting as heads of households and assuming leadership positions—a status hierarchy.[42] This mindset is promoted not only in pulpits but also in frames offered by conservative advocacy organizations. For example, the website for Focus on the Family, a staunchly conservative advocacy organization, firmly places gender hierarchy at the center of Christian belief:

> For decades, radical feminists have characterized the Bible as patriarchal. Sadly, the church has not rejected this thinking and radical feminism has impacted the way the Bible is interpreted in many Christian marriages. While every relationship will have its own unique dynamics, the biblical marriage model calls for a man to lead his home. That leadership is to be balanced by love for his wife and children. But because radical feminism calls for the overthrow of male leadership in society, the seeds of conflict in a relationship are present from the moment the biblical approach is replaced with radical feminism.[43]

Beyond the family, gender inequality has been deeply rooted in politics throughout American history. At the nation's founding, most states limited voting rights to property-owning white

men. Closely adhering to republican ideology that was prominent at the time, the nation's property-owning men believed
that republican governance required excluding participation of
those in a state of dependency.[44] According to this line of thinking, workers are dependent on their employers and women are
dependent on men. They, therefore, are vulnerable to manipulation from those who hold power over them and cannot rise above
their own self-interest to act on behalf of the collective good. In
hindsight, of course, the irony of republican theory is obvious. In
the real world, the rich and powerful in the United States have
always engaged in politics to protect and advance the interests
of the rich and powerful, rather than the collective good.[45] Yet
the idea that women are ill-equipped for participation in politics
went largely unquestioned until early rumblings of the women's
suffrage movement in the mid-1800s (see figure 4.3).[46] Many
western states granted suffrage rights to women in the late 1800s
and early 1900s, beginning with the state of Wyoming, where
women voted for the first time in 1870. Yet it was not until rati-
fication of the 19th amendment to the Constitution in 1920 that
women were able to vote in every state.

Even with the franchise, men and women at the time were
broadly seen as playing different roles in politics. Indeed, early
arguments in support of women's suffrage appealed to notions
that women's specialized roles as homemakers and mothers
equipped them with moral virtues that would guard against
political corruption.[47] Interestingly, this kind of reasoning
was even deployed by the Ku Klux Klan in the early 1920s. As
McVeigh points out in earlier work, Klan leaders grappled with
the twin tasks of keeping women confined to subordinate roles
while also encouraging them to vote to offset the increase in
female Catholic voters, who cast their ballots for the first time
in 1920.[48] A common rhetorical strategy used by Klan leaders of

FIGURE 4.3 The National Association Opposed to Woman Suffrage formed in New York in 1911. Getty Images.

the time involved heaping praise on women for fulfilling subordinate roles delegated to women: "We find woman as a home-builder, an important and never-failing ally in times of greatest need; we note with ever-increasing gratitude that she has not been found wanting in places of trust, and has proved that her patriotism and loyalty are above reproach"[49]

Securing the franchise did little to increase women's access to positions of political power. By the early 1960s, only two out of a hundred United States senators were women and there were only eighteen women in the House of Representatives. Even in the 118th Congress (2023–2025), women made up only 25 percent of the Senate, and only 124 (28.5 percent) of members of the House of Representatives were women. These figures lag far behind many other nations in terms of women serving in parliaments—nations as diverse as Rwanda, Mexico, Sweden, Spain, and Namibia. As of this writing, the United States has yet to elect a woman as president, and it was not until 2020 that a woman was elected vice president.[50] Without question, social construction of gender and broadly shared beliefs about the role of women in politics have been and continue to be consequential in politics and in the maintenance of a privileged position for men.

A gendered status hierarchy holds important implications for unequal treatment that extend far beyond voting and holding political power. In 1984, Kristin Luker wrote what is now a classic book titled *Abortion and the Politics of Motherhood*.[51] Luker conducted in-depth interviews with women who were pro-choice and anti-abortion activists in the wake of the *Roe v. Wade* ruling that made abortion legal in the United States in 1973. The pro-choice activists she interviewed tended to be highly educated professionals who recognized that control over their own fertility was essential for them if they were to pursue and maintain lucrative careers more typically held by men. Through her interviews with anti-abortion activists, however, Luker noted that most of the women had already made choices in life (e.g., forgoing a college education, marrying early) that closed the door to these lucrative career paths even if they found them to be desirable. Abortion, these women felt, diminished the status that they derived from the role of motherhood. Largely dependent on a man's earnings for their own survival, they interpreted *Roe v. Wade* as a signal that society no longer valued the work they undertook serving their husbands, doing the housework, and raising children. Control over fertility represents an essential step for women, as it facilitates developing career paths that offer women autonomy in relation to men. After fifty years of legal abortion in the United States, however, the recent ruling by the United States Supreme Court in *Dobbs v. Jackson Women's Health Organization* has reinforced gendered status inequality by establishing that the nation's laws do not grant women the same bodily autonomy that men enjoy.

Societal norms pertaining to gender roles have long resulted in different treatment and different opportunities for men and women. With development of industrial economies, a gendered division of labor emerged with men engaged in paid labor, often in occupations that require physical strength, and women either tending to the home or "supplementing" the household income working in jobs deemed appropriate for women.[52] Assumptions about who is primarily responsible for securing the family income were built into the pay structures of occupations. Proponents of "comparable worth" policies have called attention to the way in which earnings linked to occupations in society have little relationship to the societal value of those occupations. Teachers are vital to society, for example, but tend to earn low salaries compared to many occupations held primarily by men that have less intrinsic value.[53]

Beginning in the 1970s, the number of women working in the labor force began to increase sharply, and gender segregation of occupations also declined steadily. It should be noted that this largely represents an increase in employment of white women because rates of labor force participation for women of color were high long before the 1970s.[54] Ling Zhu and David Grusky show that declines in occupational segregation stalled around the turn of the millennium. As recently as 2018, it was still the case that more than 60 percent of men and women would need to change occupational categories to produce a distribution in which men and women are evenly distributed across different types of occupations.[55]

Disparities in earning potential have, historically, empowered men to dictate terms in the division of household labor. Arlie Hochschild famously analyzed the "second shift" taken on by many women as they spend a hard day working in the paid labor force, typically earning less than male workers, only to come home to take on the lion's share of the housework and child-care duties.[56] Mary Jackman powerfully describes how women's economic dependence on domestic male partners leaves them vulnerable to domination, as men deploy paternalistic strategies to secure advantages in the relationship related to housework, decision-making, and expectations regarding sex. Paternalism works as a strategy, Jackman argues, because acts of domination in the guise of love and protection are built on an understanding that violence is the "backup plan" if paternalistic domination fails to produce compliance.[57] More recently, Paige Sweet has called attention to how unequal power in a relationship leaves women vulnerable to "gaslighting" by partners who mobilize gender stereotypes to alter their partner's sense of reality in a way that leaves them vulnerable to abuse and control.[58]

Although men continue to stake a claim to privileged treatment based on their gender identity, male privilege is increasingly under challenge, providing men with additional incentive to act to preserve gender boundaries and accompanying male privilege. McVeigh and Estep show that much of Donald Trump's appeal to his core supporters during his first presidential campaign was linked to his capacity to capitalize on grievances of men who are losing footing in a global economy that rewards skills derived through higher education.[59] Relatedly, as of 2021, women make up nearly 60 percent of annual college graduates, better preparing women for highly compensated positions in the global economy.[60] At the extreme, we see the rise of groups such as the Proud Boys, a violent white nationalist organization whose name is intended to signal its misogynistic goals. More commonly, men are often receptive to politicians' promises to revive the old economy and the status advantages that accrued to men through advantages in earning capacity. Notably, even lawsuits finding Trump liable for sexual abuse of writer E. Jean Carrol in 2023 and 2024—and close to 90 million dollars being awarded by juries for Trump's libelous claims against her—have not dampened support for him among his many followers.

Despite the presence of a gender hierarchy, women in the United States are divided across the two major political parties. As we have discussed above, not all women prioritize gender equality or even support it. Nevertheless, positions taken by the two dominant parties are clear in terms of the Democratic Party showing greater commitment to dismantling the hierarchy—even more so after the Supreme Court's Dobbs ruling over-turned *Roe v. Wade* and the legal right to abortion. We expect to find that gender status preservation goals, as well as race status preservation goals, play important roles in affecting responses to One America for Working People.

WHAT DO PEOPLE THINK OF ONE AMERICA FOR WORKING PEOPLE? EFFECTS OF RACE AND GENDER STATUS CONTESTATION

The previous discussion establishes historical roots and ongoing presence of status hierarchies based on race and gender—hierarchies that grant rewards and privileges to white people and men that are not available to women or to Black, Brown, or other people of color. A key question for this study is whether status hierarchies such as those based on race and gender affect support for a progressive political coalition. To address this question, we now turn our attention to our experimental findings. Are we correct? Does our experiment reveal that race and gender status preservation goals affect the way that people respond to One America for Working People? The answer, as we will show, is an unambiguous yes.

We reemphasize here that we are taking a nontraditional approach in our analysis. We are not interested in simply assessing whether men are less likely than women to support a particular version of our organization or whether white people are less likely than people of color to offer support. Many of these types of relationships are self-evident and not very enlightening. We are instead using an experimental design to assess the extent to which the organization may gain or lose support depending on its commitments to combatting particular status hierarchies in addition to combatting economic inequality.

As we present our findings, we separate respondents by their political party affiliations.[61] This allows us to better assess the ways in which status contestation goals shape the political environment. We begin by presenting a "common sense" explanation for what we are showing in the analyses below. Those who are interested in technical details can turn to the methodological appendix at the back of the book. We asked participants in our study whether they support or oppose the content of the web page under the heading "Fighting for a Better Future." Recall that this is the only section of the web page that we altered across the different versions. Some respondents saw only a paragraph about the need to address economic inequality. Others were assigned a web page that had an additional paragraph indicating that the organization is also committed to promoting one of the following: racial equality, gender equality, LGBTQ equality, immigrant equality, and religious equality. Respondents were able to view that content while answering the question. They chose from the following response categories: 1 (strongly oppose), 2 (somewhat oppose), 3 (neutral), 4 (somewhat support), and 5 (strongly support.). In this chapter, we compare responses from those who viewed the "economics only" version to those who viewed a version that also included a paragraph on racial equality or gender equality. In chapter 5, we focus on how responses to the economics version compare to those who viewed web pages that included a commitment to fighting LGBTQ, immigrant, or religious inequalities.

We use ordinary least squares regression to calculate the mean score (1 through 5) reflecting levels of support for the content under the heading "Fighting for a Better Future." Random assignment to our different treatment groups should ensure that the composition of each group is similar regarding attributes that might affect support for One America—except, of course, in terms of their exposure to our different versions of the web page. However, as an additional precaution, our analyses control for several individual attributes that could potentially influence support or opposition to the organization's equality goals. These include measures of our respondents' gender identity, racial identity, age, marital status, income, educational attainment (college graduate or not), the importance they place on religion, and whether they indicate that they are Catholic or Protestant. In figure 4.4, we present our results.[62]

The graph displays the average marginal effects of our experimental treatment for those who identify as Democrats, Republicans, and Independents, depending on which web page they viewed. The horizontal line at the bottom, corresponding with a value of zero, represents the Republican respondents in our sample, who serve as our basis of comparison. The dots for Democrats on the graph represent the average difference between

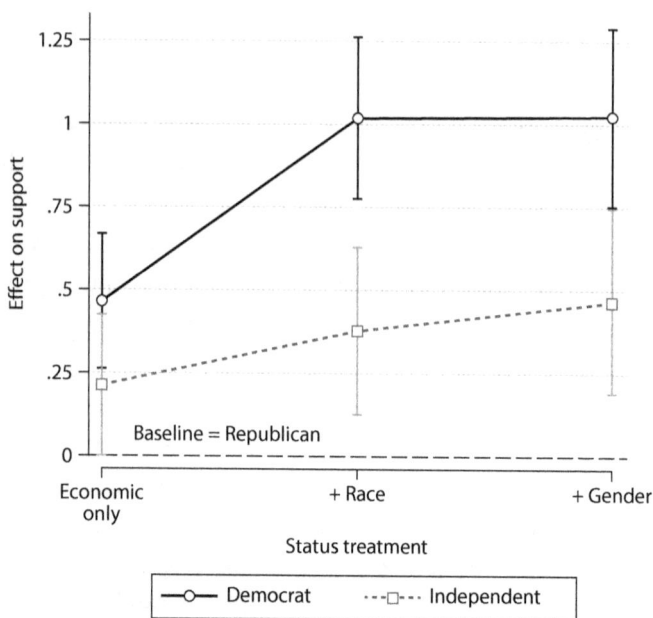

FIGURE 4.4 Support of Fighting for a Better Future content: class, race, and gender equality

Democrats and Republicans within each treatment group. Similarly, the dots for Independents represent the average difference between Independents and Republicans within each treatment group. For example, if we look at the left side of the graph, we see that among those in the "economics only" group, average support among Democrats is almost half a point higher than the average support among Republicans. Independents, on average, were almost a quarter of a point more supportive than Republicans.

When assessing these differences, how confident can we be that these represent "real" differences between adherents of the different political parties? The bars extending from each dot on the graph represent 95 percent confidence intervals. These intervals indicate that if we were to redo our experiment a hundred times, using the same sample but with a new random assignment to treatment groups each time, only 5 percent of the time would we expect to find an average marginal effect value falling outside of the range covered by the confidence intervals. Because the confidence interval for the Democrat score does not overlap with the line representing Republicans, we can conclude that it is highly likely that our findings represent a true difference between Republicans and Democrats. In other words, the relationship is statistically significant. However, because the confidence interval for Independents overlaps with the line for Republicans, we cannot conclude with confidence that support among Independents is actually higher than it is among Republicans. In other words, the average difference between Republicans and Independents is not statistically significant among those who viewed the economics only version of the web page.

Although it is interesting to examine differences between Republicans, Democrats, and Independents who viewed the economics only version of the web page, the power of the experiment comes from our ability to compare across treatment groups. If we look to the center and to the right of the graph, we see that Independents, and especially Democrats, are much more supportive of the organization's equality goals than Republicans among those who were in the racial equality or gender equality treatment groups. In both cases, Independents are almost a half a point more supportive than Republicans while Democrats, on average, are approximately a full point more supportive than Republicans. That represents a sizable difference—one that is approximately twice as large as the gap between Democrats and Republicans who were exposed to the economics only version of the web page. We also note that the larger gap between Republicans and Democrats for both the racial equality and gender equality treatments results from the way in which Republicans find the content less attractive when it addresses either race or gender equality, while Democrats find the content more attractive under those same conditions. Equally noteworthy, if we compare differences across the treatments, we see that the gaps between Democrats and Republicans who viewed the race and gender equality versions of the web page are significantly larger than the gap between Democrats and Republicans in the economics only group. Interestingly, Independents also, on average, are more supportive than Republicans if they were presented with a web page that advocates addressing both economic equality and racial equality or economic equality and gender equality. Their support, however, does not rise to the level of support among Democrats. Overall, the results confirm our argument that different preferences pertaining to race and gender status hierarchies sharply distinguish Republicans and Democrats in our sample.

Mobilization Potential for
One America for Working People

Our results clearly demonstrate that combining a struggle for status equality (in this case based on race and gender) with a struggle for economic equality is very attractive to Democrats and to a lesser extent Independents. At the same time, these coalitions make the organization less attractive to Republicans. But what happens if we consider actions rather than just words? It is important to keep in mind that the vast majority of people who are in favor of any particular cause never engage in collective action to bring about desired change. Indeed, a puzzle at the heart of social movement scholarship is why people participate in collective action to bring about change when they could instead rationally coast on the efforts of others.[63] The number of people who participate in collective action is almost always a small fraction of those who would potentially benefit from that action.[64] Yet, under the right conditions, people do organize and often achieve at least partial victories if conditions are favorable and enough people are willing to sacrifice on behalf of a shared goal.[65] To assess our participants' willingness to act, we asked them two questions. First, we asked them to indicate how willing they would be to volunteer time to work for the organization. Second, we asked them about their willingness to oppose the organization. By combining responses to these two questions, we obtain a fuller range of people's orientations toward acting in support of, or in opposition to, the alliance. Many people in our sample, for example, are unwilling to volunteer for the organization but they are not willing to actively oppose it. We constructed an index by adding responses from these two questions together. Willingness to volunteer is measured as 1 for very unwilling, 2 for somewhat unwilling, 3 for somewhat willing, and 4 for very willing. Willingness to oppose is coded as 1 for very willing, 2 for somewhat willing, 3 for somewhat unwilling, and 4 for very unwilling. Our measure, therefore, ranges from 2 to 8 with higher scores indicating greater willingness to take positive action in support of the organization and lower scores indicating greater willingness to actively oppose it.

Results presented in figure 4.5 are very similar to those we presented in our prior analysis. Again, we see that Independents are not significantly different from Republicans, on average, among those who viewed the economics only web page. They are significantly more supportive, however, if they viewed the racial equality or gender equality versions. Again, we also see that the Democrats are significantly more supportive than Republicans

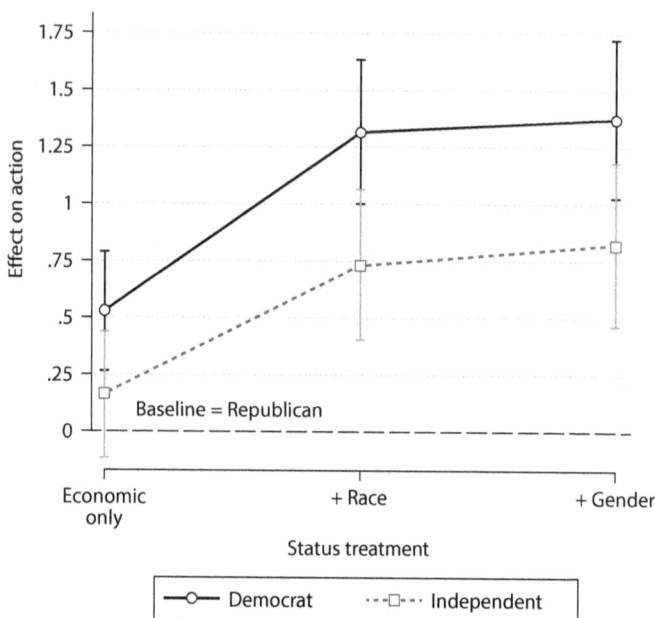

FIGURE 4.5 Willingness to act in support of One America for Working People: class, race, and gender equality

Note: Dependent variable is an additive index using questions about respondents' willingness to donate time to the organization and willingness to oppose the organization (reverse coded so that those who are very unwilling are given a high score and those who are very willing are given a low score).

when considering respondents in each of the three groups. The gap between Democrats and Republicans, once again, is much larger when we consider the respondents who viewed versions of the web page that commit the organization to addressing racial equality and gender equality in addition to economic equality. Once again, this gap results from Democrats in the race and gender groups being more supportive than other Democrats in the economics only group, while Republicans in the race and gender groups are substantially less supportive than Republicans in the economics only group. In other words, Democrats are significantly more supportive than Republicans of the economics only version of One America. That difference in support is significantly larger, however, among respondents in the racial equality and the gender equality treatment groups, compared to those in the economics only group.

CONCLUSION

Our results should be understood in relation to dramatic changes in American politics that have taken place over several decades. As we noted earlier, prominent political scholars once characterized party politics as a democratic class struggle, with the Democratic Party serving the interests of the working class and the Republican Party appealing to those who aim to preserve their wealth. That characterization is no longer true. Instead, as our analyses indicate, the two major parties are multiclass coalitions held together by shared interests in either preserving or overturning economic and status hierarchies.

Data recently presented by the Pew Foundation indicate that in 1994, white non-college graduates comprised 57 percent of Democratic voters. That percentage declined to 30 percent by 2019 while 57 percent of Republican voters in 2019 were non-college graduates.[66] Those figures are similar to what we find in our sample—white non-college graduates make up 50.7 percent of self-identified Republicans and only 26.7 percent of Democrats. It is no longer accurate to think of the Democratic Party as the blue-collar party because the working class is divided across both major parties and to a great extent the split represents a racial divide. In our sample, 86 percent of Republican non-college graduates identify as white, while only 56 percent of similarly educated Democrats identify as white.

In this chapter, we have discussed historical construction of race and gender hierarchies and how these hierarchies are meaningful even today in terms of the way that people are treated and the respect (or disrespect) granted to them in society. In recent decades, the Republican Party has sent increasingly strong signals to potential voters that it is committed to preserving race and gender status hierarchies. Democrats continue to favor progressive economic policies while also strongly opposing maintenance of status hierarchies based on race and gender. As a result of the way that the two parties forged alliances, the Republican Party is faced with a pressing dilemma. Republican voters, regardless of education levels, mainly differ from Democrats in terms of a desire to preserve status hierarchies rather than the class hierarchy. The tail, in other words, is wagging the dog, incentivizing Republican politicians to display their bona fides as defenders of race and gender privilege while also promoting economic policies that harm many of their core constituents.

As important as race and gender hierarchies are in structuring politics in the United States, we expect that other status hierarchies also affect efforts to form a progressive coalition to combat inequality. As with race and gender, this represents a constraint but also an opportunity. In the next chapter, we will focus on status hierarchies that are based on sexual orientation and gender identity, citizenship, and religion.

5

LGBTQ, IMMIGRATION, RELIGION, AND STATUS PRESERVATION

onsistent with status contestation and politics theory, in the last chapter we found that status interests based on race and gender are important factors limiting Republicans' support for a diverse progressive alliance even though Republicans, as we showed in chapter 3, are largely supportive of One America's mission statement that focuses on coming together to reduce economic inequality. Importantly, for Democrats the promise to address race and status inequalities makes the alliance to combat economic inequality much more attractive. Independent voters were also significantly more supportive of the organization than Republicans but only if they viewed a version that was committed to fighting for either racial equality or gender equality, in addition to economic equality. While we argued that status conflict resulting from race and gender hierarchies are important, other forms of status inequality also matter. In this chapter, we consider status hierarchies based on sexual orientation and gender identity, citizenship, and religion.

LGBTQ INEQUALITY

On March 2, 2023, Governor Bill Lee signed a law making public drag shows illegal in the state of Tennessee. At the time of the signing, similar bills were working through legislatures in numerous other states. Many of these same states were also proposing laws that, they argued, protect children by banning gender-affirming treatment for transgender youth and, in some cases, for transgender adults. For those familiar with the nation's history, this anti-LGBTQ performative politics and oppressive legislation is all too familiar. Perhaps most famously, on the morning of June 28, 1969, police raided the Stonewall Inn in Greenwich Village in New York. The Stonewall was a shabby building owned by the mafia that had become a popular hangout for LGBTQ people in the city at a time when social and legal oppression limited venues where queer people could socialize. During this particular raid, police confiscated alcohol, roughed up patrons, and made several arrests including those of patrons accused of violating New York's "gender appropriate clothing statute."[1]

Stonewall became a symbol of resistance and a launchpad for a gay rights movement that emerged in the early 1970s. What made Stonewall different, in this instance, is that while people in the LGBTQ community were accustomed to threats, violence, and harassment from the police and other members of society, this time they fought back in a way that attracted widespread media attention. The spirit of rebellion is captured in a 1974 letter penned by Morty Manford, president of the Gay Activist Alliance, in which he reflects on what came to be known as the Stonewall Riots:

> There is no question that the bar was illegal, dirty, dingy, and exploitative: in 1969 it was virtually all we had. . . . Crumby as it

was, it was ours. . . . The raid was like a number of other raids I'd been in with the important exception that we fought back. A spirit of pride encapsulated in anger was articulated for the first time in modern history by homosexuals as a group. That spirit said both explicitly and symbolically: "We are sick of being pushed around; we are sick of being denied our Constitutional rights; and we will persevere until injustice, exploitation, harassment, and discrimination end."[2]

Much has changed since the Stonewall rebellion, but much has stayed the same. The current conservative political assault on equal rights for LGBTQ people, notably, is being carried out at a time when support for LGBTQ rights has been steadily increasing for decades in the general population.[3] Popular support for LGBTQ equality in the United States is somewhat lower than in Canada and in most Western European countries. Nevertheless, a Pew survey conducted in 2019 indicates that 72 percent of Americans say that "homosexuality should be accepted in society."[4] Another Pew poll taken in 2021 indicates that 70 percent of Americans approve of marriage equality for LGBTQ couples.[5] While this level of support is encouraging, it is important to keep in mind that LGBTQ people throughout the nation continue to be at great risk for discrimination and violence. Indeed, data provided by the Human Rights Campaign Foundation (HRCF) identify 256 cases of fatal violence victimizing transgender and gender nonbinary people from 2013 to 2021, and 66 percent of the victims were Black transgender women.[6] In 2021, the FBI's Uniform Crime Report listed 1,132 hate crimes based on sexual orientation.[7] Importantly, these figures represent massive undercounts since many law enforcement agencies do not enforce hate crime laws or do not fully cooperate with the FBI's hate crime reporting program, and many bias-motivated crimes go unreported by victims.[8]

Public opinion polls regarding LGBTQ rights can also be deceptive because they typically reflect levels of "acceptance" or "tolerance" in the general population—phrasing that assumes heteronormativity and cisnormativity while assessing "tolerance" for deviance, rather than strong support for equality. What's more, a significant subset of the population prefers to maintain status hierarchies based on sexual orientation and gender identity (see figure 5.1). As a result, many conservative politicians find it useful to appeal to their bigotry by manufacturing threats posed by LGBTQ people. It is worth remembering that it was only a few decades ago that almost every state in the nation had anti-sodomy laws on the books. While these laws initially referred to any type of sex unrelated to procreation, they were for the most part reinterpreted in the 1960s and 1970s to target the LGBTQ population. These laws even applied to sex within the home and

FIGURE 5.1 Proud Boys protesting Drag Story Hour outside of a library in Queens, NY. December 29, 2022. Getty Images.

included harsh penalties.[9] Strikingly, antisodomy laws remain on the books in sixteen states, although a 2003 Supreme Court ruling in *Lawrence v. Texas* rendered the laws unconstitutional. In that ruling, Chief Justice William H. Rehnquist dissented along with the conservative justices Antonin Scalia and Clarence Thomas.

Scalia wrote the dissenting opinion, and his logic reflects a view that status based on sexual orientation or gender identity *should* be arranged hierarchically. As Scalia expressed it,

> One of the most revealing statements in today's opinion is the court's grim warning that the criminalization of homosexual conduct is "an invitation to subject homosexual persons to discrimination both in the public and in the private spheres." It is clear from this that the court has taken sides in the culture war, departing from its role of assuring, as neutral observer, that the democratic rules of engagement are observed. Many Americans do not want persons who openly engage in homosexual conduct as partners in their business, as scoutmasters for their children, as teachers in their children's schools, or as boarders in their home. They view this as protecting themselves and their families from a lifestyle that they believe to be immoral and destructive.[10]

This statement is remarkable in that three Supreme Court justices (including one still serving on the court) so openly articulate a belief that LGBTQ people do not deserve equal treatment under the law and their rights and privileges are of secondary importance when compared to upholding people's rights to discriminate against them. Scalia chastises the majority on the court for "taking sides in the culture war." Yet Scalia certainly would have responded differently if members of society chose to discriminate against people because they are heterosexual and cisgender. Scalia appears to be saying that the numerical majority in society should be free to define a category of people they disdain and deny them rights and privileges enjoyed by the numerical majority—directly contradicting the founding fathers' concerns about guarding against the tyranny of the majority.[11]

Scalia's dissent, written in 2003, is noteworthy today in that it resembles the way in which many Americans continue to feel about sexual orientation and gender identity. For many, this bias is rooted in religious beliefs.[12] However, as we noted previously when discussing gender inequality, religious doctrine and sacred texts are malleable. People often draw selectively from them to support their positions on various issues while ignoring doctrine of their own faith tradition that contradicts their positions.[13] We argue that it is important to view disdain for LGBTQ people, much like racism and sexism, as structural. People use socially constructed boundaries based on sexual orientation and gender identity to delineate who is deserving of societal esteem and special treatment. Those who are accustomed to deriving benefits from displaying traits associated with traditional gender roles are highly motivated to maintain status boundaries. For men, those traits evolve from displays of masculinity that have traditionally been rewarded in society within interpersonal interactions as well as in popular culture.[14] For women, traditional markers of femininity have also been rewarded and reinforced in the larger society. Indeed, unequal status treatment based on sexual orientation is so severe, as C. J. Pascoe points out, that boys learn early in life that they must avoid being labeled as gay at all costs so that they won't be subject to bullying and harassment.[15] Adolescent girls feel pressure to meet idealized standards of femininity, too, which can lead to depression, eating disorders, and other mental health problems including suicide ideation.[16]

A focus on children seems to be particularly potent when conservatives seek to maintain status boundaries. In Nicola Beisel's study of the antivice movement of the late 1800s, to which we referred in chapter 2, Beisel emphasizes the importance of social reproduction as a motive for status defense activities. By that, she means that many who supported the antivice movement were particularly receptive to appeals that Anthony Comstock made suggesting that if their children were exposed to vice (which Comstock defined very broadly to include deviation from heteronormativity), they ran the risk of destroying their own reputations and bringing shame on their families.[17] Indeed, Comstock himself wrote that gay people "are not fit to live with the rest of mankind. They ought to have branded in their foreheads the word 'Unclean.' Instead of the law making twenty years' imprisonment the penalty for their crime, it ought to be imprisonment for life." He went on to write, "Their lives ought to be made so intolerable as to drive them to abandon their vices."[18]

While this draconian view is shocking, contemporary conservative politicians have taken a page out of Comstock's playbook. Recognizing that direct rhetorical attacks against LGBTQ people can be counterproductive because of generalized support for equal rights, conservative activists and politicians have resorted to raising hysteria about alleged dangers posed to children. The state of Florida, led by the Republican governor (and former presidential aspirant) Ron DeSantis, has been at the forefront of the fearmongering campaign, but it is a battle fought on many fronts. In 2022, Florida passed the Parental Rights in Education Act with overwhelming support in the state legislature. The law, dubbed by opponents as the "don't say gay bill," prohibits classroom discussion of sexual orientation or gender identity in kindergarten through grade 3 and in other classroom settings where the content may not be age appropriate. It has since been extended to apply to grades K–12. The vagueness of the proscription is more chilling than would be the case if specific forbidden topics of discussion were spelled out, as it leaves teachers fearful that they might violate the law by saying anything that might provoke accusations that they are corrupting the minds of young children. Indeed, DeSantis's press secretary, Christina Pushaw, tweeted in response to opponents of the bill that the law should have been called the "anti-grooming" bill.[19]

Generating fear about threats to children has, thus far, produced desired results for conservatives who are looking for a way to reinforce status boundaries at a time when society at large has become more accepting of equal rights for LGBTQ people. Homophobic framing spreads quickly through social media and provides fodder for right-wing news programming. Drag Story Hour events, for example, are intended to break down stereotypes and provide role models that allow children to become comfortable with gender fluidity rather than absorb the bigotry in society. Yet the events have come under attack (at times literally) from conservative politicians, conservative media, religious groups, and often hate groups such as the Proud Boys, who hurl accusations of grooming—suggesting that children are being prepared for sex by pedophiles.

Although public opinion has shifted substantially in favor of equal rights for LGBTQ people, it is clear that a substantial number of Americans feel strongly about preserving heteronormativity and cisnormativity in society. Progressive activist organizations have helped generate support for equal treatment.[20] Kinship ties can also undermine bigotry. LGBTQ people are distributed somewhat randomly across families. When LGBTQ people do come out, it can dispel misconceptions held by friends and loved ones, making them more likely to support equality. However, many Americans embrace heteronormativity and cisnormativity even over the health and well-being of family members and their own children.[21] What's more, growing support for

LGBTQ equality in society at large can lead beneficiaries of the status hierarchy to patrol boundaries based on sexual orientation and gender identity even more strictly.[22]

When considering how status hierarchies based on sexual orientation and gender identity structure politics, we once again are not approaching the issue in terms of any specific policy preferences. Instead, we see beneficiaries of the hierarchy incentivized to resist encroachment on group boundaries that undermine special treatment gained by displaying traditional gender roles and adhering to traditional norms. In party politics, the divide between the two major parties is relatively recent. Indeed, the Democratic presidents Bill Clinton and Barack Obama initially resisted marriage equality in the 1990s and into the 2000s. Yet over the last decade, the divide has become clear, with the Democratic Party strongly supporting LGBTQ causes while many Republican legislators have taken conservative positions, calculating that it will help them to maintain and acquire power in conservative states and districts or in a Republican presidential primary. Later in the chapter, we assess the extent to which this status hierarchy structures politics in a way that is similar to hierarchies based on race and gender. First, however, we consider how hierarchies based on citizenship can also structure politics.

BUILD THE WALL! IMMIGRATION AND STATUS

Klansmen believe that the time is at least near when American citizenship must be protected by restricting the franchise to men and women who are able through birth and education to understand Americanism: A restriction of franchise to

native-born children who have had the benefit of the train-
ing given by the American educational system, and who are
by breeding and education fundamentally equipped for the
responsibilities of citizenship and the right of the franchise, is
the thought that is entitled to careful consideration.

—*Imperial Night-Hawk* (national newspaper of the Ku Klux Klan),
December 19, 1923

I think this will be the last election that the Republicans have a
chance of winning because you're going to have people flowing
across the borders. You're going to have illegal immigrants com-
ing in, and they're going to be legalized, and they're going to be
able to vote. And once that all happens, you can forget it.

—Donald Trump, 2016

In a democracy, one person equals one vote. If you change the
population, you dilute the political power of the people who live
there. So every time they import a new voter, I'd become dis-
enfranchised as a current voter. So I don't understand. I mean,
everyone wants to make a racial issue out of it. "Oh, the White
replacement." No, no, no. This is a voting rights question.
I have less political power because they're importing a brand
new electorate. Why should I sit back and take that? The power
that I have as an American, guaranteed at birth, is one man,
one vote, and they're diluting it. No, they're not allowed to do
that. Why are we putting up with this?

—Former Fox News host Tucker Carlson, April 12, 2021

The quotations above represent variations of replacement theory,
an idea popularized in the United States by white supremacist
groups. It is rooted in centuries-old antisemitic tropes alleging

that Jews are plotting to destroy or dominate white Christian civilization. Here, we take note of the central role that citizenship plays in the racist and antisemitic narrative. The 1920s Klan writer, for example, speaks of protecting American citizenship, arguing that those born outside of the United States are not worthy or capable of assuming responsibilities that come with citizenship. Restricting the franchise to those who "understand Americanism" would ensure that power remains in the hands of those who, by birthright, are deemed to be deserving of special privileges. Suggesting conspiratorial intent, Donald Trump and Tucker Carlson accuse Democrats of deliberately allowing the country to be flooded with undeserving immigrants who would, as Carlson expresses it, dilute "the power that I have as an American, guaranteed at birth." As Trump campaigned for a second term as president in December 2023, he even began paraphrasing Adolf Hitler, claiming that immigrants in the United States were "poisoning the blood" of the country.[23]

In the preceding chapter, we noted the historical coupling of immigration and racism in the United States. Here, we focus on how citizenship can, itself, be the basis of a status hierarchy.[24] People define and construct citizenship boundaries and connect those boundaries to social esteem and privileges. They also grant differential privileges based on whether they define an immigrant as "legal" or "illegal" (undocumented). In the United States, undocumented immigrants live in constant fear of deportation, harsh treatment from law enforcement or border patrol agents, and abuse from employers, landlords, and others who find that they can exploit immigrants' legal vulnerabilities.[25]

Opposition to immigrants in the United States has ebbed and flowed historically. In debates about immigration, proponents often raise the point that we are a nation of immigrants. Except for Indigenous Americans as well as many Latinos, United

States citizens need not climb too far up the family tree before they reach ancestors who migrated to the United States from another land (or were taken here by force and enslaved). Opposition to immigrants has varied, to a great extent, depending on the immigrants' nation of origin. As we noted earlier, immigration laws passed in the 1920s overwhelmingly (and by design) favored immigration from Western Europe. In 1965, however, Congress passed the Immigration and Nationality Act, which opened the country to immigration from all over the world. The new bill prioritized acceptance of skilled immigrants but also opened a path to immigrants who had family members residing in the United States. Limits imposed on the number of documented immigrants taken in each year, however, have incentivized undocumented immigration across the southern border as families hope to escape violence and poverty by securing work in the United States.[26]

As Edna Bonacich points out, business owners historically have sought to encourage immigration to facilitate exploitation of labor and maximize profits—the larger the pool of vulnerable workers, the easier it is for employers to keep wages low and thwart worker unity. Employers have been malleable, however, jumping on anti-immigrant bandwagons when labor is not in short supply and when anti-immigrant sentiment gains traction in the political arena.[27] The Bracero Program that operated in the United States from 1942 to 1964 provides a telling example of how business interests have sought to obtain inexpensive exploitable labor while minimizing political backlash. The United States and Mexico established the program as a guest worker initiative. Initially justified as a means of addressing short-term agricultural labor shortages during World War II, workers (or Braceros) obtained legal permits to work on US farms, primarily in the southwest. The benefits of the program for American agribusiness, however, kept the program in place long past the end of the war. It provided agribusiness with a cheap source of labor—laborers who did not enjoy legal protection from employer abuse that would otherwise be granted to citizens. Importantly, business owners could simply import and export labor to meet their needs, relying on vulnerable and powerless men, women, and children to work the fields. The program left Braceros defenseless from health risks that came with working long hours in the hot sun, exposing themselves to dangerous pesticides in the process. What's more, the program undercut efforts to unionize and mobilize farm workers who were not part of the Bracero program.[28]

Scholars have noted that differential treatment of vulnerable immigrant labor can be a source of conflict between immigrants and native-born laborers because exploitation of immigrant labor often undercuts wages of native workers.[29] To counter this process, a central goal of the labor movement has been to "decommodify" workers. In other words, in a capitalist system, workers become commodities and must sell their labor power to survive. Decommodification occurs when labor market demand no longer determines workers' fates, and workers instead receive protection granted by a government that provides all citizens with at least minimal economic security, thus breaking their dependence on business owners in a capitalist economy.[30] Social Security is an example of transferring economic survival needs of the elderly to the state, rather than forcing their participation in the labor force. While immigrant workers in the United States pay social security taxes, they are not eligible to receive benefits if they are not citizens. Nations vary substantially in terms of how much support people receive as a right of citizenship. Those nations with more expansive citizen-based rights tend to have lower levels of income and wealth inequality.[31]

Notably, Nordic nations including Finland, Denmark, Iceland, Sweden, and Norway have expansive welfare states and consistently score at the top of surveys measuring general happiness in the population.[32]

Although the welfare state is underdeveloped in the United States and workers' fates are largely determined by their value in the labor market, citizenship nevertheless grants important rights that are denied to those without citizenship. These can manifest in access to government issued documents (such as passports) as well as to many government-run social programs. Citizenship is required to vote or run for a political office and to work in government jobs. Citizenship also grants people eligibility to work in any job for which they are qualified.

Differential status granted to citizens relative to immigrants can be important not only in terms of access to benefits and resources but also in terms of esteem or disrespect. Many people react negatively to what they perceive as "foreign values" or customs that undermine what they think of as "American values." Movements have organized, for example, to promote English as the official language in the country or in their state.[33] In the early 1900s and beyond, battles over temperance were largely fought along native-born and immigrant lines.[34] Although status hierarchies based on citizenship often overlap with those based on race and ethnicity, there is an added dimension that can energize racism when citizenship is also in the mix. Much of Trump's popularity with his core supporters during his first presidential campaigns and beyond is related to his denigration of immigrants. Not coincidentally, he was one of the most vocal "birthers" who attacked President Obama by calling his citizenship into question. When Trump launched his bid for the presidency, he famously characterized Mexican immigrants as rapists, criminals, and drug smugglers. At his rallies, his

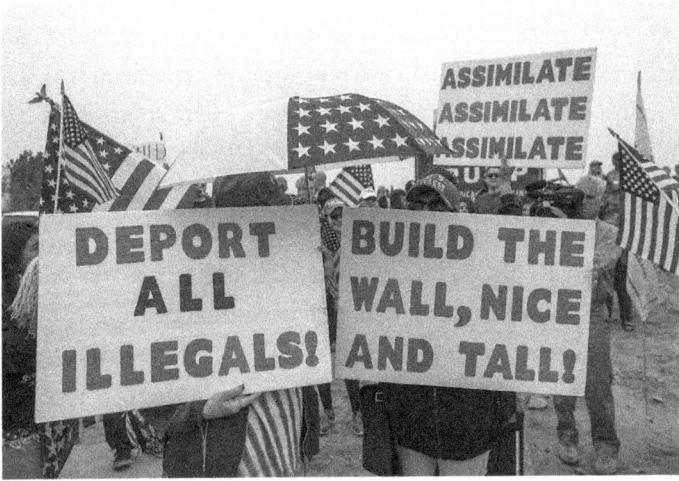

FIGURE 5.2 Anti-immigrant protesters in San Diego in advance of Donald Trump's arrival for a political rally, March 13, 2018. Getty Images.

supporters without fail vociferously chanted "build the wall," referring to Trump's promises to build a physical barrier along the nation's entire southern border (see figure 5.2). During his first term as president, Trump failed to construct his wall as he had planned. However, he continued to score points with many of his followers through displays of cruelty. The Trump administration is responsible for separating more than five thousand immigrant and refugee children from their families and, astoundingly, had no plan in place for eventually reuniting them. Even today, despite efforts of the Biden administration to right the wrong, hundreds of children remain separated from their families.[35]

Other Republicans jockeying for the limelight have also determined that cruelty to immigrant families represents a winning political strategy. In 2022, the Republican Texas governor

Gregg Abbott initiated a practice of busing migrants to northern cities, with no coordination with authorities in those cities. The busing was not an attempt to solve a problem. It was a political ploy to garner support from voters who approved of his inhumane actions. Not to be outdone, DeSantis got in on the game, flying migrants to destinations such as Martha's Vineyard or dumping them in the street in front of Vice President Kamala Harris's Washington, DC, residence to display his "get tough" approach to immigrants (many of whom entered the country legally seeking asylum in the United States). As the nation came out of the COVID-19 pandemic, a severe labor shortage was one factor contributing to sharp rises in inflation. Yet Republicans legislators refused to work with Democrats to craft legislation to find a solution for the flood of immigrants seeking entrance into the United States in hopes of securing employment. Republican legislators' actions instead reveal that citizenship represents a status boundary that many Americans wish to preserve. Inhumane treatment of immigrants reinforces that boundary and serves as a reminder of the material and status benefits that come with citizenship.[36] Before examining how this status hierarchy structures politics in the United States, we first consider a status hierarchy based on religion.

ONE AMERICA UNDER
(A CHRISTIAN) GOD

At a campaign rally in South Carolina on December 7, 2015, presidential candidate Donald Trump made headlines with the following announcement: "Donald J. Trump is calling for a total and complete shutdown of Muslims entering the United States until our country's representatives can figure out what the hell is going on."[37] Trump was speaking in the aftermath of a mass shooting that had taken place in San Bernardino, California, five days earlier. The shooters, Rizwan Farook and his wife, Tashfeen Malik, opened fire at a meeting of the San Bernardino County's Environmental Health Department, killing fourteen people and wounding twenty-two others. The Federal Department of Justice labeled it as a terrorist attack, but it appears that the two acted alone after having been radicalized by online content.[38]

Trump seized on the attack carried out by a Muslim couple to, once again, capitalize on anti-Muslim sentiment to attract political support. Just a few weeks previously on the campaign trail, he offered an unsupported and implausible claim that he had witnessed thousands of Muslims cheering and celebrating in New Jersey when terrorists attacked the World Trade Center on September 11, 2001. When elected, Trump quickly attempted to deliver on his promise to ban Muslims. He issued an executive order on January 27, 2017, that prohibited entry to the country from seven predominantly Muslim nations—an act that immediately created chaos at American airports because the executive order was issued while many people from the prohibited nations were airborne and on their way to the United States. Lawyers and advocacy organizations rushed to the airports to represent the travelers. Two days later, a federal judge granted a nationwide temporary injunction requested by the American Civil Liberties Union that blocked deportation of travelers stranded at American airports. After months of legal wrangling, the United States Supreme Court ultimately allowed Trump to implement a ban if it was not limited to nations that are predominantly Muslim and nonreligious criteria serve as justification. Six of the original Muslim nations remained on the list, but it was topped off by the addition of North Korea and bans on particular government officials from Venezuela.[39]

Core Republican voters (and beyond) cheered Trump's actions largely because of preexisting animus toward Muslims held by many Americans. When a group of Islamic terrorists brought down the World Trade Center in 2001, then president George W. Bush pointedly discouraged Americans from blaming all Muslims for the attack. While helpful, it was not enough to prevent a spike in hate crimes directed toward individuals perceived to be Muslim or to quell suspicions that many Americans hold regarding Islam and other religious faiths often perceived to be dangerous or "un-American."[40]

Deep Roots of the Christian-Led Status Hierarchy

When we speak of a religious status hierarchy in the United States, we are referring to the way in which adherents of Christian faiths enjoy higher levels of esteem in the population and often benefit from privileges denied members of other faiths. As we discussed in the previous chapter, Catholics once faced discrimination in the United States and native-born Protestants viewed them with suspicion. No presidents elected in the United States were Catholic until 1960, and John F. Kennedy's Catholic faith was a central controversy during his successful 1960 campaign. Kennedy had to overcome long-standing prejudice often expressed in terms of a belief that Catholics have divided loyalties and cannot simultaneously exhibit loyalty to the nation and loyalty to the pope. In the present day, however, it would be hard to make a case that Catholics face discrimination in the political arena or national governance. Former president Biden is Catholic, six of the nine Supreme Court justices are Catholic, and Catholics are well-represented in legislative branches of government at the federal and state levels. In contrast, a Muslim has never headed the executive branch in the United States or served on the Supreme Court. At the time of this writing, only three members of Congress are Muslims. When we think of religion in terms of status hierarchies, however, it is not simply a matter of underrepresentation or discrimination. In the United States, those holding the Islamic faith experience different treatment—fear, suspicion, disrespect, hatred, and violence (see figure 5.3). This low level of esteem for Muslims in the United States is consequential for Muslims in myriad ways.

The number of Americans identifying as Christian, or more generally as religious, has been declining sharply in the United States. Yet Americans remain generally comfortable with preferential treatment given to Christianity in the public square. Few object, for example, to children reciting the Pledge of Allegiance

FIGURE 5.3 A Trump supporter outside of the Republican National Convention in Cleveland, July 2016. Getty Images.

in public school, a pledge intended to be a commitment to service to "one nation, under God." Similarly, workers and schoolchildren typically receive time off for Christian holidays such as Christmas or Easter but not for holy days observed by members of other faiths. A recent poll from the Pew Research Center indicates that 60 percent of respondents believe that the founding fathers intended for the United States to be a Christian nation and 45 percent indicated that it *should* be a Christian nation. The same poll, however, showed that respondents generally favor a separation of church and state and would prefer it if churches and religious institutions stayed out of politics.[41] Yet Christianity serves as the default when it comes to thinking about the role of religion in public life, and the decline of religiosity in the United States seems to have radicalized a segment of the Christian population that seeks to blur boundaries between Christianity and government and has reinvigorated religious extreme biases, including antisemitism.[42]

A long history of antisemitism throughout the world incomparably highlights the danger of status hierarchies based on religion. A force that fueled the rise of a brutal dictator who put in motion the unimaginable horror of the Holocaust demands resistance whenever it surfaces. Antisemitism indeed has resurfaced in force in the United States and has even found entry into mainstream politics. The resurgence of antisemitism has been aided by the growth of social media and perhaps especially the growth of the "dark web" and imageboard sites like 4chan that allow people to post anonymously in an uncensored space.[43] Yet antisemitism spills beyond the borders of these shady spaces, even finding expression in Congress and in the White House during Trump's first term in office. The Republican representatives Paul Gosar and Marjorie Taylor Greene, for example, have expressed antisemitism in public statements and on social media and have even attended meetings headlined by well-known white supremacist and neo-Nazi figures. In August 2017, thousands of white supremacists marched in Charlottesville, Virginia, with many wearing or displaying Nazi symbols and chanting slogans such as "Jews will not replace us." The Nazi supporter James Fields Jr. killed a counterprotester at the rally when he drove his car into a crowd at high speed. Trump was roundly criticized when he initially spoke of good people "on both sides," equating neo-Nazis with those who stood up against them. Later, Trump attracted attention when he hosted the neo-Nazi Nick Fuentes and the antisemitic musician Ye (formerly Kanye West) for dinner at his home in Florida. Trump's political rallies attract many supporters who openly display antisemitic, pro-Nazi, and racist sentiments on signs, -T-shirts, and bumper stickers.

Trump's presidency, his overtly racist and sexist statements and tweets, and his tacit support for white supremacy, neo-Nazis, and purveyors of conspiracy theories such as QAnon have undoubtedly emboldened individuals and groups on the extreme right. In October 2018, Robert Bowers opened fire in the Tree of Life synagogue, just outside of Pittsburgh, killing eleven worshipers. Police later discovered that Bowers had been spewing antisemitic slurs on the social media platform Gab before the killings. Among these slurs was a reference to elite Jews organizing migrant caravans traveling toward the United States border from Central America—an issue that Trump had been using in his own fearmongering rhetoric.[44] A couple of years later, after Trump lost his bid for reelection, insurrectionists who stormed the capital building on January 6, 2021, were populated with a large smattering of white supremacist and neo-Nazi groups and individuals.

We also note that hate crimes directed toward both Jewish and Muslim Americans spiked sharply in the aftermath of an attack on Israeli civilians on October 7, 2023, by Hamas terrorists. Israel responded with a massive military assault that resulted in the deaths of an astounding number of civilians, while also destroying countless buildings and forcing Palestinians in Gaza to abandon what was left of their homes, while promoting a humanitarian crisis as food and other supplies entering Gaza fell far short of what was needed to meet even the most basic subsistence needs.[45] These events took place after we collected our data and therefore are not reflected in the results that we present. Yet the violence and hatred directed toward Jews and Muslims strongly reflects long-standing biases against non-Christians in the United States.

Again, our approach in this study is not to focus on particular policies that voters might favor as they pertain to religion. Instead, we argue that people consider the extent to which political parties signal support or opposition to maintaining a status hierarchy. Tight coupling of religious bigotry and Republican politics is a relatively recent development—both major parties once shared it. The link between conservative Christianity and the Republican Party began to take root during Ronald Reagan's presidency and as abortion became a hotly contested issue in the 1980s. Conservative Christian leaders such as Jerry Falwell and Pat Robertson mobilized their followers into politics, and the Christian right provided Republicans with a dependable source of support from voters who responded positively to courting by Reagan and other Republicans.[46] Emboldened by the Trump presidency, we have more recently seen a rise in white Christian nationalism. White Christian nationalists are committed to the idea that the nation should be controlled by white Christians and they are called upon to take the nation back from their perceived enemies.[47]

Although the rise of white Christian nationalism might be viewed as a sign of strength for the Christian right, recent trends suggest that it is more of a response to the declining influence of Christianity in the nation. Data from the Public Religion Research Institute indicate that the percentage of white Americans identifying as evangelical Protestant has declined from 23 percent of the total population in 1986 to 14.6 percent in 2021. At the same time, the percentage of white Americans who identify as religiously unaffiliated has risen from 16 percent of the total population in 1986 to 25.1 percent in 2021.[48] Given these trends, the religious status hierarchy should be more difficult to maintain in the years ahead, but the shifting trends provide conservative Christians with a strong incentive to try to secure the boundaries at this historical moment.[49]

EFFECTS OF LGBTQ, IMMIGRATION, AND RELIGION STATUS GOALS

In the last chapter, we used an experimental research design to capture support and opposition pertaining to status hierarchies based on race and gender. We showed that support for One America for Working People differed substantially when we added a short paragraph that condemns discrimination and violence motivated by race and gender and argues that fighting racism and sexism is necessary to form an alliance to combat economic inequality. We found that Republicans were less supportive than Independents and especially less supportive than Democrats, with the differences being much larger among participants who viewed web pages addressing race and gender equality. Importantly, we found that the increased gap between Democrats and Republicans when evaluating web pages committed to racial and gender equality reflected the way that the organization's equality goals became more attractive to

Democrats (compared to the economics only version) and less attractive to Republicans. This suggests that much of today's polarization between the two major parties revolves around efforts to either defend or dismantle status hierarchies.

We now return to our experimental findings to see if our study participants responded similarly when exposed to web pages that pledge to dismantle the status hierarchies described in this chapter based on sexual orientation and gender identity, immigration, and religion. Our findings presented in this section come from the same data analysis used in the last chapter, but here we focus on results pertaining to the other status hierarchies. In figure 5.4, we reproduce the key section of the web page as a reminder of the experimental manipulations that we made. Recall that everything else on the different versions of the web pages is identical.

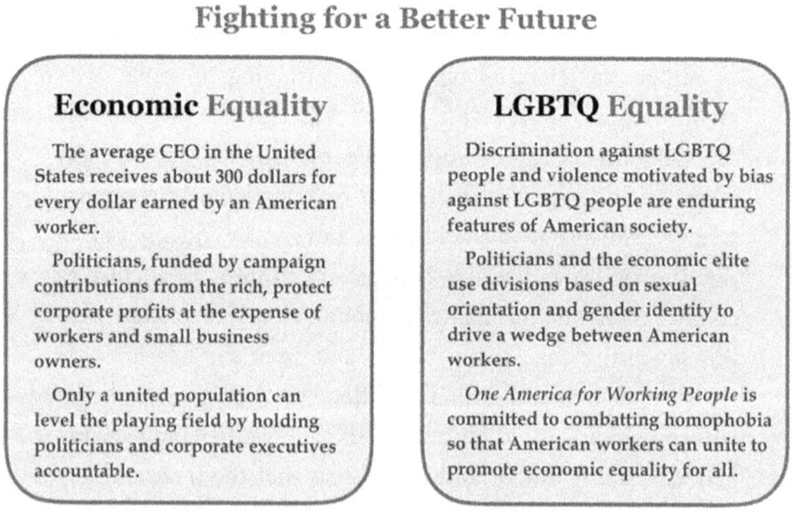

Fighting for a Better Future

Economic Equality

The average CEO in the United States receives about 300 dollars for every dollar earned by an American worker.

Politicians, funded by campaign contributions from the rich, protect corporate profits at the expense of workers and small business owners.

Only a united population can level the playing field by holding politicians and corporate executives accountable.

LGBTQ Equality

Discrimination against LGBTQ people and violence motivated by bias against LGBTQ people are enduring features of American society.

Politicians and the economic elite use divisions based on sexual orientation and gender identity to drive a wedge between American workers.

One America for Working People is committed to combatting homophobia so that American workers can unite to promote economic equality for all.

FIGURE 5.4 Experimental manipulations pertaining to LGBTQ, immigrant, and religious equality

As the figure shows, we took care to follow the same format when introducing the content related to the different status hierarchies. The first sentence establishes that discrimination and violence are enduring features of American society. The second asserts that politicians and the economic elite use the particular form of status inequality to divide workers. The third sentence commits the organization to fighting the particular form of status inequality so that all workers can unite to promote economic equality for all. As before, we start by examining responses to a question about respondents' level of support for goals specified under the heading "Fighting for a Better Future." Recall that the response categories were 1) strongly oppose; 2) somewhat oppose; 3) neutral; 4) somewhat support; and 5) strongly support.

The results we present in figure 5.5 indicate that we would be missing quite a bit if we did not also consider the roles of status hierarchies based on sexual orientation and gender identity, citizenship, and religion. Indeed, the results we present here are strikingly similar to those that we presented in the last chapter when we considered status hierarchies based on race and gender. We should note that since we are reporting results from the same analysis that we used in the last chapter, the graph simply reproduces the results pertaining to those who viewed the economics only version of the web page. We are using that version as the basis of comparison, to see how reactions to the web page are different when comparing the economics only version to a version in which the organization commits to dismantling a particular status hierarchy. So, what happens when we make those comparisons? We can see clearly that Independents and especially Democrats are much more supportive than Republicans if they were in a treatment group in which they evaluated a web page that includes the commitment to fight for LGBTQ equality, immigrant equality, or religious equality. As we saw in

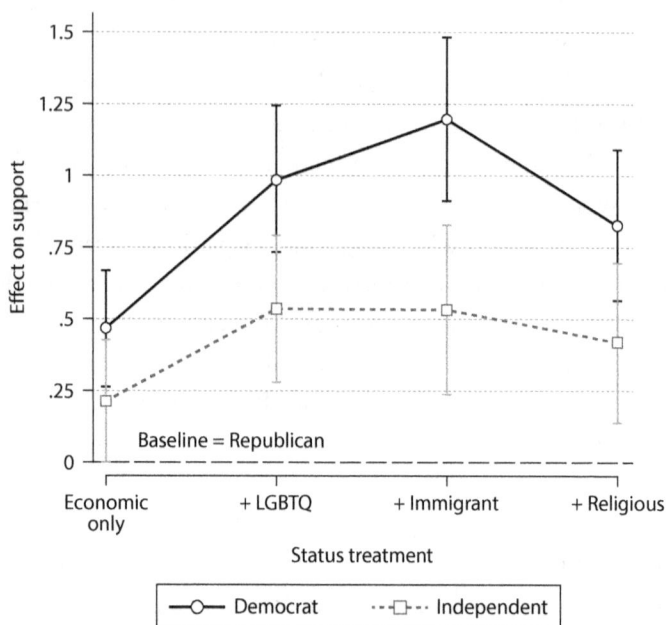

FIGURE 5.5 Support of Fighting for a Better Future content: class, LGBTQ, immigrant, and religious equality

the last chapter, the gap between Republicans and Independents and the gap between Republicans and Democrats results from Independents and Democrats finding the organization's equality goals to be more attractive when it addresses status inequalities and Republicans finding it less attractive.

To be more specific, the results indicate that among those who viewed the page committed to fighting LGBTQ equality, Democrats on average were a full point more supportive than Republicans. The gap between Democrats and Republicans is particularly large among those who viewed the immigrant equality version (almost a 1.25-point difference). The gap is somewhat more modest when we consider the religious equality version (just over .75 points). In each comparison, the differences are statistically significant. Although the Independents were not as supportive as the Democrats, it is nevertheless noteworthy that the average difference between Independents and Republicans is also statistically significant among those who viewed pages addressing LGBTQ equality, immigrant equality, and religious equality. In each case, Independents were approximately a half point more supportive than Republicans. We also see that the average difference between Democrats and Republicans is significantly higher when respondents viewed the LGBTQ and immigrant versions of the web page, in comparison to those who viewed the economics only version.

Next, we consider people's willingness to take action to support the organization. Recall that this represents an index made by adding the scores in response to a question about participants' willingness to volunteer for One America for Working People and their response to a question about willingness to oppose it. The higher the score, the more willing the participant is to act in support of the organization. Our results are presented in figure 5.6.

When examining willingness to act, we see a now-familiar pattern. The difference between Democrats and Republicans is statistically significant for all four treatment groups and the gap between Republicans and Democrats is significantly larger when considering their responses to versions of the web page addressing LGBTQ equality, immigrant equality, and religious equality compared to economic equality only. Independents, as we pointed out previously, are not significantly different from Republicans when considering the economics only treatment group. However, Independents on average are significantly more supportive than Republicans when viewing the LGBTQ, immigrant, and religions equality versions.

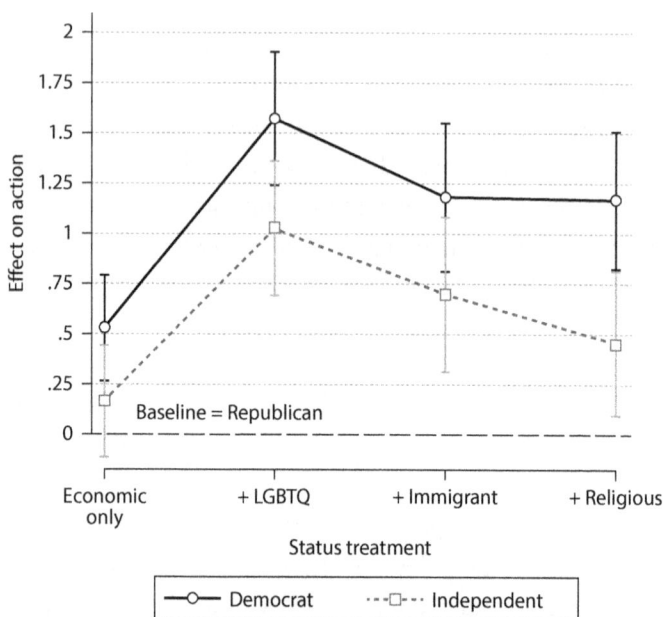

FIGURE 5.6 Willingness to act in support of One America for Working People: class, LGBTQ, immigrant, and religious equality

CONCLUSION

In the last two chapters, we examined one path of the theoretical model that we presented in chapter 2. As part of a broader argument about durable economic inequality in the United States, we argued that one key factor to consider is the extent to which peoples' perceived threats to status privileges reduce their support for a progressive alliance that would fight to reduce economic inequality. There are a number of ways to test such an argument. We could have, for example, conducted a survey and directly asked people if they feel that their status privileges are being threatened. The obvious problem with that approach is

that most people would not acknowledge that they are beneficiaries of status privilege, or they would be unaware of the many
ways in which they are beneficiaries. Another approach, which
is common in the social sciences, is to examine correlations
between attributes of people and their support for a coalition and
draw tentative conclusions from those correlations. For example,
we might expect that white respondents would show less support
for an organization designed to fight both economic inequality and racial inequality. Or, men would be less supportive of an
organization that pledges to combat economic inequality and
gender inequality. The problem with that approach is that many
people do not think in ways that correspond with the presumptions social scientists might make based upon their categorical
attributes. In our sample, for example, many white men actually
supported One America for Working People, even if they viewed
versions of the web page that commit to fighting race and gender
inequality. Not all white men, in other words, approve of discrimination and violence even if they benefit from favored treatment in society. At the same time, not all women or people of
color were supportive of the organization even though support
correlates positively with those individual traits.

We opt for a different approach by using an experiment to
directly observe the extent to which an organization's commitment to challenging a status hierarchy reduces support for the
organization. The web pages people observed were identical in
every way. The only difference appears in one section of the web
page in which the content pledges commitment to combatting
discrimination and violence directed toward one of the following: racial and ethnic minorities, women, LGBTQ people, immigrants, and adherents of non-Christian religious faiths. When
we examined the data, we found that simply opposing discrimination and violence made the organization more attractive to

Democrats and less attractive to Republicans. Those who identify as Independents were, on average, more supportive of the organization than Republicans and less so compared to Democrats. In a sense, then, our findings reveal processes underlying political polarization—different responses to status hierarchies push Republicans and Democrats in different directions. We will give more consideration to political polarization in the next chapter.

In this chapter, we argued that (as was true with race and gender) instead of thinking in terms of issues or policies related to sexual orientation and gender identity, immigration, and religion, we should think of status hierarchies that exist in American society and how Americans are motivated to resist challenges to those hierarchies or, on the other hand, to overturn them. This approach allows us to see that although race and gender hierarchies are important, hierarchies based on LGBTQ, immigrant, and religious status play a similar role in affecting the way that people respond to One American for Working People. Our approach to analyzing political mobilization suggests that the main barrier to a progressive political coalition does not reside in any particular set of attributes that people share or any particular public policies that people may support or oppose. The problem is more fundamental. Our results indicate that a sizable subset of the American population is not motivated to reduce status-based inequalities, limiting the number of Americans willing to be drawn into a progressive coalition even if that means that they align themselves with a political party that does nothing to address their economic needs.

6

STATUS CONTESTATION AND
POLITICAL POLARIZATION

I n chapters 4 and 5, we examined the link that our theory specifies between status contestation and support for a progressive
political alliance. As we might expect, given the Democratic
Party's historical support for working-class demands, Democrats in our sample are more supportive of One America than
are Republicans among those study participants who viewed the
economics only version of the web page. Importantly, however,
the gap between Democrats and Republicans is about twice
as large when the web page commits to fighting for economic
equality *and* some form of status equality (as opposed to only
focusing on economic equality). Our theoretical argument also
specifies that status contestation affects policy preference consolidation, or political polarization. While the preceding chapters
illustrate the way that status equality goals divide Republicans
and Democrats, in this chapter we delve more deeply into the
divide by examining polarization of policy preferences.

When thinking about polarization we should keep in mind
that many Americans pay little attention to most public policies. Without signifiers—cues to voters about who is initiat-
ing a particular position on a policy—they often have difficulty
articulating their own position.[1] In other words, many voters do

not consistently support positions taken by just one of the political parties unless they are first able to interpret those polices as being favorable or unfavorable to their "political team."[2] So, what drives the polarization that at present appears to be so glaring in political discourse and legislative processes? To address this question, we consider how people's approval or disapproval of our One America coalition is related to the consistency with which study participants prefer either the liberal or conservative stances on a range of policy issues. Gerrymandered legislative districts have made politicians unusually attentive to voters who align themselves against positions taken by opposing parties—those who show little interest in finding common ground for bipartisan legislation. Before examining our data, we discuss how the voters at the ideological extremes in both political parties became so important in driving the legislative process.

CAN'T WE ALL JUST GET ALONG?

On January 20, 2009, Barack Obama became the first Black president in United States history. For many, his election was a cause for celebration. Just a couple of months before, on the evening after Obama's November electoral victory, nearly a quarter million supporters packed into Grant Park, in Obama's home city of Chicago, to share in the historic moment and to hear from the newly elected president. More than seventy-one million others watched on television.[3] Obama's speech was a call for unity. His election, he proclaimed, was an answer to all of those who doubted the dreams of the founding fathers and the power of American democracy. Obama went on, "It's the answer spoken by young and old, rich and poor, Democrat and Republican, black, white, Latino, Asian, Native American, gay, straight, disabled and not disabled—Americans who sent a message to the world that we have never been a collection of red states and blue states; we are, and always will be, the United States of America."[4]

Before Obama's celebration in Grant Park, John McCain delivered a gracious concession speech in Phoenix, acknowledging the historical significance of Obama's victory. After quelling initial boos among his supporters in response to his conciliatory words, McCain pushed forward: "I urge all Americans who supported me to join me in not just congratulating him, but offering our next president our goodwill and earnest effort to find ways to come together, to find the necessary compromises, to bridge our differences and help restore our prosperity, defend our security in a dangerous world, and leave our children and grandchildren a stronger, better country than we inherited.[5] This goodwill and spirit of unity was short-lived. Indeed, neither Obama's nor McCain's words matched the underlying reality. Our politics had become polarized. Democratic and Republican elected officials saw the world in sharply different ways and could find few important issues on which they chose to form common ground.

To make matters worse, Obama inherited a mess when he assumed the presidency. A recession that began in December 2007 intensified in the fall of 2008, leading into the election. It was both the steepest and the longest recession the nation had experienced since the Great Depression. Unemployment rose from 5 percent to 10 percent. The recession was particularly notable in that a housing price bubble had been building, driven in large part by lenders pushing subprime mortgages on consumers—high-interest-rate mortgages given to borrowers considered to be credit risks. When the bubble burst, loan defaults soared, the average value of houses plummeted, and many of the nation's banks teetered on the brink of insolvency.[6]

As Obama began to take action to address the crisis, conservatives quickly mounted a campaign of resistance. Despite the collapsing economy, conservatives, backed by right-wing think tanks and right-wing media, organized a Tea Party movement dedicated primarily to aggressive advocacy on behalf of limited government spending and reduced taxes.[7] No economists worth their salt, of course, would recommend restricting government spending as a remedy for a severe recession. Elite conservatives were clearly less concerned with the strength of the national economy than they were with fears that the new Democratic president would respond to the crisis in ways that redistributed wealth to their personal detriment. The faux populism of the Tea Party symbolism helped to attract grassroots support from many middle- and working-class (overwhelmingly white) Americans who also feared that the new Black president would salvage the economy by directing more money to those who were in more desperate need.[8]

Tea Party protests began to appear across the nation and picked up steam as the Democrats introduced legislation that would ultimately become the Affordable Care Act, or Obamacare—legislation intended to address significant shortfalls in health care coverage for millions of Americans.[9] As Democratic legislators returned to their districts in the summer and fall of 2009 to promote the plan in town hall meetings, they were frequently met by angry, vociferous conservative protesters (see figure 6.1). Republican lawmakers and conservative media spread disinformation about Obamacare, adding fuel to the fire. Perhaps most famously, they embraced a term used frequently by McCain's running mate, Sarah Palin, who insisted that Obamacare legislation contained "death panels" made up of bureaucrats who would determine patients' eligibility for life-saving care. Eventually, Obama signed the legislation into law

PHOTO 6.1 Opponents of Obamacare protesting outside of the Supreme Court, June 28, 2012. The court ruled that Obamacare is constitutional but prevented the federal government from requiring states to expand Medicaid. Getty Images.

in March 2010. To pass the bill, Democratic legislators had to push it through a budget reconciliation process to avoid a certain Republican filibuster in the Senate.

Polling from the Kaiser Foundation shows that rhetorical attacks on Obamacare were effective. When the bill passed, only 46 percent of Americans had a favorable view of the legislation, and its popularity declined even further in the years ahead. Indeed, by July 2014 only 37 percent of Americans approved of Obamacare and 53 percent had an unfavorable opinion. It was not until much later, after several failed Republican attempts to repeal the legislation, that public opinion began to shift. Oddly, Republicans vowed to repeal and replace Obamacare but never offered a realistic replacement. Republican failures, as well as sharp enrollment increases in Obamacare, likely contributed to its growing support. Data show that by October 2021, 58 percent of those surveyed had a favorable view of Obamacare and only 41 percent had an unfavorable view.[10] Notably, however, even as Obamacare has become generally popular, public opinion is deeply divided along partisan lines. It is currently highly popular among Democrats while the vast majority of Republicans continue to oppose it. For example, a Pew poll conducted in late 2017 indicated that 64 percent of Republicans believed that Obamacare has had mostly a negative effect on the nation while 67 percent of Democrats said it has had a mostly positive effect.[11]

The Rise of the Freedom Caucus

Although leaders of the Tea Party initially tried to present the movement as being only concerned with promoting conservative fiscal policy, it nevertheless became apparent that supporters tended to hold racist views and conservative positions on a host of other issues.[12] This broad support for a conservative response to Obama's agenda came together at the ballot box in the 2010 midterm elections. Limited public support for Obamacare, combined with generally low approval of the Obama presidency at that time, set the stage for a Republican rout. Republicans gained seven seats in the Senate, eliminating the Democrats' substantial advantage in that body. Even more impressively, Republicans assumed control of the House of Representatives, gaining a whopping sixty-three seats. Republicans gained six state governors' seats and flipped control of twenty state legislatures.[13] Republicans capitalized on these state-level victories to gerrymander congressional districts in ways that minimized Democratic candidates' chances of winning future races in those states. Wherever possible, they placed Republican lawmakers in increasingly safe districts while diluting Democratic strength by redrawing district lines to add conservative rural communities into previously competitive districts. This extreme manipulation incentivized Republican officeholders and candidates to appeal to the most conservative voters in their districts to secure victories in primary campaigns, knowing that it protects them in a general election against a Democratic candidate.[14]

Only two years after Obama's historic victory—when he assumed the presidency with Democratic control of both the Senate and the House—the president faced a wall of new Republicans in the House who were energized and prepared to block all Democratic initiatives. Dozens of newly elected Republicans formed a Tea Party Caucus in the House that was united behind all conservative causes, not limiting itself to fiscal policies. Eventually, the caucus ran its course, but a Freedom Caucus emerged in its wake in early 2015. The caucus represents a relatively small, cohesive group of House Republicans who are particularly vocal, pressing an extreme conservative agenda that focuses more on ginning up anger and resentment toward progressive causes than enacting any legislation. For example, when House Democrats passed the Respect for Marriage Act in 2022, to protect marriage equality through legislation rather than relying solely on the Supreme Court's 2015 ruling, the Freedom Caucus issued a statement in opposition. The "radical left," according to the statement, "has launched an all-out campaign on America's traditional values and sacred institutions. It has weakened the nuclear family, attacked the norms of masculinity and femininity, and now it wants to further erode the sacred institution of marriage."[15]

Freedom Caucus members have led the charge on behalf of other extremist causes such as efforts to ban critical race theory from classrooms—a disingenuous appeal because critical race theory was not being taught in K–12 classrooms. In practice, Republicans aim to restrict any teaching that references racial inequality in the United States.[16] Meanwhile, Freedom Caucus members strongly promote efforts to remove protections, or enact new restrictions, on the rights of transgender people and of LGBTQ people more generally.[17] It would be a mistake, however, to overemphasize the role of the Freedom Caucus. Safe congressional districts and incentives to appeal to the most conservative Republican voters have radicalized almost all Republican legislators—particularly in the House of Representatives. Indeed, Republican lawmakers unite in opposition to progressive economic and social policies and against almost anything that Democratic lawmakers propose, even in cases where their positions run counter to preferences of most Republican voters.[18] Republicans politicians have more to lose, politically, by angering conservative base supporters than they do by alienating moderate or liberal voters. Strong loyalty toward Donald Trump among Republican base voters has made it particularly perilous for Republican legislators to appeal to more moderate voters.

Polarized Citizens or Polarized Politics?

Political parties are in the business of building coalitions and persuading their supporters that there actually is consistency across political positions on issues that might otherwise appear to be unrelated.[19] If Republican candidates attract some voters based on their opposition to abortion, for example, those candidates can strengthen voters' commitment to the party and solidify their hold on power if they can persuade the same voters that their position on abortion aligns with other positions promoted by the party. In a now-classic 1960 book titled *The American Voter*, the political scientist Angus Campbell and several colleagues argued that political party identity shapes the ways that voters interpret policy issues, which produces consistency among voters in their preferences—an alignment with the full range of positions taken by their party.[20] That characterization is consistent with more recent research that seeks to explain "affective polarization"—or the tendency for voters to be driven more by their animosity toward candidates and supporters of an opposing party, rather than their well-thought-out positions on a range of public policies.[21] Political parties, in other words, seek to promote a shared identity among supporters that situates them in strong opposition to supporters of other parties.

Recent research on polarization has raised an important set of questions. Are Americans' opinions on important issues moving farther apart? Or does it merely appear that way because people's opinions on issues are better aligned with the positions of the two major parties? Although some evidence suggests that, at present, Americans are moving into separate camps on some issues, most research indicates that tighter alignment between peoples' attitudes and party affiliations is the primary driver.[22] Doug McAdam and Karina Kloos have argued that much of the current state of political polarization resulted from the way that a number of progressive and conservative social movements pressed their claims on political parties, with the competing agendas ultimately refining and redefining party agendas to accommodate movement demands.[23] Consistent with this argument, scholars have proposed that the political polarization we see today largely results from political parties and their supporters more effectively sorting different policy positions along ideological lines.[24] For example, over the past thirty years, acceptance of equal rights for LGBTQ people has increased substantially in the general population, meaning that Americans are becoming less polarized on that issue.[25] However, proponents and opponents of LGBTQ equality now divide neatly into opposing parties in ways that highlight the sharp differences between progressives and conservatives.[26] Republicans can promote policies that limit freedom and jeopardize safety for LGBTQ people because they know that these appeals to bigotry can energize their core supporters.

In previous chapters of this book, we argued that political parties send strong signals indicating whether they side with those who wish to dismantle particular status hierarchies or those who wish to preserve them. We propose that it is these signals, more so than any particular policy goals or animus for particular groups aligned with the other party, that forge strong attachments to a political party. Again, we emphasize the value that many people place on preserving the preferential treatment that they receive by virtue of their positions in status hierarchies. This motivates a broader swath of voters than does individualized traditional expressions of bigotry. Voters' desires to preserve or overturn status hierarchies, in turn, structure the way that people interpret issues and policy proposals. We think this is true for a couple of reasons. First, those who are the most invested in preserving or overturning status hierarchies should have the strongest commitment to the overall strength of the party that is on their side in status conflicts. If a man enjoys status based on his gender identity and wants to preserve that status, he has a stake in the Republican Party's capacity to appeal to a unified block of voters and win elections. That same man comes to understand that the opposing party is committed to overturning gendered status hierarchies from which he benefits. Second, and perhaps just as importantly, if a party's "base" voters demonstrate both intense commitment to issues and unity across a range of issues, party leaders and candidates have an incentive to pay attention to them and send even stronger signals about efforts to either preserve or dismantle status hierarchies. Indeed, as recent political campaigns in the United States illustrate, political parties can attract strong support even when candidates do not discuss specific policies they favor. At the 2020 Republican National Convention, the Republicans took the unusual step of neglecting to draft a party platform. In a sense, it was unnecessary. Republican Party leaders can speak in broad terms, signaling commitment to preserving status hierarchies—for example, using vague terms like "wokeness" to condemn any effort to challenge status privilege boundaries pertaining to race, gender, sexual orientation, gender identity, immigration, religion, or any other salient status hierarchy.

VISUALIZING POLITICAL POLARIZATION AND STATUS CONTESTATION

We began this chapter by describing key contextual factors that characterize political polarization in the United States today. We argued that the issue sorting that characterizes the chasm between the two major parties in the United States was possible and even likely because of the way in which voters prioritize status when thinking about political issues. We proposed that status contestation is the key mechanism that aligns policy preferences with political parties. Those most committed to preserving or overturning status hierarchies have a strong incentive to form a united block within one of the major political parties and to resist compromise with the other side.

In the remainder of this chapter, we use our data to explore the relationship between status goals and political polarization. We make use of our respondents' answers to the question we asked about the content under the web page heading "Fighting for a Better Future." Recall that this is the part of the web page where we experimentally manipulated the content to see how people respond when we paired a call for addressing economic inequality with a commitment to fighting various forms of status inequality. Support and opposition to our fictious One America coalition's goals, we expect, form the progressive and conservative polarized "wings" of the two major parties.

After our study participants completed the experimental component of our survey, they answered a series of questions about their preferences on a range of policy issues. We loosely modeled the questions on those used in the American National Election Study. We examine the distribution of voter preferences across these issues to assess the extent to which these preferences consolidate—or hang together—in terms of consistent preference for a conservative or progressive position.

Table 6.1 shows that there are clear differences in opinion on the policy issues depending on the respondents' party affiliation. For simplicity's sake, in this table we only include the percentage of respondents indicating that they "strongly agree" with the statement about policy. It is worth keeping in mind that when it comes to public policy, the details really matter. Many Americans, regardless of political party affiliation, are likely to offer at least some level of agreement with general claims about the need for government to take action related to a particular problem or issue of concern. Nevertheless, the table shows clear differences among those who identify with different parties.

It is notable, first, that Democrats in our sample are particularly supportive of government action to provide some economic help to families or individuals through childcare, health care, and provision of a living wage. Even among Republicans, approximately 30 percent of respondents are strongly supportive,

TABLE 6.1 PERCENTAGE OF RESPONDENTS WHO STRONGLY AGREE WITH VARIOUS POLICY ISSUES BY POLITICAL PARTY AFFILIATION

Policy issue	Republican (n=764)	Democrat (n=990)	Independent (n=610)	Other (n=47)
Government should do more to make childcare affordable	25.9	61.8	39.3	53.5
Government should do more to make quality health care affordable to all Americans	31.8	77.0	53.6	64.0
Government should do more to assure that all Americans receive a living wage	29.5	69.9	44.4	59.2
The legal system and police departments should do more to hold police officers accountable when they kill unarmed civilians who do not pose a threat	25.2	70.9	48.9	52.8
Law enforcement agents and legal systems should do more to enforce and prosecute hate crimes	30.8	64.7	43.4	45.9
Government should invest more funds in local law enforcement to keep communities safe	56.9	39.0	37.7	33.9
Government should invest more funds to strengthen the military to protect American interests	51.3	20.7	25.1	21.6
Congress should enact laws to place strict limits on money people or corporations can donate to political campaigns	40.0	56.8	52.5	43.6

(continued)

TABLE 6.1 (*continued*)

Policy issue	Republican (n=764)	Democrat (n=990)	Independent (n=610)	Other (n=47)
More restrictions should be placed on access to abortion	38.0	8.0	14.3	16.4
Government should devote more resources to prevent immigrants from illegally crossing the southern border	71.4	17.8	37.1	25.7
Congress should enact laws that make it harder for people to obtain firearms	11.2	56.5	27.1	26.7
The federal government should be required to have a balanced budget every year	54.3	30.4	44.5	44.0
Employers and legal authorities should do more to stop sexual harassment in the workplace	39.0	65.7	52.6	52.5
Government should take stronger action to enforce affirmative action laws to address unfair hiring practices	14.3	44.0	24.1	33.2
Storeowners and employees should be allowed to deny service to gay or lesbian people if providing service to them conflicts with their religious beliefs	28.6	7.3	11.6	9.7
Government should do more to require businesses to reduce their production of greenhouse emissions linked to climate change	12.5	54.9	29.3	31.7

yet that percentage is much lower when compared to the Democrats. When considering these issues, and most of the other issues, respondents who identify as Independent fall somewhere between Democrats and Republicans. The fourth column includes respondents who indicate that they identify as something other than Republican, Democratic, or Independent, as well as those (8.4 percent of all respondents) who said that they do not affiliate with any party.

Democrats in our sample also show substantial support for stricter enforcement of hate crime laws, stopping sexual harassment, election reform, holding police accountable for killing unarmed civilians, and limiting greenhouse emissions. As would be expected, Democrats show little support for discriminating against gay or lesbian people based on religious beliefs, spending more money on the military, cracking down on illegal immigration, or placing more restrictions on abortion. On all issues, Democrats were more likely than Republicans to be strongly supportive of what are viewed as the more progressive or liberal stances and less supportive of conservative stances.

These differences in positions by political party should be expected. However, it is not yet clear as to whether our survey respondents display political polarization. That would involve Republicans and Democrats consistently holding conservative and liberal positions across the range of issues under consideration and rarely holding positions that tend to be favored by the opposing party. For our analysis, we want to account for not only the support or opposition to policy related goals but also the intensity of their support or opposition. Our respondents expressed their opinions by selecting one of the following choices for each issue: 1) strongly disagree; 2) somewhat disagree; 3) neutral; 4) somewhat agree; and 5) strongly agree. We constructed a simple index that captures this level of intensity about particular issues but also the consistency with which respondents sided with the liberal or conservative positions on the various issues. For each respondent we added up their responses (1 through 5 as described above) for each of the sixteen policy issues under consideration. If, for example, someone strongly disagrees with the liberal position on all sixteen issues, they receive a score of 16 (16 × 1), or one point for each issue. On the other hand, if someone strongly agrees with the liberal position on all issues, their score is 80 (16 × 5), or 5 points for each issue. The vast majority of our respondents fall somewhere in between. Importantly, in constructing the index we reverse-coded responses to some of the questions to ensure that a higher score indicates the respondent favors a more liberal position.

Figure 6.2 shows the distribution of our policy preference index. On the x-axis, the value of zero represents the mean value of the policy index score (51.7). Values of 1 and –1 indicate

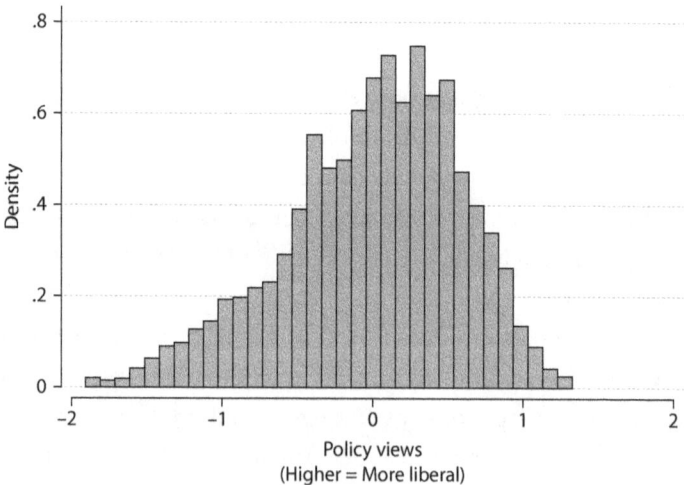

FIGURE 6.2 Distribution of scores on public policy index

respondents are one standard deviation above (61.7) or below (41.7) that mean value. A value of –2 means they are two standard deviations below the mean (31.7). The graph should offer some comfort to those who worry about Americans being hopelessly far apart in terms of their preferences on policy issues. Notably, most of our respondents fall in the middle—or just to the "liberal side" of the middle—reflecting the way in which most of our study participants agree with the liberal position on some issues and the conservative position on other issues, and many also do not feel intensely about the issues. Importantly, this distribution does *not* indicate that the respondents in our sample are polarized. Polarization would be represented in a graph showing large proportions of respondents bunched up at the extreme ends of the distribution—a large group that consistently prefers the liberal position on policies and a similarly large group that consistently prefers the conservative position—and relatively few people in the middle of the distribution.

Digging a bit deeper, in figure 6.3 we display the distribution of our policy preference index with respondents who identify as Republican shaded gray and Democratic identifiers shaded white. The dotted line represents the distribution when all respondents (including Independents and others) are included. The graph clearly displays differences between Republicans and Democrats, but these differences should be expected. The Democrats are clustered at the right of the distribution's center, reflecting greater support for liberal positions on the policy questions, while Republicans are clustered at the left of center, leaning more toward the conservative positions. However, the peaks in Democratic support and peaks in Republican support are not far apart, and there is a considerable amount of overlap between those peaks of Democratic and Republican voters. In fact, when we compare the total variation in policy preferences among

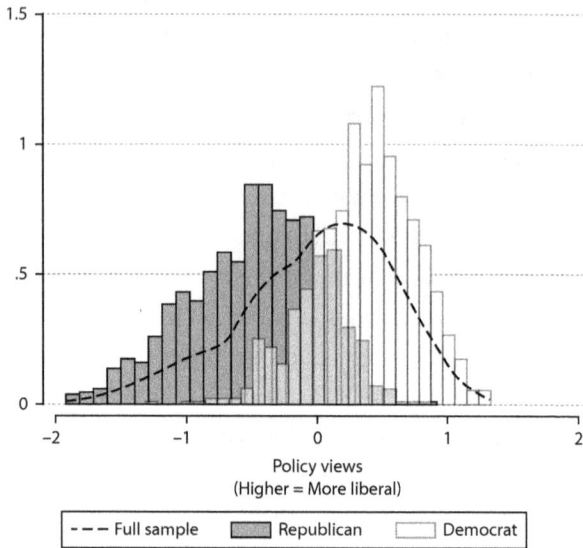

FIGURE 6.3 Distribution of scores on policy index by party affiliation

Democrats and Republicans, more than half of the variation (53 percent) in respondents' preferences is among members of the same party. Relatively few Democrats or Republicans appear in the tails of the distribution, which would indicate that they consistently and strongly favor either the liberal or conservative positions. Indeed, this distribution resembles that described by the economist Anthony Downs in his influential 1957 book, *An Economic Theory of Democracy*. Downs reasoned that because most American voters fall close to the middle of an ideological continuum, in a two-party system you would expect political candidates to strategically advocate moderate policies, positioning themselves close to the center so that they can appeal to the most voters.[27] This pull toward the center, according to the theory, contributes to the stability of American democracy—a

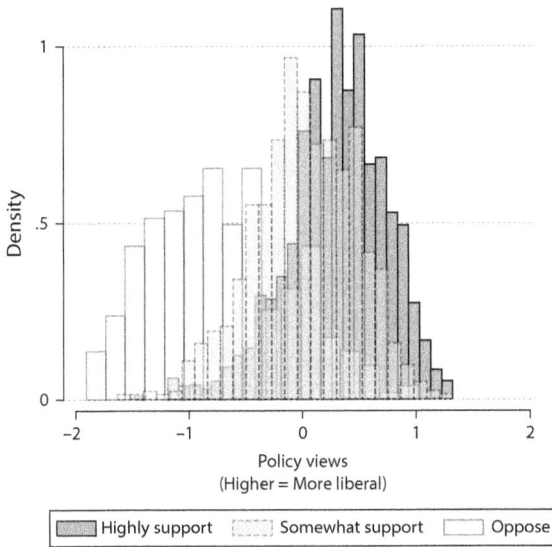

FIGURE 6.4 Distribution of scores on policy index by support and opposition to One America goals.

scenario far removed from the interparty animosity displayed by contemporary legislators.

As we show in figure 6.4, polarization that we observe among respondents in our sample has less to do with party affiliation than it does with their support or opposition to the goals of One America for Working People. In the graph, we can see that those who are highly supportive of our fictitious political alliance (One America) make up the "liberal" end of the distribution. These respondents most consistently support liberal positions on a full range of policy issues that we asked them to consider. We also see that those who oppose One America (either strongly or somewhat) are clustered much more to the conservative side of the distribution. Those who are only "somewhat supportive" serve as something of a buffer, as they are likely to support some liberal policy positions but also some conservative positions. The distance—or the polarization—is characterized by those who enthusiastically support a progressive coalition promoting both status and economic equality pitted against those who oppose that coalition.

The role that status contestation plays in shaping policy preference consolidation (or polarization) becomes even clearer when we break down the distribution of the policy preference index by political identity. At the top of figure 6.5, we see that respondents' views of One America's coalition also divide Republican voters. Among Republicans, those who oppose One America's goals overwhelmingly comprise the conservative tail of the distribution. Republicans who approve of One America's goals, on the other hand, tend to cluster around the sample mean. Policy positions among Independents, as shown in the middle panel of the graph, are also clearly divided according to their support or opposition to One America. Independents who support the coalition promoting economic and status equality are bunched up just to the liberal side of the mean value. Perhaps most notably, the distribution has a formidable tail on the left side, showing that those who oppose One America, as was true of the Republicans, tend to consistently favor conservative policy positions. Among Democrats, the small number of respondents who oppose One America tend to be bunched around the mean value of the overall distribution, indicating that they tend to favor some Republican positions and some Democratic positions on the various policy questions. Most Democratic respondents, however, approve of the content of One America and are found on the liberal end of the policy preference continuum.

By examining the distributions of our policy preference index, it becomes clear that in our sample it would be hard to

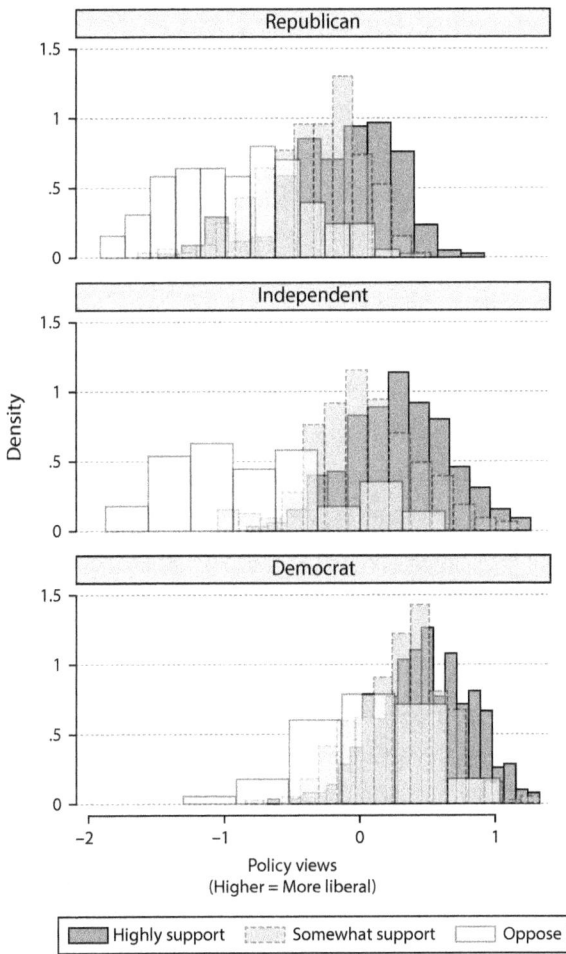

FIGURE 6.5 Distribution of scores on policy index by support and opposition to One America goals, broken down by political party identity

make a case that when it comes to public policy issues Democrats and Republicans are highly polarized. Upon closer examination, however, we see that the extreme ends of the policy preference distribution are overwhelmingly populated by those who strongly support and those who oppose the goals of One America for Working People—an organization that aims to build a coalition among those favoring greater economic equality and those supporting status-based equality. Supporters and opponents are, indeed, far apart in terms of the consistency with which they adopt the liberal or conservative positions across a broad range of issues. We see this when we examine the distribution of our entire sample but also when we look separately at those who identify as Republican, Independent, or Democrat. We should note, however, that the graphs we have displayed thus far include responses from those who were exposed to the "economics only" version of the One America web page as well as those who viewed a web page pairing economic equality goals with status equality goals. If our argument about the importance of status contestation is correct, we would expect to find that the gulf between those who support and oppose the organization on the policy preference index would be ill-defined among those who viewed the economics only version of the web page and would be much more apparent if we only considered those who viewed a version of the web page that featured an alliance between economic inequality and status inequality.

Graphs presented in figure 6.6 strikingly illustrate our point. In the top row of the figure, we display the distributions for Republicans, Independents, and Democrats among those who viewed the economics only version of the web page for One America. The bottom row shows the distributions when the economics only group is excluded. To appreciate the importance of status contestation, it is useful to compare the graphs in the top

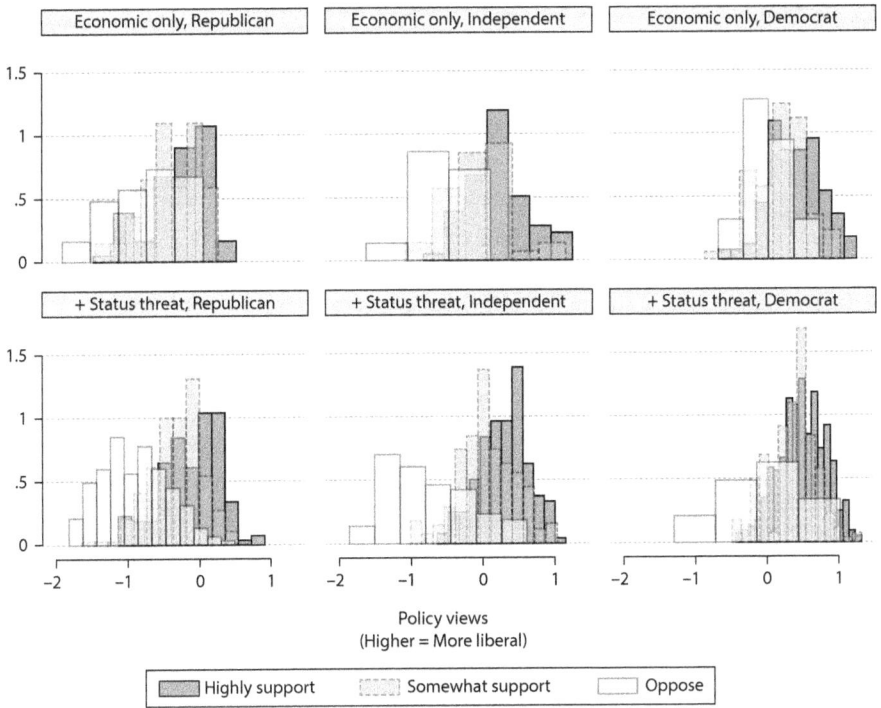

FIGURE 6.6 Distribution of scores on policy index
by support and opposition to One America goals,
broken down by political party identity

Note: The top row represents respondents who viewed the economics only version of
the web page, and the bottom row represents those who viewed a web page advocating both economic and status equality.

row to those immediately below them. Among Republicans who
viewed the economics only version of the web page, those who
oppose One America are spread across the policy index distribution. It is only when Republicans viewed a web page that com-
bines advocacy for economic equality and status equality that we
see opponents of One America clustered in the conservative tail

of the distribution. The same is true when we compare Independents who viewed the economics only version to those who viewed a version of the web page that also commits to fighting status inequality. In the first group, opponents of the economics only version of One America are spread across the distribution. Independent opponents of One America, however, make up the extremely conservative tail of the distribution if they viewed a version of the web page that addresses status inequality in addition to economic inequality. Finally, Democratic opponents of the economics only version are spread across the policy index distribution. However, among those who viewed a web page addressing status inequality, the Democratic opponents cluster more toward the conservative side of the distribution as well. In short, political polarization exists in our sample, but it reflects a gulf between those who strongly support the One America coalition goals and those who oppose them, with the two groups comprising the extreme tails of the overall distribution as well as the tails within the parties.

CONCLUSION

According to our status contestation and politics theory, political polarization is one of the primary ways in which defense of status hierarchies sustains economic inequality in the United States. Analyses presented in this chapter show that our respondents' views about the goals of One America for Working People tend to push them toward the two ends of a continuum when it comes to conservative or liberal views on a range of policy issues. Those who support the organization's goals tend to be much more consistent in their support for liberal positions on a broad range of policy issues. Those who are not supportive of the organization's

goals are substantially more likely to be consistently conservative on those same issues. Because of this polarization, many
voters who might otherwise favor progressive economic policies
align with a political party (Republicans) that works to maintain
both economic and status inequalities and strongly resists compromise with Democrats. In our sample, just under 60 percent
of Republicans do not have a college degree, making it difficult
for them to achieve economic security in today's global economy. They nevertheless align with a political party that opposes
expansion of a safety net and instead prioritizes tax savings for
wealthy voters. Many respond to conservative populist appeals
coming from Trump and other Republicans, but Republican
officeholders, unlike many Democrats, do not propose actual
policies that would reduce economic inequality.

Perhaps the most notable thing about the analyses presented
in this chapter is that our focus on status hierarchies takes us far
beyond factors that we tend to think of as structuring political
behavior—in particular, political party identity. Neither Democrats nor Republicans in our sample—not to mention those who
do not identify with the major parties—show much consistency
in their alignment with positions taken by the parties, meaning that there is substantial within-group variation in policy
preferences. Yet consistency emerges when we consider peoples'
responses to One America for Working People—an organization that seeks to reduce both economic and status inequalities. Rather than weighing policy preferences on economic
issues against particular policy preferences on social issues when
choosing parties or candidates, we show that something else is
going on. When considering our entire sample, for example,
77.4 percent of respondents, regardless of party affiliation, who
strongly support One America's agenda strongly agree that the
"government should do more to assure that all Americans earn

wages that allow them to cover normal living expenses for their families." Only 15 percent of respondents who oppose the organization's goals (strongly or somewhat) strongly agree with that statement. At the same time, 75.4 percent of those who strongly support the organization's goals strongly agree with the following statement: "The legal system and police departments should do more to hold police officers accountable when they kill unarmed civilians who do not pose a threat to the officer or a bystander." Only 19.6 percent of respondents strongly agree with that statement if they do not support the organization's goals.

By focusing on policy preferences in this chapter, we emphasize our view that they are not the starting point for many people when making voting decisions. In fact, we instead show how policy preferences and their role in politics are best understood as being formulated within a broader battle being waged over status hierarchies. Those who are the most invested in preserving or dismantling status hierarchies can easily identify which party most closely aligns with status preservation goals. With that accomplished, their status goals provide a structure they can use to make sense of political issues and policies. The high stakes of status conflict produce an active, vocal, united block of voters ("the base") that candidates for political office cannot ignore. This is especially true because political candidates operate in an environment with gerrymandered legislative districts and spatial clustering of partisan loyalties.

7

HEATED STATUS BOUNDARIES

U p to this point, our experiment has been extraordinarily revealing. By gauging peoples' responses to different versions of the web page for One America for Working People, we have been able to isolate the ways in which status goals drive political behavior. One version focuses only on economic inequality and stresses that all people must unite to bring about change. The other versions add a paragraph that accurately states that a particular group experiences discrimination and violence in American society and commits the organization to combatting this differential treatment so that everybody can act together to fight for economic equality. As discussed previously, bringing about significant change in economic inequality requires a large, forceful coalition willing to press demands on elected officials at the ballot box and in the streets. Our experimental manipulations display the practice of "frame extension." The additional paragraph pertaining to status inequalities represents an attempt to broaden support for the organization by persuading people that the goals of fighting for economic equality and status equality are compatible and in fact are both necessary to bring about success.

Findings discussed in preceding chapters have revealed a dilemma when it comes to political mobilization to remedy economic inequality. Mobilizing to combat economic inequality alone does not appeal to a broad enough segment of the population to be effective. Linking economic inequality to status inequalities can make the organization considerably more attractive to Democrats. This is important because Democratic voters (even those who are highly educated and economically prosperous) are the most committed to reducing economic inequality, meaning that an organization like One America for Working People would have no chance of succeeding without strong support from Democratic voters. Yet the very thing that energizes Democrats in our sample (the added commitment to fighting status inequalities) makes Republican voters less supportive—including a large swath of voters who seemingly would benefit from reductions in economic inequality. Those who identify as political Independents, on average, seem comfortable with commitment to status inequality. They are not as supportive of One America as are Democrats, but they are more supportive than Republicans. Importantly, the added paragraphs about fighting status inequality does not diminish average support among Independents.

The power of an experimental design, such as the one we have administered, comes from the way that it allows us to say, with confidence, that we have discovered cause and effect relationships. Random assignment to our different treatment groups makes our groups, in the aggregate, very similar to each other. Therefore, any differences that we observe in the groups' support for, or opposition to, One America are *caused* by the one thing that is different about the groups—their exposure to different versions of the web page. It is difficult to overstate the importance of that fact. People often are not fully aware of the way in which they benefit from status hierarchies and how they act in ways that support those hierarchies. As a result, we can't get a good read on how important status defense goals are in politics by simply asking people about them. With our experiment, we can instead show that inclusion of a goal to reduce status inequalities alters the way in which people perceive a social change organization and provides us with an opportunity to assess possibilities for progressive coalition formation.

We have argued that most people do not fully acknowledge or recognize the ways in which status concerns motivate their political beliefs and actions—especially for those who defend status privileges rather than those who seek to secure equal status treatment. It is more socially acceptable, for example, to state that you want to be treated fairly by others than it is to state that you prefer to benefit from unfair arrangements. Nevertheless, we think that our analysis can be enriched if we do provide people with an opportunity to explain, in their own words, why they support or oppose different aspects of One America. Certainly, we expect some people will openly express bigotry that motivates their behavior. Many others, however, will draw on different logic to explain their choices while many others, perhaps the majority, will struggle to construct a coherent argument explaining their responses. Indeed, Eduardo Bonilla-Silva found that it is very common for white people to struggle to form and articulate coherent thoughts when trying to explain their views on race in the United States.[1] Importantly, as we found in the preceding chapters, many of our respondents did not strongly object to any particular version of One America but also gave no strong indication that they would be willing to actively support it or embrace its agenda.

We gathered additional data to examine people's qualitative reactions and responses to the organization. We developed a short version of the survey that displays the varied versions of the web page but excludes many of the questions that we used to perform the quantitative analyses presented in previous chapters. We worked with Qualtrics Experience Management to obtain a sample of participants for this supplementary analysis. Instead of asking respondents to indicate their approval, disapproval, and willingness to support the organization, we provided them with a single open-ended question inviting them to describe what they like and dislike about it. We required them to provide an answer containing at least a hundred words. We found that this approach seemed to encourage participation from those who strongly opposed the organization as well as those who supported it.

We administered these surveys in June 2023. We dropped cases if the respondent, for whatever reason, failed to write a hundred-word response relevant to the question that we asked, and replaced them with new respondents. We obtained a final sample of 324. It is important for us to emphasize that these responses cannot be used to make any generalizations to populations beyond the small sample. For example, if we were to find that 20 percent of respondents provided a similar answer to the question, that tells us nothing about the percentage of people in society at large who share that sentiment. Our goal in this chapter, instead, is to identify a range of ways that people articulate the rationale behind their varying levels of support for the organization. When directly quoting respondents, we do light editing, correcting grammar when necessary, in order to clarify the message conveyed. We feel that it would be unfair to respondents to retain grammatical errors when they were writing under conditions that are not conducive to crafting perfect sentences. Importantly, we restrict our editing to grammatical errors and do not make any substantive changes in their comments. We approached this endeavor with no preconceptions about what we expected or hoped to find. We were instead attentive to the patterns and commonalities that emerged in the data when people tried to make sense of One America for Working People.

STICK TO ECONOMICS?

Republican Voices

We begin by considering responses from those who viewed the web page that only addresses economic inequality under the heading "Fighting for a Better Future." Recall that Republicans consistently favored this version of the organization both in terms of approval of the content and their propensity to support it. They also tended to view the organization as more ideologically moderate compared to Republicans who viewed other versions of the web page that committed to fighting status inequalities. Part of that attraction is clearly related to the flexibility that this version of the web page offers when it comes to supporting the economic agenda but making no sacrifices regarding status privileges. One respondent, for example, described himself as a very conservative forty-two-year-old Republican with a bachelor's degree. Despite his professed conservatism, he approved of the organization's efforts to secure higher wages and employment. This goal, for him, was consistent with his belief that "in the working world, most white guys cannot get jobs in the United States anymore." He adds that it is "impossible for a white guy to get a job, especially over a black woman."[2] Relatedly, a self-identified conservative Republican—a white man in his late forties with some college education—indicated that One America has a "very positive project and mission." Yet again, the sole focus on economic inequality on the web page gave him room to make sense of the organization through a conservative lens. He saw the organization as one that is promoting work, rather than letting people "be lazy and selfish and live off others and the government." He added, "This entitlement type of thinking needs to stop. No one is owed a thing. They need to wake up and go to work, not sit on their butts and draw checks. I'm so sick of this."[3]

Some Republican respondents did, in fact, express negative views about the economics only version of One America. A white man in his sixties with advanced education, for example, offered his own counteranalysis. He agreed that money in politics is a problem but expressed deep distrust in organizations that will "take money from hard workers to share with others." He expressed support for term limits for politicians and stressed the importance of fair elections. He added, however, that organizations like One America should not "let Democrats steal elections. Fight against all of the woke issues. I don't want it affecting my family and especially my children. Sounds like Communism."[4] Another white Republican man in his fifties dismissed One America's entire agenda. He reported having completed some college but also indicated that he has a relatively high income and identifies as being part of the upper class. Inequality, in his view, is a result of differences in merit and work ethic. As he expressed it, "If you want to have my lifestyle, then put in the effort. These views to make everything equal are not realistic because in the world things are not equal. In the animal kingdom the weak get eaten. If you don't want to get eaten, then exercise the way the other animals do and run."[5]

Although some Republicans clearly perceived that One America for Working People directly opposes their own understanding of the causes of inequality, most were at least sympathetic to the message conveyed on the web page. For several

Republicans, the web page's emphasis on the politics of division resonated strongly. A Latino man in his early sixties with some college education characterized himself as very conservative. Nevertheless, he wrote of the importance of politicians working for the people, rather than their benefactors. Regarding the need for unity, he wrote, "Divided we lose our freedoms. It is good for a group to raise our voices to get our share of the good prizes we are owed for our work."[6] A Latina Republican in her early sixties expressed dismay over the state of American politics: "Sadly, our government resembles the dictatorships our soldiers helped fight against in previous wars." She didn't think that One America could do much to solve the problem but ended by saying "I wish, with all my heart, we could repair our broken country."[7]

Several Republicans, college graduates as well as those with less education, showed awareness of growing inequality in the United States, at times drawing on their own experiences and economic struggles. A white man in his early sixties latched onto the language on the web page about CEO earnings, recalling the amount of time he spent doing IT work for a company. "The pay I received for the work I did was so out of proportion compared to the CEO who wasn't at work half the time that it was ridiculous."[8] A white woman in her early forties with a bachelor's degree shared the assessment of corporate greed. She wrote, "Americans are treated as disposable while corporate executives make record-breaking profits each year only to gain more and more wealth while the people they employ do not have a chance to get ahead."[9] One white man in his mid-fifties with a high school degree drew on his Christian faith to connect with the goals of One America: "I don't care for the disparity between the poor and the rich. We are created equal. I am a firm believer in what the Bible says, and the inequality between the wealthy and the other people in this country is ridiculous."[10]

Other Republicans had no quarrel with the web page's diagnosis of inequality but expressed either distrust or fatalism. A white man with a bachelor's degree in his early seventies wrote that One America for Working People appears to be a "worthwhile organization." He added, however, "It's a sad fact that nonprofits are often cash cows for their organizers, while the people whom they are supposed to be helping languish in neglect. Hopefully, this organization will actually be beneficial to the workers and not just for the organizers."[11] Another college graduate, a white woman in her early seventies, recalled the past failure of the Equal Rights Amendment. Referring to One America, she surmised, "Unless attitudes have changed, there is still deep resistance to this type of effort. The rich will always find a way to control the masses, if you will, and unless we can find a way to make it beneficial for that elite, it will stay that way. I say good luck to them (referring to One America)."[12]

Democratic Voices

To a remarkable degree, responses from Democrats to the "economics only" version of the web page for One America for Working People resemble those given by Republicans. A key difference, however, is that no Democrats opposed the organization. This reflects the broad support that Democrats gave to the organization in the larger sample we used in earlier chapters. Indeed, the sense of fatalism communicated by some Republicans also tempers the enthusiasm of some Democrats. For example, one white man, a college graduate in his early seventies who describes himself as very liberal, expressed support for the goals of the organization. Yet he lamented, "I am doubtful that they will be very successful in carrying out all of their very laudable goals. I believe this because, unfortunately, far too many of the legislators in this country are dependent on the contributions of the wealthy."[13] A young Black woman with a high school degree viewed the organization favorably, indicating that there wasn't anything on the web page that she disliked. However, she added, "It's America, what do you expect? Life isn't fair so you have to deal with it. You have to pray until something happens, but you also have to put that work in."[14]

Democratic respondents, like Republicans, bemoaned the politics of division. A young Black woman with an associate's degree wrote that "politics separates us and divides our country and it is time to come together as one rather than letting our differences divide us into sides of hatred and evil."[15] A seventy-seven-year-old white man with a bachelor's degree commented specifically on the Supreme Court's Citizens United ruling, which places no dollar limits on political contributions to political action committees (PACs) as long as the PACs do not coordinate activities with candidates. As he expressed it, "Politicians have been taking money from large donors who have now bought themselves a congressman. They don't want us united and are keeping us separated so we don't fight together for what we should be receiving."[16]

Although many Republicans endorsed One America's critique of corporate greed, Democratic respondents were more likely to embellish on the critique, drawing on their own personal experiences or discussing broader implications of unfettered capitalism during a time of economic transition. A seventy-year-old white woman with an associate degree, for example, commented on her own precarious circumstances: "I bought a business website in 2012 and found out how difficult it is to survive working independently. I lost my business later on. It is hard for us all."[17] Several respondents offered a critique of exploitation under capitalism. A white man in his mid-thirties with a high school degree, for example, writes, "The only thing that the company leaders care about is profits. Meanwhile, the workers struggle. Too many people are just getting by."[18] A middle-aged man who identifies as Native American concurs: "Big business in America makes a lot of money off of the backs of the small business owner and workers." He concludes, "We need to get back to the roots of what made the United States of America great and that is the hard work and dedication of the people."[19] The almost Trumpian nostalgia for a return to better days is hard to miss. Yet his longing is rooted in a real or imagined world in which hard work is justly rewarded, rather than resentment of constructed images of foreigners or outsiders threatening his way of life.

For one white man in his early seventies, the decline in union power helps explain the plight of today's workers. "Organized labor does a good job representing working people, but the vast majority of working people are not organized. Without the support of a union, these people are very much at the mercy of large corporations."[20] A Black woman in her late thirties focused her response on community-wide devastation in the modern economy. She writes that One America for Working People "could help improve the quality of life for many individuals, reduce stress and displacement of families." She expresses particular concern for the homeless and shared her hope that the organization "would positively benefit many people in the community as well as the economy."[21] Interestingly, even though this version of the web page did not explicitly mention racial inequality, one respondent, a white woman in her early forties with some college education, saw economic inequality and racial inequality as deeply intertwined. On the survey she reported that her religious faith is very important to her, and that is reflected in the answer she provided about inequality. "Everyone is made equally, and people should work together no matter what race. . . . This is America, home of the free."[22]

Other Voices

Many of our respondents, when asked about their political affiliation, indicated that they were Independent or were not affiliated with one of the two major parties. Analyses presented in earlier chapters indicate that Independents, on average, fall between Democrats and Republicans in terms of their support for One America for Working People. Simply stating that fact, however, overlooks the extent to which these respondents represent a "mixed bag." By that, we mean that they choose not to identify with either the Republicans or the Democrats for a variety of reasons with many of those reasons being at odds. For example, some progressives may view both major parties as being too conservative or corrupt and may respond enthusiastically to One America. On the other hand, some lean toward libertarianism, possessing moderate or progressive views on most social issues but conservative views on the economy. Clearly, One America for Working People would be unattractive to Libertarians because of the critique of free market capitalism. Others are simply disengaged from, or are not interested in, politics.

One America's message did resonate strongly with some Independent or unaffiliated respondents. A Black man in his thirties with a high school degree responded, "Well, I'm one of those working people who is just getting by because pay is cheap and the price of everything is shooting through the roof.

That makes it hard on people like me who have to pay the bills and try to provide for my family."[23] A number of the responses were less personal, resembling the way that many Republicans expressed agreement with the critique offered on the web page without much embellishment.[24] While most of the Independent and unaffiliated respondents were at least somewhat supportive, some strongly opposed the organization. A white man in his seventies with a bachelor's degree, for example, accused One America of pitting workers against workers. "CEOs are also workers and earn their money based on their performance." He emphasized the extent to which executive salaries must be competitive to attract and retain the best people.[25]

While it in no way reflects majority opinion, the strong sense of anger and alienation expressed by some of the Independent or unaffiliated respondents is striking. One Latino man in his early fifties with some college education, for example, indicates that he is "all for this organization" even though he self-identifies as a conservative. He added, however, that "it will remain to be seen if this actually works. It is my honest opinion that these greedy politicians are protected by the same laws they lobbied to get passed. It seems to be one big circle of corruption."[26] Perhaps most strikingly, a white man in his late thirties who self-identifies as ideologically moderate said that he also agrees with the goals of One America for Working People. Yet he is even more skeptical about what such a civic organization can accomplish. In his words, "I feel it is far too late for any peaceful change. The corporations wield too much power for peaceful resolutions. They have too much money, too many bloodsucking lawyers, and when it comes to it, the police/military will back them against any and all opposition. The politicians will never care as long as they continue to bilk the average citizen of everything they have and get away with it. The politicians don't even need to be in office that long. One term and they get a lifelong paycheck at the taxpayer's expense. It will never end until they are all held accountable by force."[27]

RACE MATTERS

Republican Voices

The responses to One America for Working people that we have presented so far help to expand the experimental findings we presented in chapters 4 and 5. Notably, although there were a few Republicans who objected to the "economics only" version of the web page because it challenged their understanding of capitalism, the majority had no quarrel with the critique of capitalism and corrupt politics featured on the web page. Democratic respondents were uniformly supportive and their responses tended to suggest that the organization's message largely resonated with a view of the economy and polity that they already held. Responses to the web page that features an additional paragraph on racial inequality, however, reveal a sharp divide that largely aligns with party affiliation. We should note, however, that several Republicans did indicate moderate support for the organization. Their responses tended to be somewhat bland, mainly reiterating points made on the web page. Interestingly, all of these supportive Republicans simply ignored the content on racial inequality. In that sense, their responses were indistinguishable from those of Republicans who responded to the "economics only" web page.

The status threat that we introduced with the paragraph about racial equality, however, did provoke many negative reactions among Republicans, corresponding with our experimental findings reported earlier. The negative responses are largely of two kinds. Some respondents took care to avoid making direct statements about opposition to racial equality, yet their responses reflect the kind of "color-blind" racism that is common in contemporary American society.[28] Unlike most of the Republicans who opposed the "economics only" version of the web page, their responses are not limited to a defense of capitalism over socialism. For example, a man in his fifties with an associate's degree who identifies as Hispanic or Latino avoids mentioning race in his evaluation: "I just can't wrap my mind around it being something that will be beneficial for everyone because there's going to be winners and losers to everything, but this (One America) makes more losers than it does winners."[29]

Other Republicans indicated support for economic goals but downplayed the significance of racial inequality. An Asian American college graduate in her early thirties, for example, acknowledged "here in the U.S. there are some issues about racism, but I know most companies impose some punishment for it."[30] A white woman in her mid-thirties with some college education indicated she supports the organization but expressed qualifications. She observed that the economy "has gone to shit in the past few years" and added that it has been "a struggle finding decent paying jobs for the average people in America." While not specifically mentioning race, she wrote, "We are focusing on things that are not of any importance. Let's make America great again like Donald Trump once said."[31] A twenty-four-year-old woman with some college education also did not speak directly to race but seemed to draw on racist tropes in her assessment of the situation. For her, poverty in America is mainly due to laziness. She concluded her statement by writing "Sometimes I wish I could live off the government, but then I know it's not right." Everyone needs to work or "they won't make it in the world."[32]

Nothing in the web page refers to welfare policies, but that was clearly on this respondent's mind.

Other Republican respondents were more comfortable openly expressing anger over racial equality goals. A fifty-nine-year-old white woman with some college education linked a critique of socialism to her opposition to efforts to address racial equality. One America's agenda, she argued, "sounds too much like socialism, or at the very least, control." She adds, "Racial equality is discrimination in itself. Everyone should have the right to work, go to school, etc. In the United States, rights are protected and we are already equal."[33] Another white woman in her forties with some college education concurs. "I believe that people yelling about racism are really the racist ones. If you want to change racism, quit asking about race on the application." A fifty-eight-year-old white man with an associate degree left no doubt about how he feels about racial equality. He liked the way in which One America seems to be for the little guy against the rich who generally have all the power. He added, however, "I don't like racial equality. I believe that races are not equal even though we really may want it that way." He concludes by saying "I don't think we will truly achieve economic equality. The world needs ditch diggers. What I mean is we need low-income jobs for the masses such as service jobs."[34]

Democratic Voices

Consistent with the results of our experiment, Democrats who offered qualitative evaluations of One America for Working People were particularly enthusiastic if they viewed the version that pledged to address racial inequality. Indeed, strong support was nearly universal. Several respondents commented directly on the benefits of pairing economic and racial equality. A young Black woman with a college degree stressed the importance of simultaneously addressing race and class. She added, "People putting an effort into making change will benefit so many innocent people who need help."[35] Unlike Republicans, white Democrats did not see economic and racial equality in zero-sum terms. A white woman in her early sixties with some college education explained, "As a person who is in a very low-income range, I could benefit from this type of advocacy." Speaking directly to the pairing of economic and racial equality, she added, "We have been advocating for these two issues for so long and they don't seem to be going anywhere. We need a strong force of people who will get representatives to listen to them as a voice for others."[36] A white man in his late seventies with some college education strongly endorsed the logic of the web page content regarding the necessity of fighting for racial equality in order to also bring about economic equality. "Racial equality is a must to address. I think that would increase our chances of economic equality." He concludes, "We should all come together as one. If we could really get together and work things out, we would have a great opportunity for both economic equality and racial equality."[37]

Unlike supportive Republicans, Democrats did not ignore racial equality when expressing their views, nor did they overlook class inequality. The pairing of the two seems natural and beneficial in their evaluations of the organization. But some Democrats, while supportive, did express a sense of fatalism. More commonly, they wanted to know more about the specific actions the organization would take, or they indicated that the organization needs to take more aggressive action. One white man in his late sixties said that he strongly supports the organization. He indicated, however, that money, power, and corruption inevitably win out. He lamented, "The problem with an organization like this is, if it gets to be a powerful force, it will be infiltrated by the outside and destroyed from within by petty invented issues."[38] A white woman in her mid-sixties agrees: "Unfortunately, I don't think an organization like this will make a big difference. The division in this country has been going on for years, and it won't end with one group promising to bring people together."[39]

For others, however, recognition of the power of the opposition led them to call on the organization to focus more on action than words. A young Latino with some college education supported the organization but pressed for details, particularly regarding the kinds of actions that would reduce racial inequality. To illustrate his concerns, he recalled an academic study that "has proven that in low-income jobs in the fast food industry there is a large gap between tips that Black people get compared to White people."[40] A Latina in her thirties also pressed for more details and for more active resistance: "It doesn't seem like this organization is doing anything beyond providing information. It would be nice to see what direct actions are taken to help workers gain economic and racial equality. Do they organize protests or petitions or other things like calling legislators and encouraging others to contact?" She concluded by saying, "It's a great idea, but I feel like there needs to be more action than words."[41]

As was the case with those who responded to the economics only version of the web page, Democratic respondents tended to display a sophisticated understanding of racial, as well as economic, inequality. One white woman in her mid-thirties with some college education, for example, expressed appreciation for the pairing of economic and racial inequality. She summed up the situation by focusing on the structural aspects of racism: "Racism is rampant in America and it needs to change. It's systemic, and the systems need to be recreated to make sure it's inclusive and equitable for everyone." She concluded, "Without changes, we will keep going in circles and repeating the same mistakes. It's time to stop dividing ourselves and unite to make this country the place it is supposed to be; 'the land of the free and the home of the brave.'"[42]

Other Voices

As was true of those who viewed the economics only version of the web page, Independents and unaffiliated respondents showed a diverse range of responses to the version that commits to addressing racial inequality. One woman, white and in her mid-twenties who holds a bachelor's degree, seemed to suggest that focusing on economic and racial inequality undermines One America's claim that it is nonpartisan (or bipartisan, as she expressed it).[43] However, several Independent voters showed strong support. Like some of the Democrats, a white woman in her thirties with a doctorate or professional degree appreciated the linkage of class and race but, like several Democrats, pushed the organization to take things further. In particular, she called for an extension of the focus on intersectionality—in particular by thinking about gender. She also pushed for more detail about what the organization would do and for a more comprehensive argument detailing the problems to be overcome.[44]

A young white woman with a high school degree articulated intersectionality in more personal terms. "As someone who is currently unemployed and looking for a job, I have been pretty unlucky as of late trying to find anything. I've seen, firsthand,

FIGURE 7.1 A demonstration against teaching critical race theory in the classroom in Leesburg, Virginia, June 12, 2022. Getty Images.

lesser wages for women or for people of color and it hurts my heart." She adds, "I love that this organization wants to speak up for people who are otherwise discouraged or have no voice."[45] Yet opponents also frequent the ranks of Independents (see figure 7.1). For example, a white woman in her late sixties who indicated that her Catholic faith was very important to her characterized One America as "another scam to get money by blaming race instead of just working hard to earn a salary. (I'm) tired of all these excuses people keep conjuring up so they can get money without earning it the way people should be by working hard, learning a trade." She complained, "There seems to be one excuse after another why companies should just hand over money to certain races. It should be for all and not a few, so that you can receive just what you actually earn, not just have it handed to you for some idiotic political excuse or 'woe is me' scam."[46]

CHALLENGING SEXISM

Republican Voices

The gender hierarchy is somewhat unusual in that men and women are in frequent contact with one another through kinship ties, and they each comprise roughly half of the total population. These facts may have implications for the way in which gender inequality is discussed, but they do not remove the incentive for many men, as well as some women, to strongly defend male privilege or a "traditional" unequal relationship between men and women. As we discussed in chapter 4, the emergence of a global economy has implications for gender equality because the traditional "male as breadwinner" model has become hard to sustain with the decline of domestic manufacturing in the United States, while highly educated dual-income couples are able to enjoy a high standard of living that gives both members of the couple a stake in promoting gender equality.

Very few of the Republicans who provided qualitative reactions to One America for Working People showed strong support. The organization was quite appealing, however, to a young unmarried woman with a bachelor's degree who identifies as Hispanic or Latina. As she put it, "While some may think that there is equal opportunity for men and women, it has been proven that women are more likely to make a lower salary for the same work as their male counterparts. I have seen this in my own life as well."[47] Her views are largely shared by a high-earning white man in his sixties who also has a bachelor's degree. He endorsed the simultaneous goals of fighting for gender and economic inequality, while also introducing a critique of racial inequality and mass incarceration.[48]

Among Republicans, however, it is much more common for respondents to directly counter the claims on the web page about discrimination that women face. A white man in his sixties who self-identified as working class, for example, expressed tentative support for the organization. He quickly pivoted to describing his own situation, however, upset about how his company is giving higher wages to new employees with no experience after he has developed skills at the company for more than a decade.[49] A white woman in her sixties with an associate degree indicated she opposes One America for Working People. She interprets efforts to fight gender discrimination as giving special treatment to women. "I believe everyone should be paid what he or she is worth in the business. It should not be by gender, color, nor race. It should go by experience."[50] An Asian American man in his fifties echoes this response: "I agree that pay is unequal among different cultures. However, I also believe that people should be paid for what they are worth and not because of the color of their skin or gender."[51] Responses like these are based on an understanding that attempts to remedy discrimination are illegitimate, interfering with merit as the ultimate determinant of economic rewards. Indeed, one white woman in her early fifties with an associate degree and a modest income blames victims of discrimination and exploitation for stirring up trouble. As she put it, "I think we should all be able to work together to get along. Fighting against each other helps nobody. We are supposed to be Americans so we should be able to set aside any differences, whether age, race, wealth, etc., and work together to make America great and keep it great."[52]

Democratic Voices

Democrats who provided qualitative feedback on the "gender version" of One America for Working People almost uniformly operated from a different set of assumptions about the extent to which gender discrimination and other forms of discrimination are pervasive in the economy. It is worth repeating that we should not assume that these responses are numerically representative of Democrats and Republicans in the United States. However, the pattern that we observe in our sample does strongly reflect the way in which views on gender equality are developed within the context of the emergence of a global economy that rewards higher levels of education. Republicans most staunchly opposed to the gender equality goals tended to be white, older, and with relatively low levels of education. Democratic supporters, on the other hand, are diverse in terms of gender and race, younger, highly educated, and well off financially. While most responses focus on gender in the workforce, it is important to keep in mind that gender inequality operates strongly outside of the workplace, including violence within families and within society.[53]

A white woman in her late fifties, currently unmarried but with a relatively high income, noted "ever changing gender identity roles," making specific mention of transgender people. "We must ensure that every individual has protection under the law."[54] Another white woman in her mid-sixties with a bachelor's degree likewise expressed concern about LGBTQ people as well as women specifically. She was highly critical of (presumably Republican) Congressmen and -women enacting laws that go against public opinion. The Supreme Court, she argued, "seems to be making laws instead of judging whether court decisions are based on laws currently on the books. One America could encourage Congress and the Supreme Court to represent America."[55]

Several of the most outspoken supporters were young to middle-aged white men with college degrees and high incomes. A thirty-five-year-old married man with no children praised the organization's goals and pitched his endorsement in terms of restructuring work in ways that can reduce stress and hardships in broader society.[56] An unmarried white man with a bachelor's degree endorsed the fight for income equality, adding, "In regard to sexism, it is still a rampant problem and needs to be addressed so that we can truly lift up everyone."[57] A married man in his mid-forties with two children, who holds a master's degree and reports a high household income, suggested that One America could unite Americans "irrespective of creed, religion, or social class." He adds, "Women would be able to have a say in a world where men shut them up; they would be able to achieve what men achieve through a suitable platform that enables growth for all."[58]

Several young women voiced strong support grounded in their personal experiences. A Black college student, for example, linked the content on gender equality to the struggle for voting rights. She wrote (in all caps), "WE CAN GIVE ALL AMERICANS THE RIGHT TO SPEAK UP FOR THEIR OWN RIGHTS, women, Black people, native American." She adds, "Not everyone has the voice to speak out, which makes it really important for us to do it."[59] For many respondents, the link between economic inequality and gender inequality was clearly apparent. A young woman with a bachelor's degree who identifies as Hispanic or Latina spoke of the difficulties that Americans have making ends meet. While strongly endorsing One America, she indicated that the organization should do more to emphasize the intersection of income and gender inequality (as well as the intersection with race).[60] A Latina in her late forties who has four children of varying ages reported a firmly middle-class household income but discussed the difficulties of making ends meet in the face of rising costs. As the head of her household, she also stressed her experiences with gender discrimination.[61]

Interestingly, two respondents with high school degrees and relatively low incomes—one man in his forties and a woman in her thirties—expressed support for the organization but limited their discussion to the class equality goals. Another man in his late thirties with some college education said he supports the organization but offered a striking caveat. "When it comes to heavy labor, I believe most women would use their gender as a ticket to not work these jobs." He added, "It is rare to see a female in my profession, and even more rare to see a woman who could match my skill level. So as good as it sounds, I believe it is an excuse and caters to women who have their eyes set on higher positions of power such as management, supervisor, and CEO positions with higher salaries."[62]

Other Voices

Once again, responses from Independent or unaffiliated people display strong emotions both for and against One America. As is true of Republicans and Democrats, many of the supporters clearly see the ways in which their own lives are affected by gender inequality. One woman in her upper twenties identifies as multiracial. She is unmarried, with a child in the household, holds a high school degree and reports a low household income. Her comments are most notable for their emphasis on safety in the workplace, serving as an important reminder that for many Americans who are struggling to make ends meet, working conditions can be at least as important as low wages when considering hardships faced. "Everybody should feel safe, no matter their race or gender."[63] Another young woman in similar circumstances made the case that economic hardships faced by so many Americans puts tremendous pressure on women as well as men, and both need higher wages and better working conditions to survive and form stable families.[64]

An unmarried Black man in his thirties with a high school degree approved of the gender equality goals while extending the organization's agenda to a host of other pressing social problems in the country. His response appears rooted in his religious faith, calling for unity to bring about justice for all.[65] A young college student who identifies as Latina or Hispanic approaches the nation's problem from a different angle. She argues, "Regardless of who you are, you are entitled to a job in order to achieve your dreams. I dislike racist or hate comments about 'YOU GUYS TAKE OUR JOBS' or 'GO BACK TO WHERE YOU CAME FROM.' These are simply made by racist hillbillies who can't accept that the world is diverse and that this country should be open to ANYBODY who wants a better life. This country has gone to shit and should do better by accepting everyone as a whole and allow EVERYONE to achieve their dreams."[66]

Many other Independent and politically unaffiliated respondents, however, drew very different conclusions. One white woman in her late fifties, for example, claims that too many people are unmotivated to work and are looking for government handouts. She wrote, "Everyone needs to stand together and be accountable for their own actions and decisions concerning their own lives and quit relying on everyone else to take care of them."[67] While there is some irony in the call to stand together and quit relying on others, it is a similar sentiment as that expressed by the Republican woman described earlier, where standing up for equal treatment is seen as a source of disunity.

Two young men, one in college and the other with a high school degree who is married with two children, offer similar responses in that they come close to acknowledging that gender discrimination exists but nevertheless argue against efforts to address it. The married man grapples with the problem in a unique way: "I agree with equality strongly. I also feel like we need to work more on economic issues than gender issues. Economic issues will affect the U.S. long term, whereas gender identity and equality issues do not directly affect the economy in a way that is of major concern."[68] The college student also seemed to be debating himself to some extent: "I like equality. However, financial equality is another question. That's not completely impossible, but I don't think it will work out. Gender-based economic equality is good, though. No matter your gender, you should receive the same wage for your level of work. It makes sense, but I don't believe it will be beneficial for anyone. It may help with some issues around poverty, but people who gained a high rank they deserve will receive less for their efforts."[69]

As we have seen before, the gender equality version of the web page also draws accusations about its promotion of socialism. In this case, a seventy-eight-year-old married man states, "Putting every working person's paycheck in a pot and then giving everyone, including the unemployed, an equal share is totally wrong."[70] Importantly, as we have noted previously, gender inequality extends far beyond discrimination in the labor force. A man in his mid-twenties with a high school degree indicates that he is a fundamentalist Christian. He sums up what remains a common sentiment in American society: "I like how they (One America) are supporting equality, but there are only two genders and men and women are super different. Gender inequality is usually mixed up with sexism and is something that most people don't actually understand. A woman is supposed to be caring and loving while the man is supposed to be protective. Even in nature, the males compete for their woman and protect families through danger. This generation is stupid and needs to realize Mother Nature doesn't care about their feelings and doesn't need to comply. Life isn't fair and they can cry about it for all I care."[71]

CHALLENGING HETERONORMATIVITY AND CISNORMATIVITY

Republican Voices

Thus far, rationales offered for support or opposition to One America for Working People provide us with a sense of how status hierarchies shape people's political positions. Perhaps most notably, the largely positive comments from Republicans and Independents when they viewed the economics only version of the web page are few and far between (especially for Republicans) when they view the additional paragraph about race or gender equality. With Independent voters and others who are unaffiliated with a major party, it is rare to find respondents who have mixed views. They tend to either like both the organization's economic and status goals or dislike them both. The pattern continues as we consider responses from those who viewed the web page that includes a paragraph on LGBTQ equality. The pattern suggests that, especially among Republicans, an economic agenda that they might otherwise embrace is viewed with suspicion when it is paired with a threat to status hierarchies. Democrats, on the other hand, consistently express positive views of both the economic message and the challenge to status hierarchies.

As was true of respondents' views on gender equality, differences across age groups are hard to miss. For many of the Republicans, inclusion of LGBTQ equality seems to powerfully distract them from the economic agenda of One America. One seventy-year-old white woman with an advanced degree feels that when the web page mentions CEO earnings, it causes "undue tension." She interprets the economic message as one in which people are calling for a "free ride," rather than working and saving to succeed in life. This blame-the-victim approach is also found in her comments on status hierarchies: "As far as LGBTQ members of our society, I say live and let live but respect others and don't throw it in our faces or those of our children."[72] Such a statement denies the importance of status inequality, essentially saying that people can do what they want but shouldn't ask for equal treatment.

A seventy-nine-year-old white man—a devout Catholic with a high school degree—similarly, but more forcefully, links the economic and status agendas to immorality. He bemoans what he sees as a move toward becoming a "socialist communist nation" while blaming the government for permitting other activity that he finds despicable. He concludes by writing, "We have lost our way and I do not see any hope. Respect and morals are a thing of the past. Sorry we have to leave our children this mess."[73] A sixty-year-old white man with a bachelor's degree was so incensed that he ignored the web page's discussion of economic inequality (which is the primary focus) and jumped directly to expressing his feelings about LGBTQ equality:

> Lifestyles being forcefully pushed on me and my family. Schools are for learning, not to be used for gender reassignment classes. I also feel that it's everybody's right to be who they want to be but I don't believe it's correct that you have to turn around, stop what you are doing, and recognize somebody and applaud them when you totally don't agree with their lifestyle. I think gender reassignment LGBTQ should be taught at home. I don't think school teachers should be pushing it. I don't think a politician should make you have to take it and especially don't think it has to be pushed at your employment.[74]

A common thread running through all of the resistance to status inequality is simple denial of inequality claims. Conservative respondents do not acknowledge the call for an end to discrimination and violence that appears on the web page and instead characterize calls for equal treatment as demands for special treatment. As we have argued throughout this book, this represents deep commitment to preserving status privileges that are typically not acknowledged by beneficiaries. A white man in his early forties, for example, wrote, "There are already laws about discrimination on people of the United States of America, so I don't think it (the organization) would do much of anything." Indicating annoyance about having to offer a hundred words on the topic, he concluded his remarks with the following advice: "I'm going to try to say they just need to get a better job and stop crying about life. Life is hard sometimes. Suck it up buttercup and just go for the ride. It might get better or not, but that's not up to me, that's up to you."[75]

Perhaps more than any of the other status hierarchies, LGBTQ equality provoked animated responses. One white woman in her mid-twenties with some college education indicated that her Pentecostal faith is very important to her. From her perspective, "Everyone is over the LGBTQ community. They are selfish and don't respect those who don't share their same opinions. They keep talking and talking without any regard about the people (unintelligible) them. They want everyone to bend to the delusions." Without considering the dominance of Christian religion in the United States, she continues, "If Christians shoved religion down everyone's throat the way they shove their delusions down everyone's throat, there would be an uproar."[76]

Democratic Voices

Unlike Republicans, Democrats overwhelmingly acknowledge unequal status treatment as objectively true and of great importance. The vast majority also make a relatively seamless connection between economic inequality and status inequality. Indeed, several of our respondents discussed LGBTQ equality in terms of fundamental human rights. A Latina in her early twenties emphasized freedom of expression. "People should be able to truly show off who they really are and could be."[77] Another Latina from a different generation—in her early sixties—shares similar sentiments. "People have a right to decide what they do with their lives."[78] This, she added, is a matter of respect and of human rights. A young Latino man in his early twenties, married with two children, emphasized the importance of taking a stand, stating that we must "do the right thing regardless of how others feel negatively. We have to do the right thing positively, and that's it."[79]

Some of our respondents revealed that the organization is particularly appealing to them because they are members of the LGBTQ community. A seventy-year-old white man with an associate degree likes the way that LGBTQ equality is included in a broader call for unity. He wrote, "I am not the type of person to get involved in many causes, but this one certainly seems worthwhile."[80] For other Democrats, fighting for LGBTQ equality is naturally accepted as being part of a broader struggle against inequality. A Latina in her mid-twenties with a bachelor's degree wrote, "I like that they (One America) are fighting against LGBTQ+ discrimination because I think homophobia is disgusting and that no one should be discriminated against for who they love. I also like that they are fighting for wage equality because billionaires make way too much money without being taxed properly."[81] A Black woman in her early twenties expressed strong approval, apparently assuming the survey was being administered by One America organizers: "I love that you guys focus on battling homophobia because it should always be about that. About economic equality, too. . . . Everyone should be afforded the same opportunities regardless of economic status and I like that you guys stand for that." She concluded, "Homophobia is a pest."[82]

Another Black woman in her late twenties voiced her approval but added, "I wish it could also help fix racism. I wish it would help all people come together as one and get along so we can support one another better." She mentioned several additional issues, such as gender equality, abortion, and homelessness, that should be part of the same struggle.[83] A white man in his mid-forties with a master's degree indicated that he strongly approves of One America's goals. Zooming in on the key element of frame extension that we constructed on the web page, he points out, "The goals of economic equality are intrinsically tied to the plight of marginalized groups. I think recognizing that economic equality and social discrimination are closely aligned is a smart move."[84] Sounding much like a well-trained social scientist, however, he did offer some criticism pertaining to the use of "overly simplistic terms" to characterize the root causes of discrimination and inequality."

Unlike Republican respondents, several of the Democrats expressed concerns, in particular, for violence and persecution directed toward LGBTQ people. A Black man in his early forties with a bachelor's degree wrote that LGBTQ people "should be able to go about their business without worrying about something being said in a negative manor. It could sometimes end up in violent attacks for no apparent reason."[85] Expressing approval of One America for looking out for working Americans like himself, a Black man in his early thirties added, "I also like that this organization is trying to stand up for the rights of LGBTQ people because a lot of their rights are being taken away by the state legislatures and they need an organization like this one."[86] Specifying that point, a white man in his mid-sixies with a high school degree writes, "I think that supporting economic and LGBTQ+ equality is important throughout the community. . . . The rise of hatred in this country is at an all-time high. Politicians like Ron

DeSantis and his Don't Say Gay campaign further the extent of hate for the LGBT community, not only in Florida but throughout the country." Hate, he concluded, "has no place in today's society but Donald Trump will be sure to keep it in the forefront as he gets indicted for the second time."[87]

Reactions from Democrats to the LGBTQ equality version of the One America web page, like the other versions, showed strong support for the organization. The qualitative comments, however, show an elevated level of dismay and concern, reflecting awareness of Republican politicians' intensified efforts to scapegoat LGBTQ+ people—especially transgender people—to score political points with base supporters who, according to our theoretical argument, are appealing to voters by offering to protect status rewards that come with heteronormativity and cisnormativity. This dismay comes through clearly in the comments of a seventy-six-year-old white woman: "I grew up without a lot of prejudice (meaning that she herself did not hold prejudices) during a time when there was a lot against Blacks, Jews, and gays. It bothers me to see the divisive atmosphere that still exists in America today, and I commend your organization for trying to level the playing field and change people's feelings. However, so many people are opposed to change, and it may take generations to change people's viewpoints against the LGBTQ community. There is a lot of hatred and divisiveness to overcome. This is an issue that will be very difficult to overcome and succeed. People need to be taught more compassion in today's world."[88]

Other Voices

As we pointed out previously, people who identify as Independents or those not affiliated with a party often do not fit stereotypes related to moderate voters or disinterested citizens.

As we found when considering race and gender inequalities, when considering LGBTQ equality many of the respondents who do not identify as Republicans or Democrats speak with passion on both sides of the ideological spectrum. Among conservatives, we see many of the same ideas expressed by Republicans but often expressed with even greater rancor. One married white man in his late forties with a bachelor's degree takes issue with the web page's commentary on the need for unity. He is perhaps missing the point that the call for unity on the web page is intended to encourage people to unite *against people who hold his beliefs*. We have seen that a number of conservative respondents instead think of unity in a way that suggests that the very act of raising issues of inequality is divisive for society as a whole. Clearly, the web page struck a nerve with this respondent:

> What I like is the language of unity rather than division among American workers. Unfortunately, this kind of language has been co-opted by ideologues that in fact seek to divide people based on class, race and the diversity of their opinions. What they are saying sounds good on the surface, but the ways in which they seek "unity" takes the shape of fascism. Forcing uniform thought by way of threat is fascism. And so, as a result of this hijacking of unifying language, any organization that uses said language like that featured here is automatically suspicious to me—which is a shame.[89]

A white man in his early seventies with a master's degree similarly takes offense: "This sounds like a 21st century version of Marxism." After offering a brief critique of Marxism, the respondent raises the LGBTQ focus: "I'm also very curious why the focus is on LGBTQ equality and there is no mention of racial equality. Racism affects a far larger number of Americans and cuts across multiple races—Blacks, Asians, antisemitism, etc. The LGBTQ community is a much smaller segment."[90]

The response is somewhat unusual and may simply reflect the way in which class inequality and LGBTQ inequality are not empirically correlated and are rarely paired in political discourse. Yet the comment does rely on logic suggesting that the small size of the group diminishes the importance of unequal treatment. The response also underestimates the size of the LGBTQ community, particularly among younger Americans who are more likely to be open about sexual orientation and gender identity. For example, a recent Gallup Poll indicates that just over 20 percent of respondents from Generation Z identify as LGBT.[91]

It should also be noted that positive responses among the Independent voters outnumber the negative responses (and in the larger sample that we used for the experiment). One respondent who identifies as a gay man indicated that he is naturally supportive. As an interesting contrast to the conservative respondent quoted earlier, he writes that the organization is "perhaps even a tad socialist leaning, but I am all for the 'levelling' of the proverbial playing field."[92] Another strong supporter—twenty-six years old with some college—identifies as nonbinary. They strongly support One America, focusing primarily on the economic agenda: "I like that you know the importance of holding politicians accountable and are planning to do what you can to make sure the working person's voice is heard."[93]

Like Democratic respondents, several of the Independents see efforts to combat class and LGBTQ inequalities as part of a broader struggle. A young college student who identifies as biracial, for example, writes, "Creating economic equality between all groups will help create a better economy and equality between others."[94] While not going into specifics in ways that some Democratic supporters did, some Independent supporters of One America expressed similar levels of dismay about the persistence of discrimination. A woman in her mid-fifties, who identifies as a devout Catholic, writes, "It's time we give LGBTQ people fair treatment. We are in the 21st century and we need to evolve."[95] A white single mother in her late thirties shared similar sentiments: "Gay, straight, it doesn't matter. I'm tired of the negativity in this world. It is so uncalled for and if we all just communicate with one another we may get a better understanding and realize everyone is unique in their own way. That's what makes them special!"[96]

CITIZENSHIP AS A STATUS HIERARCHY

Republican Voices

When we designed the version of our One America web page that features a section on immigrant equality, we purposefully chose not to specify the legal status of the immigrants in need of equal treatment. This is because citizenship itself is an important privilege hierarchy. Those who claim citizenship status are granted many rights and privileges denied to noncitizens, as well as social esteem—including freedom from abuse and denigration and protections from state-sponsored violence and control.[97] It is true that many Americans specify documented status when stating their positions on immigration, giving the impression that they are supportive of immigrants as long as they have legally entered the country. That distinction certainly appears in our qualitative data. It is worth considering, however, that historically in the United States legal status has often done little to protect immigrants and even the children of immigrants from violence, discrimination, and denigration.[98] It is also notable that throughout much of United States history, business owners have tended to support immigration because a surplus supply of labor can be used to keep wages low. Strong political backlash against immigration, however, can make it difficult for employers to maintain a pro-immigration stance.[99] That is clearly the case in today's political climate, where Republican politicians use anti-immigration rhetoric to gain support from conservative base voters, while many Democratic politicians have also moved toward more conservative positions on border control.

Consistent with findings from our experiment, the mere mention of immigrant equality "triggered" many Republican respondents. One white man in his early fifties, for example, harshly criticizes the economic agenda of the web page, finding it ironic that One America calls for equality but "feeds the fires of class warfare and class envy." This respondent, like others we have mentioned, seems to misinterpret the call for action, failing to recognize that the web page is not calling for unity between workers and the elite but is instead calling for unity in opposition to the elite. The respondent adds, "The immigrant stuff is complete BS as well, making no distinction between legal immigration and those who come into this country illegally. I would never support any Marxist organization such as this and I am certainly no 'wealthy CEO.'"[100] These sentiments are shared by a white man in his late sixties with a master's degree. He also condemns Marxist organizations and advises those who "hate America" to go to Cuba. He adds, "Colleges have been corrupted by Marxist socialist agendas and will ruin the best country in the world. I have traveled the world and there is nowhere better than the U.S. These people that are coming into our country at our southern borders are not welcome and will ruin our economy."[101]

Opposition to immigrant equality appears to be motivated both by a desire to defend capitalism as well as by resentment of competition with immigrant labor. A white woman in her late sixties in a high-income household, for example, says, "I feel that 'equality for immigrants' is code for supporting illegal immigration. It seems to have a goal of increasing government interference with private companies. The woke policies supported by this organization are destroying the economy of this country."[102] On the other side of the class spectrum, a white woman in her early seventies reports, "I have not been chosen for jobs because the employer's quota of hiring minority people was not met." She adds, "It is not fair for illegal immigrants to come in and take jobs that native born Americans need to support their families, just because they are immigrants."[103]

We also see opposition to immigrant equality that is based primarily on cultural grounds. A white woman in her late forties with an advanced degree, for example, emphasizes the legal distinctions between immigrants and native-born citizens. She extends her argument: "There are language barriers with people coming in from other countries not knowing the language. Then they would most likely file for SSI, SSDI, or welfare, or SNAP benefits." She adds, "They have limited knowledge, education, and work ethics, unlike the United States citizen who was born here and knows via education what to expect and how to live within the United States." While the vast majority of Republicans in our sample are white and tend to be older, it is important to note that not all opponents of immigration are white. For example, we heard from a woman in her early fifties who contributes to a high-income household and identifies as Hispanic or Latina. Regarding the One America web page, she notes, "This seems like something that is intended for a millennial and not for the majority. It likely doesn't represent the country as a whole. Pushing equality for all is not going to go over well with those who have a job."[104]

Democratic Voices

The overwhelming majority of Democrats in our sample expressed strong support for the immigrant equality version of One America for Working People. It is clear, though, that the immigration question does give pause to some Democrats who might otherwise be more supportive. Some Democrats, for example, did specify the importance of the distinction between documented and undocumented immigrants, although they did not make their points with the kind of animosity found in Republican responses. A white woman in her late sixties with a bachelor's degree, for example, wrote, "I believe that the immigrants that come to our country should not be entitled to all benefits that they receive." She added, "Immigrants should be able to seek citizenship, just like our ancestors, but they need to earn that status."[105] A white man in his mid-fifties with a bachelor's degree approved of the organization. On the immigrant question, he wrote, "We need immigrant workers to complete work that many Americans do not want to do or in cases where not enough workers can be hired to complete the needed work." He added, "But we also need to make sure these workers are in the country legally."[106]

The idea that immigrants are needed and should be appreciated for doing the work that native-born Americans are unwilling to do turns up as a common justification for supporting immigrants. Respondents making this case, however, do not seem to recognize a need to square this framing (i.e., somebody needs to do the dirty work) with a call for equality. It is perhaps not surprising that some Democrats struggle with the immigrant question. On the one hand, immigrant equality is consistent with a more general call for human rights, equal rights, and supporting the dignity of all people. Yet, as mentioned, immigration has at times been used by the business class to undercut the leverage of organized labor. Perhaps due to this dissonance, a number of our respondents expressed their strong approval for One America but simply neglected to mention immigrant equality when they explained their support. Clearly, Democratic voters are not unanimous in their support of immigrant equality. One man in his late forties who identifies as biracial (white and Black) made his feelings clear: "As for illegal immigrants, they can stay right where they are because I don't feel as though they should be part of anything over here in America and I don't know why they (One America) should include illegals in anything as far as goals go."[107] He concluded by saying that everything else about the organization is OK.

However, for other respondents the support of immigrant equality adds to the appeal of One America for Working People. For one white woman in her early sixties, it is a matter of morality and justice: "We all are descendants of immigrants and anyone not wanting people to legally immigrate is evil, since we basically slaughtered the entire group of American natives who actually were born in this country."[108] Democratic Latinos in our sample also provided a strong counterargument to the Republican beliefs about how immigration affects the economy. A young Latino in his early twenties with an associate degree writes, "As a minority myself I am extremely happy and grateful that an organization like this exists so me and my family can be given equal rights and opportunities in the workforce." For him, the issue is not simply a matter of self interest: "It is extremely important that we take advantage of the opportunities given and expand on them so we can create wealth."[109] Along these lines, a Latina in her early thirties wrote, "I am proud that somebody is trying to create equality in the economy and for immigrants. We need equal rights. It is not a secret that bosses pay less money to immigrants or people with no documents because they don't have the same rights." She also argued that immigrant equality would benefit communities by combatting social problems associated with poverty. As she expressed it, "With less money, more people are frustrated because they have more endeudamiento (debt). Living here is expensive." Some, she suggests, look for other ways to deal with the expenses by getting involved with drugs or crime, or even by taking their own lives.[110]

Other Voices

Once again, opinions are mixed among those who identify as Independents or who do not identify with a major party. While there is some overlap with comments of Republicans and Democrats, responses from Independents seem to be somewhat removed from the well-rehearsed lines often spoken by Democratic and Republican politicians. That finds expression in statements about humanity that extend beyond national borders, as well as appeals on moral grounds. To be clear, however, there are staunch opponents among the Independents. A white man in his early sixties with an associate degree, for example, approves of most of what One America stands for. However, he pointedly adds, "I am not crazy about immigrant rights for those who came to the USA illegally."[111]

As is true among Democrats, we also find Independents who justify support for immigrants by praising them for doing work that nobody else will do. A white woman in her mid-sixties with a high school degree, for example, supports the organization and says, specifically pertaining to immigrants, "From my experience most immigrants are very hard workers and usually do work most Americans don't want to do and for much less money and with no benefits."[112] Another white woman in her early sixties observes, "I live in a shore summer tourist location. We have lots of immigrant workers. Everyone bitches about them being here. But no locals want the jobs. Nor will they work the hours the immigrants work. So, don't complain unless you want to do the work."[113]

References to hard-working immigrants to some extent preserve a sense of the immigrant as the "other." Some respondents, instead, approved of the organization while expressing a greater sense of unity and inclusion. A young Latina with a bachelor's degree, for example, wrote, "The well-being of American citizens should be on the forefront of all policy makers. It is important that someone fight for us and advocate for ALL Americans. I think One America for Working People does just that."[114] Notably, this respondent does emphasize citizenship and legal status in her construction of "we-ness." This may reflect the way in which many Latinos whose families have been in the United States for many generations often experience discrimination from those who assume they are immigrants and treat them with disrespect.[115] A white man in his early forties with a high school degree expresses support but through a more universalistic lens. He laments, "I don't know. I guess it's just hard for people to treat each other decently. All workers should be paid and treated well everywhere in the world."[116]

For other Independent voters in our sample, the immigration issue struck a chord on moral grounds. A white woman in her mid-fifties with some college education, for example, wrote, "I like the idea of people standing up to politicians and uniting to demand equality for all workers. There is too much hatred and violence in the world, especially toward immigrants and anyone who does not fit the mold. People need to stop fighting amongst themselves and stop the politicians from dividing the people."[117]

A young man in his early twenties with some college education asserts that everyone in the country deserves the same rights and protections. "These things should not be a matter of opinion and simply given rights. Simply because people exist, they deserve rights."[118]

Strikingly, a white woman in her early thirties in a low-income household powerfully drew on her experiences to explain her support:

> I believe there are systems designed to keep the working class as poor, sick, and uneducated as possible so that the wealthy few may stay comfortable where they are. I used to believe they were simply out of touch and do not know what it is like to have to live paycheck to paycheck or to be marginalized. But I have found that no matter how often we show them or try to help them understand, they simply do not want to. We cannot beg them for a better life and there should be more organizations dedicated to helping people. Everyone deserves a fair chance in life and they deserve more than just the "opportunity" for survival.[119]

RELIGION AS A STATUS HIERARCHY

Republican Voices

Responses to the religious equality version of the One America web page display a certain amount of confusion. Many respondents seem to expect the pairing of economic inequality with race or gender but are not accustomed to thinking about class inequality within the context of religion. By that, we mean that there is a tendency to think of religious differences as horizontal cleavages that may or may not be correlated with economic inequality. The One America web page, however, is based on the idea that Christianity in the United States conveys privileges and esteem that are denied to non-Christians. In designing the web page, we pointedly specified discrimination and violence directed toward members of non-Christian religious faiths.

To some extent, lack of familiarity with arguments about religious inequality and class inequality being intertwined seems to have given many respondents freedom to simply ignore the content on religion. Indeed, among Republicans we see a mixture of support and opposition to the economic goals of One America that is similar to what we saw among those who viewed the economics only version of the web page. The support tends to be passive and noncommittal—simply expressing agreement with the content of the web page. Opposition is more animated, forcefully defending capitalism against what they perceive to be socialist or communist agendas.

Respondents who indicate that they are Christians, and that religion is very important to them, however, do tend to strongly object to the content about religious equality. This squares with contemporary societal debates in which conservatives appeal to religious liberty to justify denying services to others because doing so would violate their Christian religious beliefs. The United States Supreme Court, for example, recently ruled in favor of a woman who argued that a Colorado public accommodations law protecting LGBTQ people from discrimination violates her religious freedom. She designs websites for couples to celebrate their weddings but is unwilling to design websites for LGBTQ couples because doing so, she claims, violates her religious freedom. Catholic schools have made similar religious freedom arguments, objecting, for example, to a mandate in the

Affordable Care Act (Obamacare) to cover the cost of contraception in health care packages.

We specified discrimination and violence against non-Christian groups to gauge people's responses when asked to consider violence and discrimination directed toward Jews, Muslims, and people of other minority faiths. That clearly did not sit well with a number of Republican respondents. One white Christian woman in her mid-twenties with an associate degree, for example, indicated that she liked what the One America web page had to say about economic equality, but she concludes, "The thing I disliked about the goals is when it comes to religion. This is because I'm strongly religious myself."[120] The response is striking in that the respondent apparently believes that a religious person's opposition to religious equality and protections for non-Christians should be self-explanatory.

A white evangelical woman in her late seventies indicated that she is suspicious of One America because "it is so infrequent that we see groups getting together to protect these aforementioned groups" (workers and non-Christians). She added, "At present our government is pointing to Catholics as fomenters of violence, and we know that's not true."[121] She is apparently referring to a leaked memo from an FBI agent that cautioned against the possibility of violent extremism from adherents of radical traditional Catholicism—an extremist sect with organizations categorized by the Southern Poverty Law Center as hate groups.[122] The memo sparked a broad and intense backlash, as Republican lawmakers accused the FBI of spying on ordinary Catholics. The FBI has since withdrawn the memo. The striking aspect of this episode, for our purposes, is how difficult it is for Christians in the United States, in this case Catholics, to conceive of violence and extremism initiated by any group identifying with the Christian faith.

We observed both supporters and opponents of the economic agenda voicing the same complaint about the focus on protecting non-Christians from discrimination and violence. A white Christian man in his early forties who indicates that his faith is very important to him endorses the web page content about economic inequality. Regarding religious equality, he writes, "I agree with the idea outlined in that section, but it also seems like you are saying that Christian groups are not discriminated against, which I would say is untrue." Meanwhile, a white Christian woman in her forties objects to the critique of economic inequality, as she feels that everyone has a chance to succeed in America. She adds, "The other thing that stood out is that Christian discrimination (meaning discrimination against Christians) is becoming real in the US, yet only everything but Christianity is covered here. Any kind of religious discrimination, anti-Christian or not, should not be tolerated."

Our goal here is certainly not to endorse discrimination against Christians. The comments from Republicans, however, highlight the extent to which many respondents do not recognize that Christianity has something of a taken-for-granted quality in the United States that establishes norms that others are expected to follow. While the web page intends to invoke images of hate crimes and "terrorist" stereotypes directed toward Muslims in the United States, or the rampant antisemitism we have witnessed in recent years, Republican respondents are more likely to interpret the web page as a slight directed toward Christians at a time when Republican politicians are escalating efforts to impose conservative Christian values on the entire population, as seen in legislation sharply restricting or prohibiting abortion and legislation aimed to restrict freedoms of transgender people, including limiting or restricting access to health care.

Democratic Voices

To some extent, Democrats also seem puzzled by the pairing of economic equality and religious equality. Many respondents simply voiced their support for One America while neglecting to discuss the web page's treatment of religious equality. Other Democrats, however, clearly welcomed the linkage of economic and religious equality. Their responses were strikingly different from those of the Republicans not only in terms of approval but also in terms of their recognition of the hierarchical nature of religion in the United States. A young Jewish woman with a high school degree expressed her support for the economic agenda before pivoting to religion: "I also definitely think there's a big problem with discrimination against other religions in the U.S. I feel that very strongly as a Jew. Christianity is not the only religion in the world and America is supposed to be diverse. The lack of equality and the prejudice against other religions should stop. I've encountered many Christians who blame Muslims for 9/11 but won't take accountability for any mass shootings and terror attacks done by Christians."[123] Similarly, one respondent in our sample is a white man in his thirties with an advanced degree and who identifies as agnostic. He voices his concerns about the way that religion is becoming increasingly dominant. "Religious groups are taking advantage of the lack of regulations to promote the well-being of their members, sometimes at the expense of other less represented groups of people."[124]

A man in his forties who identifies as Black and Latino applies the call for religious inequality to his own circumstances. "Being a minority in this country and a part of the LGBTQ community, this is something that has affected me personally throughout my working career. If these goals (the goals of One America) become a reality that would end inequality and we all would be able to have an opportunity to live the American Dream."[125] In this instance, the respondent appears to identify religious inequality with the broader issue of discrimination and perhaps most directly with discrimination experienced due to his LGBTQ identity. As a young white woman currently attending college reminds us, religious inequality can be experienced with a sense of terror: "As someone who is part of the LGBTQ+ community, and as a woman, I fear for my life and for my future based on the workings of the government. The influence of religion in government today is very scary and makes me feel as though extremists are pushing their own agenda at the expense of others."[126]

Clearly, it is not only members of the LGBTQ community who feel this sense of despair stemming from conservative Christianity and its influence on politics. For example, a white man in his fifties with a bachelor's degree colorfully expresses his concerns for the nation as a whole. "I'm rapidly losing faith in this country, and only through organizations like this (One America) will there be hope. But there are too many idiots out there. For the first time in my life, I'm literally afraid for this country, and would just as soon move. The Republican Party is an evil being, and Trump can kiss my ass. I'm scared more that so many people follow him than I am of him. In my 58 years I've watched boundless leaps in freedoms and newfound equalities and now it's literally going backwards. I fear a civil war of some sort is inevitable. The USA is swirling down the drain."

Other Voices

Independents and those not identifying as Republican or Democrat, once again, show a range of intense views about One America for Working People. While the Democrat just quoted feels there are too many idiots out there, one Independent voter asserts that we (the authors of the study or, more likely, the directors of One America for Working People) are the idiots. As he expressed it, "Sorry, you idiots, but not everyone should earn the same amount." He further instructs, "Get your heads out of the gutter and realize people have to work. . . . I thought you get out of life what you put in, but clearly you people want to be lazy and get paid just as much as people who work."[127] We do not intend to ridicule this respondent by including his full quotation. Yet this sentiment, not always expressed with such anger, appears time and time again in our data among Republicans and, as in this case, some Independents. Even though the respondent reports a household income well below the national average, he is strongly committed to the idea that people's earnings reflect their skills and work ethic. Not coincidentally, we think, this kind of animated response is much more likely to surface when our subjects confront an appeal for economic equality that is linked to a promise to fight status inequalities that benefit the angry respondent.

Other Independents who provided qualitative responses, however, offer enthusiastic support. As we found when considering other versions of the web page, the Independent supporters often think of the organization in terms of norms of fairness and a desire for peace and harmony. One woman in her mid-twenties with a high school degree endorsed the web page's statements about resisting divisiveness and added, "It is also refreshing to see religious beliefs included in the discussion of discrimination, as I don't see this very often."[128] Similarly, a white woman in her early forties with a high school degree states, "I feel like no matter what race or religion or sexual preference or any other personal choice a person makes, they are entitled to have equal rights and equal pay."[129]

As was true of Democratic responses to the LGBTQ equality version of the web page, here it is also easy to detect a strong sense of dismay with the current state of affairs and a deep longing for a more harmonious world. A young Latina college student, for example, writes, "This (One America) is something I believe will help people see that everyone is the same and shouldn't be looked at differently for their race, color, and religion." In the end, she added, "We all have blood in our bodies," and that is what matters.[130] A white Mormon woman in her fifties pleads, "We should be concerned with each other and help each other—not continue to fight. Judgments against others based on religion or race are wrong and everyone should stop the violence. We were put on this earth to love each other and be there for them. There is too much hate in this world."[131]

CONCLUSION

In this chapter, we have solicited feedback from Americans not just on their support or opposition to One America for Working People but also their explanations for that support or opposition. The experimental research that we presented earlier was designed to isolate the effect of status goals in affecting people's support for a progressive alliance and to show how status contestation drives political polarization. Those results strongly indicate that status matters. Simply adding a brief paragraph committing the organization to fighting for equal treatment—protection from violence and discrimination—substantially changes the way that people feel about the organization. In this chapter, we aimed to let people explain, in their own words, why they feel the way that they do. More specifically, we want to identify a range of ideas and beliefs that people draw upon to make sense of the organization.

The qualitative findings of this supplementary analysis align well with the quantitative findings we presented earlier. Few people objected to One America when they viewed the economic equality version of the organization, regardless of their party identity. Support from Republicans was a bit more reserved, but only a few Republicans disagreed with what was presented to them as a sharp critique of inequality under capitalism sustained by political corruption. We saw Republicans and Democrats sharply at odds, however, when they explained their views of the organization when status equality is in the picture. We think that the qualitative data, in many ways, provide additional confirmation of the theoretical argument that guides our work. On the one hand, it is not difficult to identify patterns in our presentation of the data pertaining to individual characteristics, or what Seymour Martin Lipset referred to as the social bases of politics. In addition to party identity, for example, younger people, people of color, and highly educated people tended to be more supportive of the organization. However, our presentation of the data also reveals quite a few exceptions to those patterns. For example, some Latino respondents opposed the organization even when they viewed versions of the web page that address racial equality or immigrant equality. Several women oppose the gender equality goals while several men support them. Many white respondents support One America's racial equality goals, while many wealthy respondents do as well. Rather than seeking out patterns reflecting the average responses of people with particular attributes, we have instead focused directly on isolating preferences to either preserve or overturn status hierarchies and to consider how powerfully these preferences drive political behavior.

The qualitative data presented in this chapter also reveal ways in which consideration of status hierarchies can evoke strong emotions that appear to intensify support or opposition to One America. It is not coincidental, we believe, that Republican views of the economic agenda of the organization tend to be hostile when the organization's economic goals are linked to challenges to a status hierarchy. We also see that expressions of support from Democrats and from many Independents are more animated when they are asked to consider the interdependence of goals to overturn class and status hierarchies. For the Republicans and some Independents, the organization's commitment to reducing status inequalities leads them to become suspicious of an economic agenda that they might otherwise endorse. Democrats, and some Independents, become more enthusiastic in support for the economic agenda as they feel that they are not being asked to sideline status equality goals that are important to them.

Critically, we must emphasize that we are presenting the voices of those who were willing to express an opinion, one way or another. The sad truth of American politics is that a very large segment of the population is disinterested, uninformed, or disinformed. We do not make this point in order to denigrate or insult the average American. Indeed, we feel that this is an unsurprising outcome in a society characterized by extreme inequality, in which people must devote their energies to making ends meet, feeding their children, and finding ways to secure enjoyment and dignity despite the forces working against them. We recognize that we are in a privileged position in that we are paid to devote our time and energy to thinking, writing, and researching politics, inequality, and other social issues. Without question, any progressive coalition with goals similar to our fictitious One America for Working People must find ways to draw more people off the sidelines and bring them into the struggle for justice. We now consider those possibilities in the concluding chapter.

8

LOOKING TO THE FUTURE

Crisis or New Coalition?

W e undertook this study with a general goal similar to that held by many scholars. We want to
understand how extreme economic inequal-
ity persists in a democratic society such as the United States.
Among American households, the overwhelming majority of
the nation's wealth is held by the top 10 percent of households
while most American families struggle to make ends meet.[1] So
why don't Americans get behind a political agenda that promotes greater equity? Rather than focusing on average voting
preferences of people who hold particular attributes (like race,
class, gender, education, religion, etc.), we instead developed an
innovative research design to assess the extent to which status
hierarchies organize political behavior in a way that transcends
individual attributes. We purposefully refrained from imputing
political interests to people based on preconceived categorical
groupings and instead considered how Americans, possessing a
range of individual attributes, engage in politics to advance or
preserve positions within status hierarchies.

We have argued that scholars have underestimated the
importance of status in motivating political behavior. Many
people derive special treatment based on their position within

status hierarchies that have been historically constructed and endure, in part, because status privileges are often taken for granted and presumed to be natural and deserved. As we saw in the last chapter, many of our study participants who most strongly opposed One America for Working People vehemently denied the existence of status inequalities.

Our status contestation and politics theory stipulates that beneficiaries of different status hierarchies oppose progressive coalitions that aim to simultaneously combat economic and status inequalities—even though they may favor efforts to reduce economic inequality. At the same time, many others embrace these same coalitions because they are harmed by status inequalities or they understand economic equality and status equality as both being desirable or as necessarily compatible goals. While it may be the case that receiving respect and admiration for group traits, behaviors, or attributes can be gratifying, we argue that people care about preserving status primarily because of the differential treatment they receive. Not everyone can be wealthy, but many hold dear the favored treatment that comes with being white, male, heterosexual, cisgender, Christian, or a citizen in American society. Our theory also stipulates that efforts to defend status privileges are central to political polarization that stymies progressive legislation. One's position in various status hierarchies offers a lens through which people interpret and organize public policy proposals, and status interests push voters toward opposing sides on a broad range of issues. This can result in people opposing policies that would promote greater economic inequality if they cognitively link status and economic equality goals.

The results of our experiment, which we have presented in the preceding chapters, offer striking support for our argument. Indeed, the findings actually exceed our own expectations in terms of illustrating how strongly status preservation goals sustain inequality. Perhaps surprisingly, our fictitious organization is broadly popular among those who participated in our study when they considered a mission statement that sharply criticizes the economic and political elite and calls for a united front to fight for economic equality. That support cuts across differences in education, gender, racial identity, political party, and even political ideology. Most people in our sample, in other words, want a more equal society when it comes to wealth and income. Our experimental manipulations reveal the heart of the problem. Those who identify as Republicans are much less likely to support the organization if it links economic inequality to status inequalities. Interestingly, the negative reaction is similar in magnitude, regardless of whether Republican study participants are reacting to calls for racial equality, gender equality, LGBTQ equality, immigrant equality, or religious equality.

Some might suggest that these findings point to a simple solution. If you want to fight for economic equality, you should not simultaneously fight for status equalities. Our results indicate, however, that such a strategy would be as ineffective as it is repugnant to opponents of status inequality. Among Democrats in our sample, One America is much more popular and perceived to be worthy of support if it links economic inequality to status inequalities. Importantly, even though One America aims its appeal at the working class, college-educated Democrats are overwhelmingly supportive of the organization and its goals, as are Democrats without a college degree. Also important, those who indicate that they are Independents are more supportive of One America than are Republicans if they evaluated a web page that commits to fighting any of the status inequalities that we considered. That holds true for Independents who are college educated as well as those who are not. Independents are not different from Republicans if they viewed the "economics only" version of the web page.

Consistent with our theory, we also find that our study participants' positions on a broad range of policy issues—in terms of the consistency with which they take the progressive or conservative stances—are powerfully shaped by their approval or disapproval of the goals of One America for Working People. We see little political polarization based solely on party affiliation, but proponents and opponents of One America comprise the extreme tails of the distribution of responses on our policy preference index. In short, the findings of our study indicate that status contestation goals are at the very center of political divisions in the United States.

We think that the importance of status contestation has been underappreciated in large part because of the way in which status is typically understood in studies of politics. Earlier scholarship treated status more in terms of efforts to gain recognition for the proposed superiority of a group's lifestyle or values. Joseph Gusfield, for example, argued that temperance activists were not particularly concerned with concrete steps taken to prevent others from imbibing alcoholic beverages. From his perspective, the state's endorsement of temperance was satisfying because that recognition served as a substitute or even a consolation prize for members of the old middle class who were experiencing declines in the class structure.[2] We, on the other hand, are focused on tangible privileges that people derive when they are situated at the top of a status hierarchy—privileges so consequential that beneficiaries will strongly oppose attempts to level the playing field, often while simultaneously denying that the playing field is tilted. Our theoretical argument borrows insights from studies of structural racism and structural sexism.[3] Consistent with these theories, we do not reduce structures of inequality to individuals' differences of opinion on cultural issues or policies. Status shapes politics because it reflects vertical rather than horizontal divisions. Resistance is strong not because people have different values but because beneficiaries of status hierarchies often feel entitled to special treatment and are highly motivated to resist any challenge to their advantaged position.

CURRENT DANGER TO DEMOCRACY

Scholars have noted that in recent decades Americans are much less likely to express attitudes (when surveyed) that reflect blatant racism or other forms of bigotry. While some have taken this to mean that levels of discrimination are declining in American society, Mary Jackman and Michael Muha threw a bucket of cold water on that rosy interpretation in a seminal paper published in 1984 titled "Education and Intergroup Attitudes: Moral Enlightenment, Superficial Commitment, or Ideological Refinement?"[4] Using survey data administered to a representative sample of adults in the United States, they first took note of the way that those with higher education were less likely to express overtly bigoted attitudes. Although such a finding is consistent with the notion that bigotry reflects a lack of knowledge and understanding, the authors drew different conclusions based on additional analyses. They noted that while the highly educated were much less likely to endorse overtly bigoted viewpoints, they were no more likely than less educated people to support policies that would reduce intergroup inequalities. They had developed more sophisticated ways of talking about race, but that did not reflect a desire to reduce inequality.

Decades later, Eduardo Bonilla-Silva explored this phenomenon in depth, publishing *Racism Without Racists: Color-Blind Racism and the Persistence of Racial Equality*. Originally published in 2003, a sixth edition of this extraordinarily popular book came out in 2021.[5] Bonilla-Silva delves into the ways that contemporary white Americans discuss race, engaging in awkward verbal gymnastics to portray themselves as "color-blind" while nevertheless struggling to conceal their underlying commitment to maintaining white advantages. A key point raised by the book is that we should not assume that declines in expressed bigotry—even an increase in statements claiming support for equal rights—correspond with a decline in the way that racism persists and continues to have real consequences for victims. More recently, Hajar Yazdiha calls attention to how both proponents and opponents of racial equality often draw on the legacy of Martin Luther King Jr. to marshal support for their positions. Conservatives selectively draw on King's famous line from his "I Have a Dream" speech, in which he expresses longing for the day when his children will be judged not by the color of their skin but by the content of their character. The conservative spin deliberately neglects the aspirational nature of the statement and instead uses it as "evidence" indicating that King favored a "color-blind" society and therefore would oppose any policies that seek redress for racial inequality.[6]

Sociologists have fruitfully studied sources of intergroup conflict, often pointing to competition and exclusion processes that deploy group solidarity to protect an advantaged position. It is important to keep in mind, however, that socially constructed status hierarchies are deeply rooted in historical processes and are more stable compared to periodic and persistent eruptions of open conflict. Women's suffrage, for example, did not put an end to status advantages and preferential treatment awarded to men. Laws prohibiting employment discrimination based on sexual orientation have not spelled the demise of heteronormativity. We are living in a time, however, in which beneficiaries of status hierarchies are openly and aggressively acting to protect their status advantages. This suggests that nonconflictual strategies to preserve status advantages are breaking down because beneficiaries of hierarchies are motivated to openly fight to preserve status privileges that had previously been taken for granted and largely went unchallenged.

The size and visibility of the uprising in defense of status hierarchies signifies danger. The sustained popularity of Donald Trump among roughly half of the American population illustrates this clearly. At the time of writing (December 2024), Trump is preparing for a second term in office after winning the 2024 election, and polls show that a little more than 50 percent of Americans have a favorable view of him. While prior Republican presidential candidates often used "dog whistle" messaging to signal their willingness to defend privilege, Trump threw away the whistle and pulled out a megaphone. He recognized early that many Americans enthusiastically responded to his campaign rhetoric that had little to do with public policy and more to do with simply denigrating the status of people of color, women, LGBTQ people, immigrants, and non-Christians.[7] Even when Trump passes from the scene, the anger and resentment that fueled his ascendance will linger for decades. Trump did not create the anger; he stoked it and rode the wave. He did offer a model, however, that illustrates how far conservatives can go to bend the rules of politics, to suppress votes of those who oppose them, to lie to the American people, to exploit the mainstream media and social media to push Americans toward conspiracy theories that undermine confidence in democratic institutions, and to issue veiled (and unveiled) threats that make people think twice before standing up for what is right because doing right can make them targets of violence and harassment.

Our analysis presented in this book offers a clear view of why this ugly brand of politics attracts so many supporters. Many

Americans sense that their taken-for-granted status privileges are being usurped. Their capacity to maintain power and status privileges through less visible and less confrontational means is breaking down as the number of people with an interest in overturning status hierarchies has grown.

In chapter 5, we discussed the way in which replacement theory resonates with many who feel disrespected and increasingly powerless. The theory places blame on a vast conspiracy orchestrated by Jews or by Democratic politicians who, according to the theory, are purposefully allowing immigrants to flood across the borders, and those people will ultimately replace "true Americans" at the voting booth, the workplace, and in society more generally. The slogan "Make American Great Again" speaks to a share of Americans who long for what they perceive to be better days when their status privileges went unchallenged—a nation where white Christian heterosexual men ran the show and were admired for doing so. Of course, no such conspiracy exists, but consensus in support of these status hierarchies is fractured. Although more than seventy-four million people voted for Trump in 2020 and more than seventy-seven million voted for him in 2024, Americans had previously elected Barack Obama, the nation's first Black president, to two full terms. And in 2020, more than eighty-one million people voted for Joe Biden, with many of them motivated more by their hatred of Trump than by love for Biden. The intense anger expressed by many MAGA supporters, and their indifference to the ongoing assault on democratic institutions, only makes sense when we recognize that a challenge to their status and privilege animates, to varying degrees, nearly half of the country.

While status contestation played an important role in placing Trump back in the White House, it is also important to consider the failure of the Democratic Party to offer an alternative to Trump that was attractive to more voters. While Democratic strategists typically devise cautious strategies in hopes of winning support from moderate voters, they may be underestimating the extent to which the Party could draw more voters from the sidelines if they offered a vision that unapologetically offers bold remedies for economic inequality while steadfastly supporting efforts to dismantle status hierarchies.

WILL ONE AMERICA FAIL?

We are living in perilous times in which many Americans display high tolerance for political violence, authoritarianism, and corruption as long as these are in the service of status preservation. Although we think this danger is quite serious in the years ahead, there is reason to think that conditions will improve in the future if democracy holds in the present. In our sample, the majority of participants approved of One America for Working People, and those who identified as Democrats and Independents showed greater approval if they were presented with a version of the web page that commits to simultaneously combatting economic and status inequalities. Nevertheless, in the country at large we have a stalemate that is increasingly contentious, as conservative forces are fighting a desperate fight. But what about the future? Will this stalemate ever end? There is reason to expect that it will.

Social movement scholars have emphasized the importance of the "political opportunity structure" when it comes to determining whether movements will emerge and whether they are likely to succeed.[8] The core idea is that for many people who are inclined to organize to bring about progressive social change, the political climate may appear to be inhospitable. For example, those holding political power may be united in opposition to significant change and prepared to use their superior resources to stifle any dissent that may surface. Or perhaps public opinion indicates broad support for the status quo and high levels of opposition to a change agenda. Under such conditions, formidable social movements are unlikely to emerge because people are afraid to act or they may sense that any action they take is doomed to failure and would, therefore, be wasted effort. In the case of the American civil rights movement, for example, Doug McAdam has shown how urbanization of the Black population leading into the 1960s, as well as the great migration of African Americans from the south to northern cities, fundamentally altered the political context for contesting racial oppression. As long as the majority of Black Americans was concentrated in rural locations in Southern states—where they were denied franchise rights—their grievances could be safely ignored by national politicians. Yet with urbanization and Black people's migration into northern states like Illinois, Pennsylvania, and New York, Black voters were critical in electing John F. Kennedy to the White House in 1960. Although Kennedy was reluctant to embrace the civil rights agenda wholeheartedly, he was vulnerable to pressure from the movement because support given in one election could be withdrawn in the next. Kennedy had to be at least somewhat responsive to civil rights demands, creating greater optimism about the chances of success if Black Americans continued to press a civil rights agenda with vigor.[9]

If perceptions of success are important in generating collective action, what do our study participants think about chances of success for One America for Working People? We asked them. Their responses offer more than a glimmer of hope for the future. Indeed, 14 percent said that they think the organization would be "very successful" and 52 percent indicated that it would be "somewhat successful." There is a substantial difference, however, when we break the responses down by age. If we only consider the responses of those who are forty years old or younger, 82 percent said they thought the organization would at least be somewhat successful. Nearly one-fourth of participants said it will be very successful. Perhaps most encouraging, white men under forty seem to be especially optimistic—31 percent say that the organization will be very successful and 47 percent say it will be somewhat successful.

This stark difference between age groups aligns with the points we have emphasized. The fierce defense of status privilege that we currently see reflects anger that many Americans feel about potentially losing the status privileges they have enjoyed during their lives. The racist backlash to the civil rights movement found a home in the Republican Party in the 1970s. The tight bond between conservative Christianity and the Republican Party (which is highly relevant when considering status related to gender, sexual orientation, and religion) took root in the early 1980s. Americans born in more recent decades have come of political age in a different context—one where various forms of status privilege were being called into question as the nation, and cultural understandings of group difference, evolved (figure 8.1). We can get a better sense of these changes by considering some polling data. A Gallup poll indicates that in 2001, 64 percent of white respondents said that they were "satisfied" with the treatment of Black people in American society. By 2021, that percentage dropped to 44 percent, indicating growing awareness in broader society of ongoing racial injustice.[10] Although some Republican politicians like Ron DeSantis are appealing to white voters by "outlawing" teaching about key aspects of the Black experience in the United States, another recent poll indicates that 79 percent of white respondents think

FIGURE 8.1 Thousands of young people engaged in an antiracism protest in front of the Lincoln Memorial, June 6, 2020. Getty Images.

that schools should teach about the history of racism in the United States, 72 percent favor teaching about current impacts of racism, and 85 percent think schools should teach about positive contributions made by Black Americas to society.[11]

Regarding gender, polling data shows that in 1998 only 45 percent of men characterized sexual harassment as a "major problem" in the United States. By 2017, that percentage had grown to 66 percent.[12] And while it may seem to some conservatives that attacking LGBTQ people is a winning strategy, given levels of homophobia in the population and the relatively small number of people who identify as LGBTQ, that is clearly a miscalculation. A Gallup poll published in 2023 indicates that while only 2.7 percent of the baby boomer generation identify as LGBT, the percentage (19.7) is strikingly higher among those in Generation Z (born from 1997 to 2004).[13] Likely reflecting the increasing visibility of LGBTQ people, another poll reports that in 2023, 64 percent of adults said that same-sex relations are "morally acceptable," compared to only 40 percent who thought so in 2001.[14] Regarding immigrant status, currently many Americans are concerned with what they perceive to be a crisis at the southern border. However, support for immigration has increased substantially over time. According to Gallup, in 2023, 57 percent of adult Americans said immigration levels should increase or remain the same. In 1993, that was true of only 33 percent of Americans. What's more, in 2023, 64 percent of respondents indicated that they are at least somewhat sympathetic toward the plight of undocumented immigrants.[15]

Since the nation's founding, many Americans derived status from their affiliation with Christianity as the dominant religion in the country. Yet conservative brands of Christianity also provided a justification for enjoying other forms of status inequality such as those related to gender and sexual orientation. Here, also, we have witnessed a decline in Christianity's hold over the population in recent decades. In 1971, 90 percent of adults in the United States identified as Christian, 6 percent as non-Christian, and only 4 percent said they did not have a religious preference. By 2021, Christian identifiers dropped to 69 percent, non-Christians remained relatively steady at 7 percent, and most strikingly, 21 percent indicated no religious affiliation. Gallup polling also shows that in 1965, 70 percent of adults surveyed said religion was "very important" to them. By 2021, that figure had dropped to 49 percent. And while weekly church attendance hovered close to 50 percent from the 1940s through the 1990s, by 2021 it had dropped to just 29 percent.[16]

By presenting these figures we do not intend to suggest that status hierarchies based on race, gender, sexual orientation and gender identity, citizenship, and religion are no longer potent and consequential for lived experiences today. Everything we presented in this book demonstrates just how consequential they are. We do think these trends are relevant, however, for explaining the desperate war in defense of status hierarchies waged by the Republican Party and in showing why the younger participants in our sample are much more optimistic about the potential success of One America for Working People. We are at a crossroads. Status defense could destroy American democracy. If democracy holds, however, politics centered on advancing both economic and status equality can usher in a more just and equitable world. Conservative beneficiaries of status privilege need not worry about a vast conspiracy that will replace them with immigrants or some other designated outgroup. As is true of many things in life, they will instead be replaced by their children.

METHODOLOGICAL APPENDIX

This appendix provides numerous details regarding our analyses for interested readers.

RANDOM ASSIGNMENT TO TREATMENT CATEGORIES

In chapter 3, we describe our experimental design, where subjects are randomly assigned to view versions of our One America for Working People web page (technically, our "treatments"). Random assignment procedures should ensure that there are no systematic differences between the groups that are exposed to the different treatments in our study. We can check this assumption based on the observed characteristics of subjects in each treatment group. Specifically, we can examine whether the proportions or means for the observed variable differ across treatment groups.

Table A.1 shows the six treatment categories as columns and the observed characteristics as rows. The first variable in the table is the respondent's self-reported political party. If we look at the first row ("Republican"), we see that the proportion

TABLE A.1 MEANS AND PROPORTIONS FOR INDEPENDENT VARIABLES BY TREATMENT CATEGORY (N = 2,540)

	Economic equality	Racial equality	Gender equality	LGBTQ equality	Immigrant equality	Religious equality	Log-likelihood ratio (p)
Political party							0.413
Republican	.31	.28	.29	.28	.31	.30	
Democrat	.39	.40	.39	.37	.38	.39	
Independent	.22	.22	.27	.25	.24	.22	
Other/None	.08	.10	.05	.10	.07	.09	
Age	52.60	53.78	54.91	54.33	54.84	54.72	0.170
Income	14.90	15.50	15.99	15.49	15.41	15.47	0.773
Male	.41	.37	.39	.40	.40	.39	0.782
Race/Ethnicity							0.390
White (non-Hispanic)	.73	.71	.75	.73	.72	.73	
Hispanic/Latino(a)	.10	.09	.08	.08	.08	.10	
Black	.08	.10	.09	.10	.06	.09	
Asian Am.	.05	.04	.04	.02	.04	.03	
Other	.05	.06	.04	.06	.09	.05	

							LLR
Education	.44	.46	.49	.44	.49	.50	0.313
Married	.55	.48	.51	.53	.50	.48	0.292
Religion							0.432
Other faith	.36	.39	.34	.39	.35	.40	
Protestant	.42	.43	.48	.39	.42	.42	
Catholic	.22	.18	.18	.22	.23	.19	
Importance of religion							0.531
Very important	.39	.37	.38	.34	.34	.32	
Somewhat important	.29	.27	.25	.29	.28	.27	
Not very important	.13	.14	.17	.14	.15	.19	
Not important at all	.19	.22	.20	.23	.22	.22	

Note: The LLR statistics are generated using a multinomial logistic regression model, where the treatment (status manipulation) is the dependent variable, and each variable in the left-hand column is the sole independent variable in the model. The probability of the LLR test is equivalent to a p value for a hypothesis test, where the null hypothesis is statistical independence in the population.

of Republicans across the six treatment categories is very similar (a high of .31 to a low of .28). The pattern is similar for the other political party affiliations. Overall, these small differences in political party affiliation across treatment categories suggest that our randomization procedures worked as expected.

We can go one step further and test whether the variable "Political Party" affiliation is related to the treatment categories. To do so, we estimated a multinomial logistical regression, where the treatment variable is the dependent variable, and each variable in the table is the sole independent variable. The Log-Likelihood Ratio (LLR) from this model tests the null hypothesis that the two variables are statistically independent in the population. In the rightmost column, we report the probability ("p value") for the LLR test, which indicates the probability that we obtained the results in the data if the null hypothesis were true. A p value less than 0.05 would indicate that it is highly unlikely that the null hypothesis is true, and our sample contains systematic differences between the treatment and political party affiliation. In this case, the p value is 0.413, which strongly suggests that the minor differences across categories observed in the table are due to chance variations in the random assignment procedures.

The remainder of table A.1 shows only minor differences on the observed variables across the six treatment categories. In addition, none of the LLR tests show a p value of less than .05, which indicates that the differences in the tables are most likely due to chance variation in the random assignment process. In sum, our random assignment procedures worked as expected on a large array of variables that are important for the outcome. To ensure that these chance differences in random assignment did not affect our main findings, we added them as controls in our regression analyses to adjust for any effects of these chance differences on the outcome. We describe these analyses in the following section.

Finally, it is important to note that we cannot test whether unobserved variables (i.e., variables that are not in our dataset) are randomly distributed across our treatment categories. However, random assignment is a powerful design that should work in the same way for these variables as it did for the observed variables in table A.1. Thus, while the assumption of "exogeneity" (the treatment variable is independent of potential confounding variables) is strong, we are confident in making it, based on our research design.

REGRESSION RESULTS: CHAPTERS 4 AND 5

Chapters 4 and 5 include our main findings regarding how the status threats affect respondents' support of the content under the Fighting for a Better Future heading of the web page (Support) and their willingness to act is support of One America for Working People (Action). In presenting these results, we highlighted the variables that are at the heart of our analysis: status contestation and political party. However, as noted in the text, we estimated ordinary least squares (OLS) regression models to generate the predictions in the figures. As noted, these regression models also included a host of control variables. We included these in our models for two main reasons. First, these controls adjust for possible confounding due to any imbalances in subjects across treatment groups, which we saw was a very minor issue in table A.1. Second, we improved the efficiency of our estimates (lowering the standard errors for our coefficients), which meant that our statistical estimates are more precise.

The full regression results are presented in table A.2. As the table shows, very few of our control variables are significantly

TABLE A.2 FULL REGRESSION RESULTS FOR MODELS PRESENTED IN CHAPTERS 4 AND 5

	Support	Action
Status threat		
Racial equality	−0.243*	−0.221
	(−1.99)	(−1.40)
Gender equality	−0.257*	−0.414*
	(−2.02)	(−2.53)
LGBTQ equality	−0.358**	−0.656***
	(−2.90)	(−4.14)
Immigrant equality	−0.425**	−0.445**
	(−3.25)	(−2.66)
Religious equality	−0.361**	−0.358*
	(−2.86)	(−2.22)
Political party		
Democrat	0.386***	0.349**
	(3.73)	(2.63)
Independent	0.217	0.114
	(1.82)	(0.75)
Other/None	−0.174	−0.284
	(−1.04)	(−1.32)
Status threat by party		
Racial equality* Democrat	0.537***	0.730***
	(3.34)	(3.54)
Racial equality* Independent	0.212	0.449
	(1.14)	(1.88)
Racial equality* Other/None	0.110	0.636*
	(0.44)	(2.01)
Gender equality* Democrat	0.563***	0.865***
	(3.32)	(3.99)
Gender equality* Independent	0.152	0.626**
	(0.80)	(2.59)

Gender equality* Other/None	0.817**	0.646
	(2.62)	(1.62)
LGBTQ equality* Democrat	0.513**	1.006***
	(3.12)	(4.78)
LGBTQ equality* Independent	0.219	0.659**
	(1.19)	(2.80)
LGBTQ equality* Other/None	0.439	0.974**
	(1.74)	(3.02)
Immigrant equality* Democrat	0.727***	0.681**
	(4.13)	(3.03)
Immigrant equality* Independent	0.300	0.540*
	(1.50)	(2.12)
Immigrant equality* Other/None	0.716*	1.020**
	(2.42)	(2.70)
Religious equality* Democrat	0.406*	0.658**
	(2.41)	(3.05)
Religious equality* Independent	0.0872	0.130
	(0.45)	(0.52)
Religious equality* Other/None	0.590*	0.409
	(2.18)	(1.19)
Demographics		
Age	−0.00869***	−0.0186***
	(−5.84)	(−9.76)
Income	−0.00231	−0.00842
	(−0.66)	(−1.88)
Sex		
Male	−0.181***	−0.255***
	(−4.12)	(−4.54)
Race/Ethnicity		
Hispanic/Latino(a)	0.0186	0.0843
	(0.23)	(0.82)
Black	0.0439	0.165
	(0.54)	(1.57)

(continued)

	Support	Action
Asian Am.	0.0934	0.0548
	(0.82)	(0.37)
Other	−0.140	−0.124
	(−1.50)	(−1.04)
Education		
Bachelor's and above	−0.0598	0.0426
	(−1.30)	(0.72)
Marital Status		
Married	−0.0103	−0.0182
	(−0.22)	(−0.30)
Religion		
Protestant	−0.0529	−0.0568
	(−0.90)	(−0.75)
Catholic	−0.170*	−0.201*
	(−2.52)	(−2.33)
Importance of religion		
Somewhat important	−0.0560	0.0474
	(−1.03)	(0.68)
Not very important	0.0379	0.238**
	(0.55)	(2.71)
Not important at all	0.0900	0.127
	(1.23)	(1.35)
Constant	4.451***	6.524***
	(33.73)	(38.43)
R^2	0.147	0.173
Observations	2,538	2,526

Notes: The models were estimated using OLS regression, and the table includes unstandardized coefficients. Standard errors are presented in parentheses.

* $p < 0.05$, ** $p < 0.01$, *** $p < 0.001$

related to the outcome, net of the treatment and political party affiliation. Older respondents, male respondents, and Catholic respondents were all less likely to show support for the Fighting for a Better Future content. Otherwise, the other covariates did not predict either outcome.

While OLS regression models are better suited for continuous outcome variables, our main analyses included dependent variables that are measured in a metric that is ordinal (ranked categories with an unknown distance between them). For ordinal outcomes, the ordinal logistic regression model is more appropriate than the OLS model because it is difficult to meet the assumptions of OLS regression when the outcome is ordinal. To check whether our results are sensitive to the model that we selected, we reestimated our OLS regression models using ordinal logistic regression models. The results are presented in table A.3. Overall, we see that the main pattern of results holds when using ordinal logistic regression: Consistent with table A.2, Democrats differ more from Republicans when they are exposed to the treatments discussed in chapters 4 and 5. Ultimately, we decided to present the OLS models in the main text of the book because they are more familiar to most readers, and the results are simpler to interpret using the graphs included in those chapters.

One downside of the ordinal logistic regression model is that it produces coefficients that are scaled in the log odds metric, which is particularly difficult to interpret. In addition, the significance tests of interactions can be very misleading in the logit model (see Mize 2019). To address these issues, the coefficients can be transformed into average marginal effects, which are much easier to interpret, and provide valid tests of interactions. For a logistic regression model, the average marginal effect of X on Y is an estimate of how the predicted probability that Y equals category m changes in response to a one-unit change in X.

TABLE A.3 OLS REGRESSIONS MODELS FROM CHAPTERS 4 AND 5 ESTIMATED USING ORDINAL LOGISTIC REGRESSION

	Support	Action
Status threat		
Racial equality	−0.399	−0.227
	(−1.92)	(−1.08)
Gender equality	−0.364	−0.447*
	(−1.66)	(−2.03)
LGBTQ equality	−0.482*	−0.792***
	(−2.23)	(−3.69)
Immigrant equality	−0.606**	−0.497*
	(−2.65)	(−2.15)
Religious equality	−0.515*	−0.435*
	(−2.33)	(−2.02)
Political party		
Democrat	0.738***	0.473**
	(4.05)	(2.70)
Independent	0.411*	0.153
	(1.97)	(0.76)
Other/None	−0.332	−0.475
	(−1.11)	(−1.66)
Status threat by party		
Racial equality* Democrat	0.995***	0.937***
	(3.46)	(3.40)
Racial equality* Independent	0.284	0.571
	(0.88)	(1.79)
Racial equality* Other/None	0.199	0.945*
	(0.47)	(2.24)
Gender equality* Democrat	0.930**	1.064***
	(3.05)	(3.66)
Gender equality* Independent	0.128	0.749*
	(0.39)	(2.32)
Gender equality* Other/None	1.400*	0.845
	(2.47)	(1.63)
LGBTQ equality* Democrat	0.677*	1.325***
	(2.32)	(4.68)

LGBTQ equality* Independent	0.155	0.833**
	(0.48)	(2.64)
LGBTQ equality* Other/None	0.622	1.241**
	(1.40)	(2.90)
Immigrant equality* Democrat	1.213***	0.834**
	(3.80)	(2.74)
Immigrant equality* Independent	0.401	0.679*
	(1.14)	(2.00)
Immigrant equality* Other/None	1.297*	1.500**
	(2.44)	(2.91)
Religious equality* Democrat	0.489	0.818**
	(1.65)	(2.86)
Religious equality* Independent	0.0244	0.184
	(0.07)	(0.56)
Religious equality* Other/None	1.047*	0.740
	(2.17)	(1.61)
Demographics		
Age	−0.0157***	−0.0238***
	(−5.88)	(−9.34)
Income	−0.00226	−0.0100
	(−0.36)	(−1.68)
Sex		
Male	−0.278***	−0.350***
	(−3.56)	(−4.63)
Race/Ethnicity		
Hispanic/Latino(a)	0.0894	0.0837
	(0.60)	(0.61)
Black	0.146	0.269
	(0.97)	(1.88)
Asian Am.	0.0521	0.00147
	(0.26)	(0.01)
Other	−0.145	−0.103
	(−0.84)	(−0.61)
Education		
Bachelor's and above	−0.0664	0.0612
	(−0.81)	(0.78)

(*continued*)

	Support	Action
Marital status		
Married	−0.0579	−0.0298
	(−0.69)	(−0.37)
Religion		
Protestant	−0.126	−0.0639
	(−1.20)	(−0.63)
Catholic	−0.369**	−0.268*
	(−3.13)	(−2.37)
Importance of religion		
Somewhat important	−0.190*	0.0433
	(−1.98)	(0.46)
Not very important	0.0120	0.309**
	(0.10)	(2.65)
Not important at all	0.126	0.178
	(0.96)	(1.42)
Cutpoint 1	−4.202***	−4.778***
	(−16.57)	(−19.02)
Cutpoint 2	−3.026***	−3.651***
	(−12.60)	(−15.49)
Cutpoint 3	−1.853***	−2.680***
	(−7.90)	(−11.68)
Cutpoint 4	−0.444	−1.249***
	(−1.91)	(−5.55)
Cutpoint 5		−0.202
		(−0.90)
Cutpoint 6		1.649***
		(7.11)
Observations	2,538	2,526

Notes: Coefficients are presented in the log odds metric. Standard errors are presented in parentheses.

* $p < 0.05$, ** $p < 0.01$, *** $p < 0.001$

To present our findings from the models in table A.3, we calculated the average marginal effects for our treatment variables by political party for each category of the outcome. After estimating these average marginal effects, we created figures A.1 through A.4 to show the overall pattern of results. Figure A.1 plots the effect of being a Democrat (relative to a Republican) on the probability of being in each of the five categories of the "Support" variable, which are presented along the x-axis of the graph. The six graphs within the figure show the results for each treatment category.

We will briefly interpret the basic logic of figure A.1 to help the reader understand our findings. In the top left graph in figure A1, we see the average marginal effect of being a Democrat (rather than a Republican) among respondents who were exposed to the "economic only" condition. The graph shows that Democrats are significantly less likely to "strongly" or "somewhat" oppose the content under the Fighting for a Better Future heading than Republicans. They are also less likely (by a decreased probability of 0.05) to be "neutral" but much more likely to "strongly support" the content (by an increased probability of 0.17) than Republicans. The remaining graphs in the figure compare the different treatments against this baseline condition. In the adjacent graph, we examine the responses among cases that were exposed to the "racial inequality" treatment. The darker line in this graph shows the average marginal effects for this group, while the "economics only" group is shown as a reference. In this graph, we see that Democratic respondents who received the "racial equality" condition are less likely to oppose or be neutral about the content, and they are much more likely to "strongly support" the content than Democrats in the "economics only" condition. Indeed, the difference from

Democrat (vs. Republican)

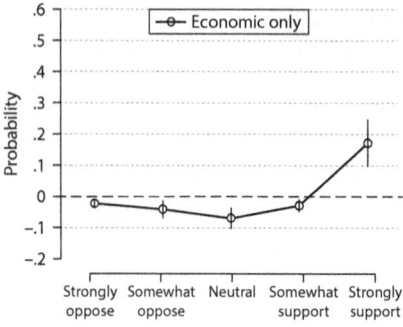

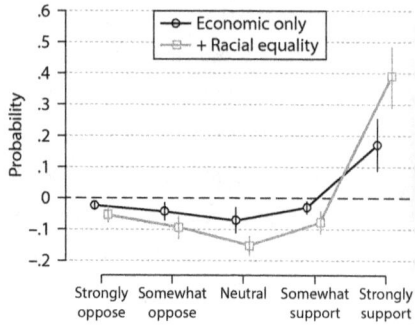

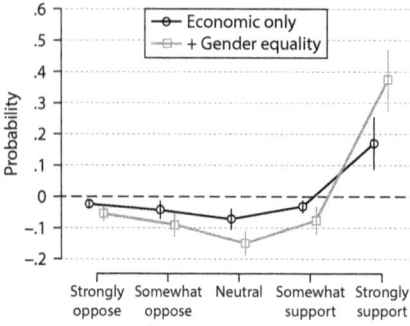

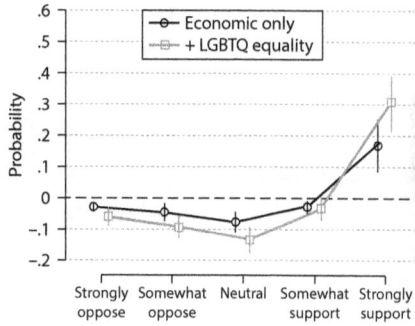

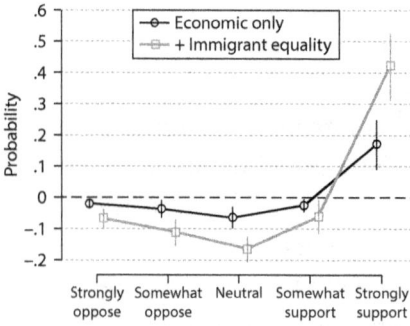

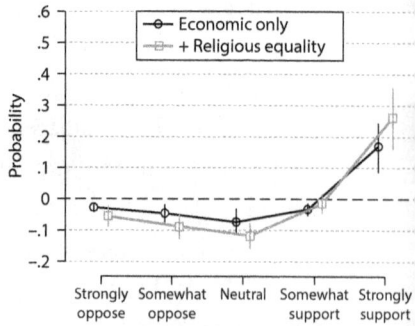

FIGURE A.1 Average marginal effects of being a Democrat (vs. Republican) on support of One America content across treatments (ordinal logistic regression)

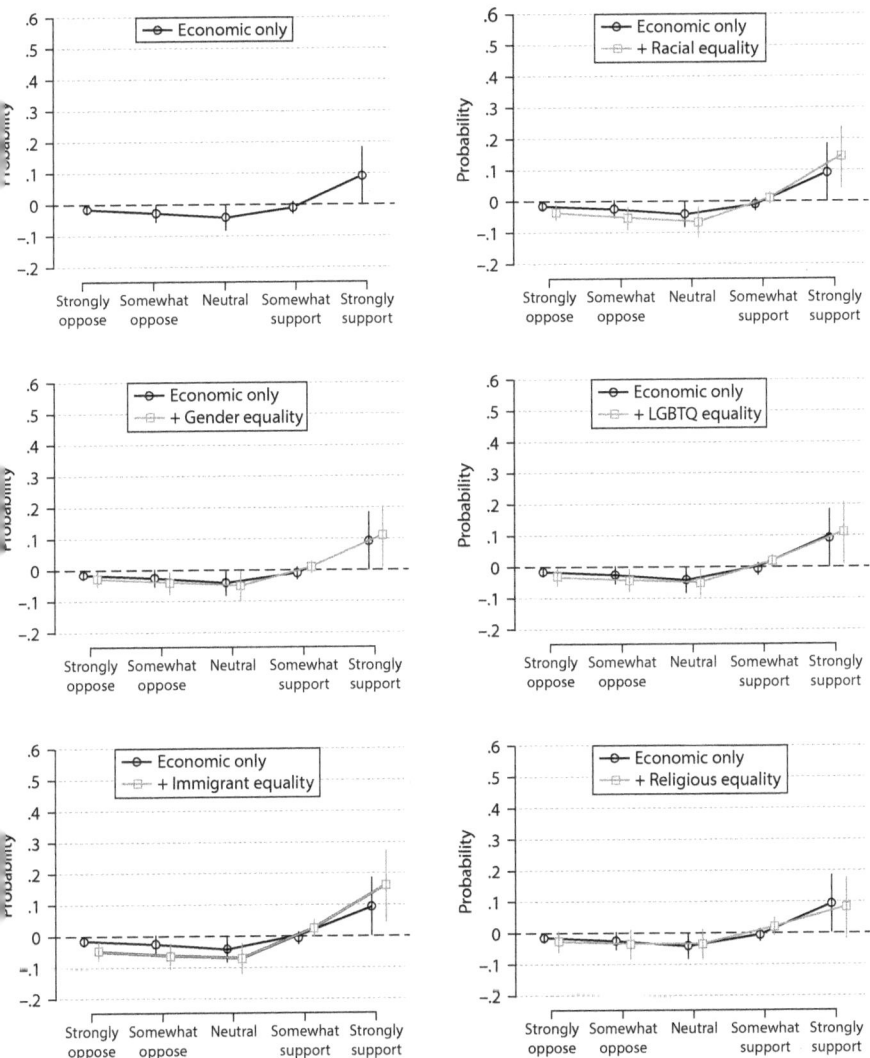

Independent (vs. Republican)

FIGURE A.2 Average marginal effects of being an Independent (vs. Republican) on support of One America content across treatments (ordinal logistic regression)

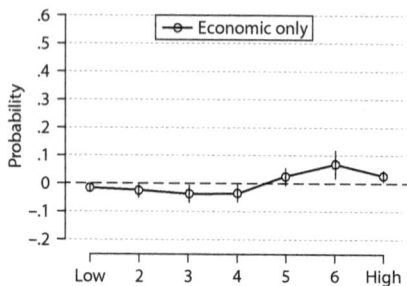

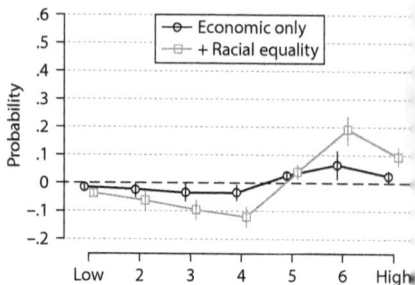

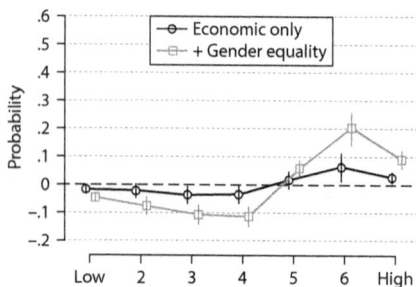

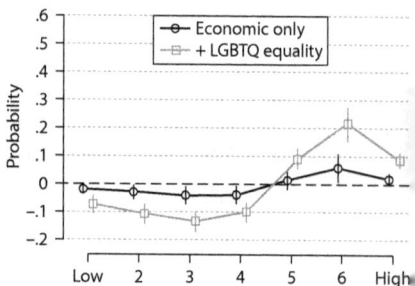

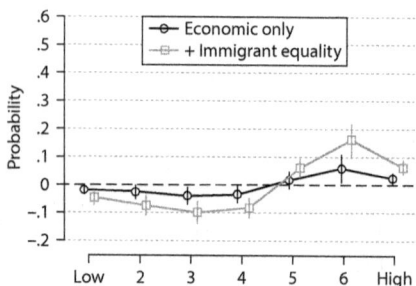

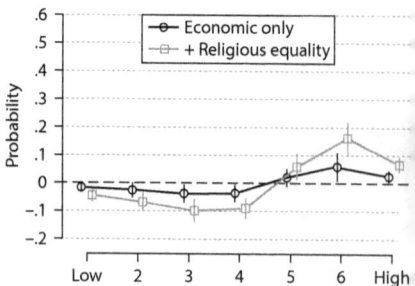

FIGURE A.3 Average marginal effects of being a Democrat (vs. Republican) on willingness to act in support of One America content across treatments (ordinal logistic regression)

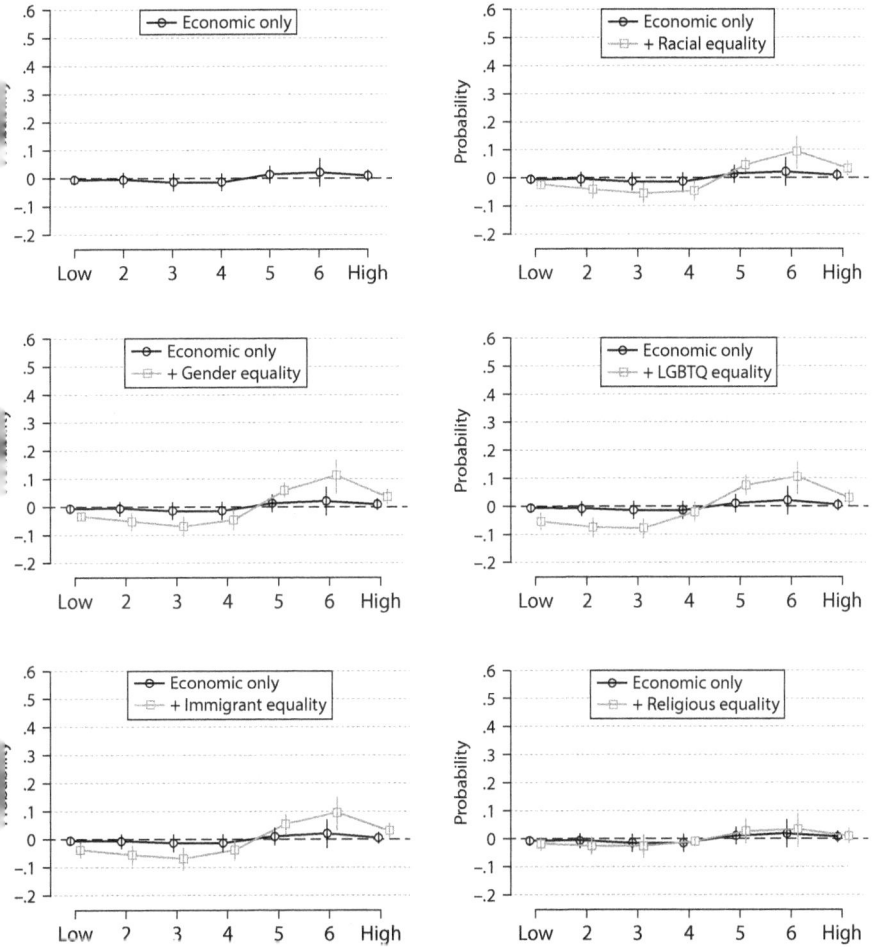

FIGURE A.4 Average marginal effects of being an Independent (vs. Republican) on willingness to act in support of One America content across treatments (ordinal logistic regression)

Republicans in predicting the "strongly support" category more than doubles (from 0.17 to 0.39). We see the same pattern for the other four treatments (although they are less pronounced for the "religious equality" condition).

This pattern of results is completely consistent with the OLS regression results presented in chapters 4 and 5, and it shows how status contestation affects how Republicans and Democrats rate the content in the Fighting for a Better Future section of the web page. Figure A.2 presents the results for Independents vs. Republicans for the same model, and figures A.3 and A.4 extend the same framework to the "act in support" outcome variable. We will let readers interpret these figures on their own, but we believe that these figures also support the main conclusions that we presented using our OLS regression models in chapters 4 and 5.

POLICY PREFERENCE SCALE: MEASUREMENT ISSUES

Chapter 6 examines respondents' policy preferences, based on their responses to a serious of questions addressing a broad range of issues. In this section, we provide some additional details regarding the scale used to measure respondents' policy preferences. Table A.4 shows the sixteen items used in the scale. It is important that our scale is reliable, which means that respondents provide consistent responses across the items. In other words, the responses to one item in the scale should help predict the responses to other items in the scale. A scale that does not have this property would have low reliability and would introduce errors into the analysis, which would make finding patterns in our data difficult.

TABLE A.4 ITEMS FOR THE POLICY PREFERENCE SCALE AND THEIR CONTRIBUTIONS TO SCALE RELIABILITY

Item	N	Sign	Correlation of item with scale (minus item)	Alpha if item deleted
Government should do more to make childcare affordable	2,591	+	0.6367	0.8584
Government should do more to make quality health care affordable to all Americans	2,591	+	0.6950	0.8557
Government should do more to assure that all Americans receive a living wage	2,595	+	0.6867	0.8561
The legal system and police departments should do more to hold police officers accountable when they kill unarmed civilians who do not pose a threat	2,590	+	0.5919	0.8604
Law enforcement agents and legal systems should do more to enforce and prosecute hate crimes	2,594	+	0.5346	0.8630
Government should invest more funds in local law enforcement to keep communities safe	2,593	–	0.1670	0.8788
Government should invest more funds to strengthen the military to protect American interests	2,590	–	0.3667	0.8704
Congress should enact laws to place strict limits on money people or corporations can donate to political campaigns	2,592	+	0.2509	0.8753

(*continued*)

Item	N	Sign	Correlation of item with scale (minus item)	Alpha if item deleted
More restrictions should be placed on access to abortion	2,593	–	0.5381	0.8629
Government should devote more resources to prevent immigrants from illegally crossing the southern border	2,595	–	0.4920	0.8649
Congress should enact laws that make it harder for people to obtain firearms	2,590	+	0.6254	0.8589
The federal government should be required to have a balanced budget every year	2,594	–	0.2454	0.8756
Employers and legal authorities should do more to stop sexual harassment in the workplace	2,589	+	0.4696	0.8659
Government should take stronger action to enforce affirmative action laws to address unfair hiring practices	2,594	+	0.6105	0.8596
Storeowners and employees should be allowed to deny service to gay or lesbian people if providing service to them conflicts with their religious beliefs	2,594	–	0.5507	0.8623
Government should do more to require businesses to reduce their production of greenhouse emissions linked to climate change	2,596	+	0.7007	0.8555
Alpha reliability (full scale)			0.8716	

To examine the reliability of our scale, we used Cronbach's alpha to measure the internal consistency among items. The alpha for the scale is high (0.87), which indicates that the scale is highly reliable. Table A.4 also provides additional information about the measurement properties of our scale. The column "Sign" indicates whether each item is coded positively or negatively ("reverse-coded") in the scale. The sign for each item is determined based on the item's correlation with responses to other items. The next column indicates the correlation between each item with the remaining items in the scale. For example, the first item (government support for affordable child care) has a correlation of 0.67 with the other fifteen items in the scale. Higher correlations for each item are desirable, since we want the items to be predictive of each other (i.e., internal consistency). There are a few items (spending more money on law enforcement, limits on campaign contributions, and requiring a balanced budget) that have lower correlations with the other items. The last column shows how removing each item from the scale would affect the scale's alpha. A higher alpha means greater scale reliability, so it is often advisable to drop items that lower the scale's alpha. If we dropped the three items with low correlations, the alpha for the scale would improve, but only very marginally (not more than .01). Ultimately, since keeping these items has a trivial effect on the scale's alpha, we decided to keep these items in the scale, in order to maximize the content validity of the scale and maintain its breadth across numerous policy domains.

NOTES

1. IT'S THE ECONOMY, STUPID! OR NOT?

1. Raymond M. Duch and Randy T. Stevenson, *The Economic Vote: How Political and Economic Institutions Condition Election Results* (Cambridge University Press, 2008).
2. Harvey Molotch, "The City as a Growth Machine: Toward a Political Economy of Place," *American Journal of Sociology* 82, no. 2 (1976): 309–32.
3. Leslie McCall and Christine Percheski, "Income Inequality: New Trends and Research Directions," *Annual Review of Sociology* 36 (2010): 329–47; Geoffrey T. Wodtke, "Social Class and Income Inequality in the United States: Ownership, Authority, and Personal Income Distribution from 1980 to 2010," *American Journal of Sociology* 121, no. 5 (2016): 1375–415.
4. Adam D. Reich, "The Organizational Trace of an Insurgent Moment: Occupy Wall Street and New York City's Social Movement Field, 2004 to 2015," *Socius* 3 (2017): 1–21.
5. Frank Newport, "Americans Continue to Say U.S. Wealth Distribution Is Unfair," Gallup, May 4, 2015, https://news.gallup.com/poll/182987 /americans-continue-say-wealth-distribution unfair.aspx.
6. Ari Pinkus, "What Do Americans Say Are the Biggest Factors for Success," American Communities Project, January 29, 2024, https://www .americancommunities.org/what-do-americans-say-are-biggest-factors -for-success/.
7. Frank Newport, "Inequality as a Voter Concern in 2020," Gallup, July 31, 2019, https://news.gallup.com/opinion/polling-matters/262439 /inequality-voter-concern-2020.aspx.

8. Karl Marx and Frederick Engels, *The Communist Manifesto*, in *Collected Works*, vol. 1 (1848; Lawrence and Wishart, 1968), 35–63.

9. Bart Bonikowski and Noam Gidron, "The Populist Style in American Politics: Presidential Campaign Discourse, 1952–1996," *Social Forces* 94 (2016): 1593–1621.

10. Rory McVeigh and Kevin Estep, *The Politics of Losing: Trump, the Klan, and the Mainstreaming of Resentment* (Columbia University Press, 2019).

11. Arlie Russell Hochschild, *Strangers in Their Own Land: Anger and Mourning on the American Right* (New Press, 2018).

12. Ana Hernández Kent and Lowell R. Rickets, "Has Wealth Inequality in America Changed Over Time? Here Are Key Statistics," Federal Reserve Bank of St. Louis, December 2, 2020, https://www.stlouisfed.org/open-vault/2020/december/has-wealth-inequality-changed-over-time-key-statistics.

13. Benjamin Sosnaud, David Brady, and Steven M. Frenk, "Class in Name Only: Subjective Class Identity, Objective Class Position, and Vote Choice in American Presidential Elections," *Social Problems* 60 (2013): 81–99; Rory McVeigh, David Cunningham, and Justin Farrell, "Political Polarization as a Social Movement Outcome: 1960s Klan Activism and Its Enduring Impact on Political Realignment in Southern Counties, 1960 to 2000," *American Sociological Review* 79 (2014): 1144–71.

14. Gerhard Lenski, *Power and Privilege: A Theory of Social Stratification* (McGraw-Hill, 1966).

15. Peter J. Katzenstein, *Small States in World Markets: Industrial Policy in Europe* (Cornell University Press, 1985).

16. Kim Voss, *The Making of American Exceptionalism: The Knights of Labor and Class Formation in the Nineteenth Century* (Cornell University Press 1993); Jill Quadagno, "Creating a Capital Investment Welfare State: The New American Exceptionalism: 1998 Presidential Address," *American Sociological Review* 64, no. 1 (1999): 1–11; Barry Eidlin, "Why Is There No Labor Party in the United States? Political Articulation and the Canadian Comparison, 1932 to 1948," *American Sociological Review* 81, no. 3 (2016): 488–516; Seymour Martin Lipset, *American Exceptionalism: A Double-Edged Sword* (Norton, 1997).

17. Clem Brooks and Jeff Manza, "Social Cleavages and Political Alignments: U.S. Presidential Elections, 1960 to 1992," *American Sociological Review* 62, no. 6 (1997): 937–46; Jeff Manza and Clem Brooks, "Does

Class Analysis Still Have Anything to Contribute to the Study of Politics?—Comments," *Theory and Society* 25, no. 5 (1996): 717–24.

18. Seymour Martin Lipset, *Political Man: The Social Bases of Politics* (Anchor/Doubleday, 1963); Walter Korpi, *The Democratic Class Struggle* (Routledge and Kegan Paul, 1982).

19. Anthony Downs, *An Economic Theory of Democracy* (Harper and Row, 1957); Robert A. Dahl, *Polyarchy: Participation and Opposition* (Yale University Press, 1972); Arend Lijphart, *Patterns of Democracy: Government Forms and Performance in Thirty-Six Countries* (Yale University Press, 1999).

20. Doug McAdam and Karina Kloos, *Deeply Divided: Racial Politics and Social Movements in Post-War America* (Oxford University Press, 2014).

21. Merlyn Thomas and Mike Wendling, "Trump Repeats Baseless Claim about Haitian Immigrants Eating Pets," BBC, September 15, 2024, https://www.bbc.com/news/articles/c77l28myezko.

22. Max Weber, "Class, Status, Party," in *Class, Status and Power*, ed. Reinhard Bendix and Seymour Martin Lipset (Free Press, 1963), 63–75.

23. Cecilia Ridgeway, *Status: Why Is It Everywhere? Why Does It Matter?* (Russell Sage Foundation 2019), 1.

24. Hubert M. Blalock, *Toward a Theory of Minority-Group Relations* (Wiley, 1967); Susan Olzak, *The Dynamics of Ethnic Competition and Conflict* (Stanford University Press, 1992); Sarah A. Soule, "Populism and Black Lynching in Georgia, 1890–1900," *Social Forces* 71, no. 2 (1992): 431–49; Lawrence Bobo and Vincent L. Hutchings, "Perceptions of Racial Group Competition: Extending Blumer's Theory of Group Position to a Multiracial Social Context," *American Sociological Review* 61 (1996): 951–72.

25. Maureen A, Craig and Jennifer A. Richeson, "On the Precipice of a 'Majority-Minority' America: Perceived Status Threat from the Racial Demographic Shift Affects White Americans' Political Ideology," *Psychological Science* 25 (2014):1189–97; Maria Abascal, "Contraction as a Response to Group Threat: Demographic Decline and Whites' Classification of People Who Are Ambiguously White," *American Sociological Review* 85 (2020): 298–322.

26. Craig and Richeson, "On the Precipice of a 'Majority-Minority' America," 1189–97; Robb Willer, Christabel L. Rogalin, Bridget Conlon, and Michael T. Wojnowicz, "Overdoing Gender: A Test of the Masculine

Overcompensation Thesis," *American Journal of Sociology* 118 (2013): 980–1022.

27. Cecilia Ridgeway, "Why Status Matters for Inequality," *American Sociological Review* 79 (2014): 1–16.

28. Ridgeway, *Status*, 151.

29. Michèle Lamont and Virág Molnár, "The Study of Boundaries in the Social Sciences," *Annual Review of Sociology* 28 (2002): 167–95.

30. Eduardo Bonilla-Silva, "Rethinking Racism: Toward a Structural Interpretation," *American Sociological Review* 62 (1997): 465–80.

31. Patricia Hill Collins, "Toward a New Vision: Race, Class, and Gender as Categories of Analysis and Contention," *Race, Sex and Class* 1 (1993): 25–45; Kimberle Crenshaw, "Demarginalizing the Intersection of Race and Sex: A Black Feminist Critique of Antidiscrimination Doctrine, Feminist Theory and Antiracist Politics," *University of Chicago Legal Forum*, issue 1 (1993): 139–67.

32. Eduardo Bonilla-Silva, *Racism Without Racists: Color-Blind Racism and the Persistence of Racial Inequality in America* (Rowman and Littlefield, 2009).

33. Victor Ray, "A Theory of Racialized Organizations," *American Sociological Review* 84, no. 1 (2019): 26–53.

34. McVeigh and Estep, *The Politics of Losing.*

35. Bonilla-Silva, "Rethinking Racism," 465–80; Ray, "A Theory of Racialized Organizations," 26–53.

36. Lamont and Molnár, "The Study of Boundaries," 167–95; Charles Tilly, *Durable Inequality* (University of California Press, 1998).

37. Bonilla-Silva, "Rethinking Racism," 465–80; Ray, "A Theory of Racialized Organizations," 26–53; Ridgeway, *Status.*

38. Shelley J. Correll, Cecilia L. Ridgeway, Ezra W. Zuckerman, Sharon Jank, Sara Jordan-Bloch, and Sandra Nakagawa, "It's the Conventional Thought That Counts: How Third-Order Inference Produces Status Advantage," *American Sociological Review* 82 (2017): 297–327.

39. Bobo and Hutchings, "Perceptions of Racial Group Competition," 951–72; Herbert Blumer, "Race Prejudice as a Sense of Group Position," *Pacific Sociological Review* 1 (1958): 3–7.

40. Stanley Presser and Linda Stinson, "Data Collection Mode and Social Desirability Bias in Self-Reported Religious Attendance," *American Sociological Review* 63, no. 1 (1998): 137–45.

41. Adam Przeworski, *Capitalism and Social Democracy* (Cambridge University Press 1985).

42. Przeworski, *Capitalism and Social Democracy*.

43. Here, we present the image in black and white. The version that study participants received was presented to them in color.

44. David A. Snow, E. Burke Rochford, Steven K. Worden, and Robert D. Benford, "Frame Alignment Processes, Micromobilization, and Movement Participation," *American Sociological Review* 51, no. 4 (1986): 464–81.

45. McVeigh and Estep, *The Politics of Losing*.

46. Emily Kasyak, Kelsy Burke, and Mathew Strange, "Logics of Freedom: Debating Religious Freedom Laws and Gay and Lesbian Rights," *Socius* 4 (2018): 1–18.

47. Ipsos directed potential participants to a link to our survey. It has tools to screen out responses from bots, as well as to remove cases when people did not complete the survey or spent so little time completing the survey that their responses would not be trustworthy. These unusable cases were replaced with new respondents and randomly assigned to one of our treatment groups. We also included questions on the survey to help us identify respondents who were not conscientiously reading the material that we presented to them (the web pages). Most importantly, we asked respondents if they could recall the specific types of equality mentioned under the subheading "Fighting for a Better Future," In the survey, we gave them multiple-choice response categories to give them some guidance. Forty-five percent of respondents answered correctly. Because this content is of central importance to our experiment (respondents need to be aware of the content in order to (potentially) be affected by it), we limit our analysis to those who answered the question correctly. If we were to include all respondents, we obtain similar results as long as we include a statistical control for "flawed memory." We also obtained data from 1,034 respondents who were randomly assigned to a seventh group. Respondents in this group received a version of the survey that did not include any web pages or questions about One America for Working People. We did this so that we could compare policy preferences and demographic attributes of those not exposed to our experimental treatment groups to those who were.

48. See the methodological appendix at the end of the book for more detail on how we assessed the effectiveness of the random assignment process for our study.

2. STATUS CONTESTATION AND POLITICS THEORY

1. For a critique of this approach, see Howard S. Becker, *Tricks of the Trade: How to Think About Your Research While You're Doing It* (University of Chicago Press, 1998); Charles C. Ragin, *Fuzzy-Set Social Science* (University of Chicago Press, 2000).

2. Seymour Martin Lipset, *Political Man: The Social Bases of Politics* (Anchor, 1963).

3. Rory McVeigh and David Sikkink, "God, Politics, and Protest: Religious Beliefs and the Legitimation of Contentious Tactics," *Social Forces* 79, no. 4 (2001): 1425–58.

4. Patricia Hill Collins, "Toward a New Vision: Race, Class, and Gender as Categories of Analysis and Contention," *Race, Sex and Class* 1 (1993): 25–45.

5. Mustafa Emirbayer, "Manifesto for a Relational Sociology," *American Journal of Sociology* 103, no. 2 (1997): 281–317.

6. Joseph Gusfield, *Symbolic Crusade: Status Politics and the American Temperance Movement* (University of Illinois Press, 1963).

7. Michael Wood and Michael Hughes, "The Moral Basis of Moral Reform: Status Discontent vs. Culture and Socialization as Explanations of Anti-Pornography Social Movement Adherence," *American Sociological Review* 49 (1984): 86–99; Ann L. Page and Donald A. Clelland, "The Kanawha County Textbook Controversy: A Study of the Politics of Lifestyle Concern," *Social Forces* 57 (1978): 265–81.

8. Nicola Beisel, *Imperiled Innocents: Anthony Comstock and Family Reproduction in Victorian America* (Princeton University Press, 1996).

9. William A. Gamson, *Talking Politics* (Cambridge University Press, 1982); James M. Jasper, *The Emotions of Protest* (University of Chicago Press, 2018).

10. William Julius Wilson, *The Declining Significance of Race: Blacks and Changing American Institutions* (University of Chicago Press, 1978).

11. Edna Bonacich, "A Theory of Ethnic Antagonism: The Split Labor Market," *American Sociological Review* 37, no. 5 (1972): 547–59; Susan Olzak and Suzanne Shanahan, "Racial Policy and Racial Conflict in the Urban United States, 1869–1924," *Social Forces* 82, no. 2 (2003): 481–517.

12. Peter M. Blau and Otis Dudley Duncan, *The American Occupational Structure* (Wiley, 1967).

13. Douglas S. Massey and Nancy Denton, *American Apartheid: Segregation and the Making of the Underclass* (Harvard University Press, 1993).

14. Mary Patillo, *Black Picket Fences: Privilege and Peril Among the Black Middle Class* (University of Chicago Press, 1999).

15. Aldon Morris, "From Civil Rights to Black Lives Matter: Protest Expert Aldon Morris Explains How Social Justice Movements Succeed," *Scientific American*, February 3, 2021, https://www.scientificamerican .com/article/from-civil-rights-to-black-lives-matter1/.

16. Devah Pager and David S. Pedulla, "Race, Self-Selection, and the Job Search Process," *American Journal of Sociology* 120 (2015): 1005–54.

17. Paula S. Rothenberg, *White Privilege*, 5th ed. (Worth, 2015); Michèle Lamont, "Addressing Recognition Gaps: Destigmatization and the Reduction of Inequality," *American Sociological Review* 83, no. 3 (2018): 419–44; Stewart E. Tolnay and E. M. Beck, *A Festival of Violence: An Analysis of Southern Lynchings, 1882–1930* (University of Illinois Press, 1995); Rory McVeigh, *The Rise of the Ku Klux Klan: Right-Wing Movements and National Politics* (University of Minnesota Press, 2009).

18. Arlie Hochschild with Anne Machung, *The Second Shift: Working Families and the Revolution at Home*, rev. ed. (Penguin, 2012); Paige L. Sweet, "The Sociology of Gaslighting," *American Sociological Review* 84 (2019): 851–75; Candace West and Don H. Zimmerman, "Doing Gender," *Gender and Society* 1 (1987): 125–51.

19. James Madison, Alexander Hamilton, and John Jay, "The Federalist No. 10," in *The Federalist Papers*, ed. Ian Shapiro (Yale University Press, 2009), 47–53.

20. Chris Leaverton, "Three Takeaways on Redistricting and Competition in the 2022 Midterms," Brennan Center for Justice, January 20, 2023, https://www.brennancenter.org/our-work/analysis-opinion/three -takeaways-redistricting-and-competition-2022-midterms.

21. Jill Quadagno, *The Color of Welfare: How Racism Undermined the War on Poverty* (Oxford University Press, 1996); Theda Skocpol, *Protecting Soldiers and Mothers: The Political Origins of Social Policy in the United States* (Harvard University Press, 1992); Gregory Hooks and Brian McQueen, "American Exceptionalism Revisited: The Military-Industrial Complex,

Racial Tension, and the Underdeveloped Welfare State," *American Sociological Review* 75, no. 2 (2010): 185–204.

22. Elmer Eric Schattschneider, *The Semisovereign People: A Realist's View of Democracy in America* (Holt, Rinehart, and Winston, 1960).

23. Harvey Molotch, "The City as a Growth Machine: Toward a Political Economy of Place," *American Journal of Sociology* 82 (1976): 6–29.

24. Delia Baldassarri and Peter Bearman, "Dynamics of Political Polarization," *American Sociological Review* 72, no. 5 (2007): 784–811.

25. Dannegal G. Young, Huma Rasheed, Amy Bleakley, and Jessica B. Lanbaum, "The Politics of Mask-Wearing: Political Preferences, Reactance, and Conflict Aversion During COVID," *Social Science and Medicine* 298 (2022): 114836.

26. Nicholas Dias and Yphtach Lelkes, "The Nature of Affective Polarization: Disentangling Policy Disagreement from Partisan Identity," *American Journal of Political Science* 66 (2021): 775–90.

27. Eli J. Finkel, Christopher A. Bail, Mina Cikara, Peter H. Ditto, Shanto Iyengar, Samara Klar, et al., "Political Sectarianism in America: A Poisonous Cocktail of Othering, Aversion, and Moralization Poses a Threat to Democracy," *Science* 370 (2020): 533–36.

28. Joshua Robison and Rachel L. Moskowitz, "The Group Basis of Partisan Affective Polarization," *Journal of Politics* 81 (2019): 1075–79.

29. For example, see James Davison Hunter, *Democracy and Solidarity: On the Cultural Roots of America's Political Crisis* (Yale University Press, 2024).

3. BROAD SUPPORT FOR WORKER UNITY

1. Edward A. Tiryakian, "American Religious Exceptionalism: A Reconsideration," *The Annals of the American Academy of Political and Social Science* 527 (1993): 40–54.

2. Edwin Amenta, Chris Bonastia, and Neal Caren, "US Social Policy in Comparative and Historical Perspective: Concepts, Images, Arguments, and Research Strategies," *Annual Review of Sociology* 27 (2001): 213–34.

3. Seymour Martin Lipset, *American Exceptionalism: A Double-Edged Sword* (Norton, 1997).

4. Douglas Rae, *The Political Consequences of Electoral Laws* (Yale University Press, 1967).

5. Susan Olzak, *The Dynamics of Ethnic Competition and Conflict* (Stanford University Press, 1992); Rory McVeigh, *The Rise of the Ku Klux Klan: Right-Wing Movements and National Politics* (University of Minnesota Press, 2009).

6. Harvey Molotch, "The City as a Growth Machine: Toward a Political Economy of Place," *American Journal of Sociology* 82 (1976): 309–32.

7. John Gaventa, *Power and Powerlessness: Quiescence and Rebellion in an Appalachian Valley* (University of Illinois Press, 1980). Also see Steven Lukes, *Power: A Radical View* (Macmillan, 1974).

8. Tali Kristal, "The Capitalist Machine: Computerization, Workers' Power, and the Decline in Labor's Share within U.S. Industries," *American Sociological Review* 78, no. 3 (2013): 361–89.

9. Ruth Milkman, "Back to the Future? U.S. Labour in the New Gilded Age," *British Journal of Industrial Relations* 51 (2013): 645–65.

10. David Brady and Michael Wallace, "Spatialization, Foreign Direct Investment, and Labor Outcomes in the American States, 1978–1996," *Social Forces* 79 (2000): 67–105.

11. Lainey Newman and Theda Skocpol, *Rust Belt Union Blues: Why Working-Class Voters Are Turning Away from the Democratic Party* (Columbia University Press, 2023).

12. Rory McVeigh and Kevin Estep, *The Politics of Losing: Trump, the Klan, and the Mainstreaming of Resentment* (Columbia University Press, 2019).

13. David Autor, David Dorn, and Gordon Hanson, "When Work Disappears: Manufacturing Decline and the Falling Marriage-Market Value of Young Men," *American Economic Review: Insights* 1 (2019): 161–78.

14. Bart Bonikowski, "Ethno-Nationalist Populism and the Mobilization of Collective Resentment," *British Journal of Sociology* 68 (2017): 181–213.

15. Bart Bonikowski and Noam Gidron, "The Populist Style in American Politics: Presidential Campaign Discourse, 1952–1996," *Social Forces* 94 (2016): 1593–621.

16. Doug McAdam, "Be Careful What You Wish For: The Ironic Connection Between the Civil Rights Struggle and Today's Divided America," *Sociological Forum* 30 (2015): 485–508.

17. Delia Baldassarri and Andrew Gelman, "Partisans without Constraint: Political Polarization and Trends in American Public Opinion," *American Journal of Sociology* 114 (2008): 408–46.

18. Mark Rank and Tom Hirschl, "Poverty Facts and Myths," Confronting Poverty, https://confrontingpoverty.org/poverty-facts-and-myths /americas-poor-are-worse-off-than-elsewhere/, accessed April 2, 2025.

4. RACE, GENDER, AND STATUS PRESERVATION

1. Robert D. Putnam, *Bowling Alone: The Collapse and Revival of American Community* (Simon and Schuster, 2000); David E. Campbell, "Voice in the Classroom: How an Open Classroom Climate Fosters Political Engagement Among Adolescents," *Political Behavior* 30 (2008): 437–54.

2. Nicole Hemmer, *Messengers of the Right: Conservative Media and the Transformation of American Politics* (University of Pennsylvania Press, 2016).

3. Hemmer, *Messengers of the Right*, 264.

4. Theda Skocpol and Venessa Williamson, *The Tea Party and the Remaking of Republican Conservatism* (Oxford University Press, 2012).

5. Mason Walker and Katerina Eva Matsa, "News Consumption across Social Media in 2021," Pew Research Center, September 20, 2021, https:// www.pewresearch.org/journalism/2021/09/20/news-consumption -across-social-media-in-2021/.

6. Rory McVeigh, *The Rise of the Ku Klux Klan: Right-Wing Movements and National Politics* (University of Minnesota Press, 2009).

7. Kathleen Blee, *Women of the Ku Klux Klan: Racism and Gender in the 1920s* (University of California Press, 1991); Nancy MacLean, *Behind the Mask of Chivalry: The Making of the Second Ku Klux Klan* (Oxford University Press, 1994).

8. Andrew Abbott, "Of Time and Space: The Contemporary Relevance of the Chicago School," *Social Forces* 75 (1997): 1149–82.

9. Robert E. Park and Ernest W. Burgess, *Introduction to the Science of Society* (University of Chicago Press, 1921).

10. Charles Hirschman, "America's Melting Pot Reconsidered," *Annual Review of Sociology* 9 (1983): 397–423.

11. Aldon Morris, *The Scholar Denied: W. E. B. Du Bois and the Birth of Modern Sociology* (University of California Press, 2015), 130.

12. Morris, *The Scholar Denied*.

13. Lawrence Bobo and Vincent L. Hutchings, "Perceptions of Racial Group Competition: Extending Blumer's Theory of Group Position to a Multiracial Social Context," *American Sociological Review* 61 (1996): 951–72; Herbert Blumer, "Race Prejudice as a Sense of Group Position," *Pacific Sociological Review* 1 (1958): 3–7.

14. Eduardo Bonilla-Silva, "Rethinking Racism: Toward a Structural Interpretation," *American Sociological Review* 62 (1997): 465–80; Victor Ray, "A Theory of Racialized Organizations," *American Sociological Review* 84 (2019): 26–53.

15. Evelyn Nakano Glenn, *Unequal Freedom: How Race and Gender Shaped American Citizenship and Labor* (Harvard University Press, 2002).

16. Aldon D. Morris, *The Origins of the Civil Rights Movement: Black Communities Organizing for Change* (Free Press, 1986); Doug McAdam, *Political Process and the Development of Black Insurgency, 1930–1970* (University of Chicago Press, 1982); Doron Shultziner, "The Social-Psychological Origins of the Montgomery Bus Boycott: Social Interaction and Humiliation in the Emergence of Social Movements," *Mobilization* 18 (2013): 117–42.

17. Stewart E. Tolnay and E. M. Beck, *A Festival of Violence: An Analysis of Southern Lynchings, 1882–1930* (University of Illinois Press, 1995).

18. Charles Tilly, Durable Inequality (University of California Press, 1998).

19. Tomás R. Jiménez and Adam L. Horowitz, "When White Is Just Alright: How Immigrants Redefine Achievement and Reconfigure the Ethnoracial Hierarchy," *American Sociological Review* 78 (2013): 849–71.

20. Glenn, *Unequal Freedom*; Rory McVeigh and Kevin Estep, *The Politics of Losing: Trump, the Klan, and the Mainstreaming of Resentment* (Columbia University Press, 2019).

21. Catherine Lee, "'Where the Danger Lies': Race, Gender, and Chinese and Japanese Exclusion in the United States, 1870–1924," *Sociological Forum* 25 (2010): 248–71.

22. Glenn, *Unequal Freedom*.

23. Luis Noe-Bustamante, Neil G. Ruiz, Mark Hugo Lopez, and Khadihah Edwards, "About a Third of Asian Americans Say They Have Changed Their Daily Routines Due to Concerns Over Threats, Attacks," Pew Research Center, May 9, 2022, https://www.pewresearch.org/short-reads/2022/05/09/about-a-third-of-asian-americans-say

-they-have-changed-their-daily-routine-due-to-concerns-over
-threats-attacks/.

24. Katayoun Kishi, "Assaults Against Muslims in U.S. Surpass 2001 Level," Pew Research Center, November 15, 2017, https://www .pewresearch.org/short-reads/2017/11/15/assaults-against-muslims-in-u-s -surpass-2001-level/.

25. Perry Stein and Devlin Barrett, "Threats to U.S. Senator Amid Spike in Anti-Jewish, Anti-Muslim Activity," *Washington Post*, October 30, 2023, https://www.washingtonpost.com/national-security/2023/10/30/fbi -threats-jewish-muslim-antisemitic/.

26. Jeffrey Ostler, "Disease Has Never Been Just Disease for Native Americans," *Atlantic*, April 29, 2020, https://www.theatlantic.com/ideas/archive /2020/04/disease-has-never-been-just-disease-native-americans/610852/.

27. Clifford E. and Michelle Lorimer, "Silencing California Indian Genocide in Social Studies Texts," *American Behavioral Scientist* 58 (2014): 64–82.

28. Glenn, *Unequal Freedom*; Jorge A. Bustamante, "The 'Wetback' as Deviant: An Application of Labeling Theory," *American Journal of Sociology* 77 (1972): 706–18.

29. Tomás R. Jiménez, *Replenished Ethnicity: Mexican Americans, Immigration, and Identity* (University of California Press, 2009).

30. Gordon W. Allport, *The Nature of Prejudice* (Addison-Wesley Brown, 1954); Peter M. Blau, *Inequality and Heterogeneity: A Primitive Theory of Social Structure* (Free Press, 1977); Susan Olzak, *The Dynamics of Ethnic Competition and Conflict* (Stanford University Press, 1992); Blumer, "Race Prejudice as a Sense of Group Position," 3–7.

31. Sara A. Soule, "Populism and Black Lynching in Georgia, 1890–1900," *Social Forces* 71 (1992): 431–49; Olzak, *Dynamics of Ethnic Competition and Conflict*.

32. Mary Jackman, *The Velvet Glove: Paternalism and Conflict in Gender, Class, and Race Relations* (University of California Press, 1994); John Gaventa, *Power and Powerlessness: Quiescence and Rebellion in an Appalachian Valley* (University of Illinois Press, 1980); Bonilla-Silva, "Rethinking Racism."

33. Blumer, "Race Prejudice as a Sense of Group Position," 3–7; Bobo and Hutchings, "Perceptions of Racial Group Competition," 951–72.

34. Arlie Russell Hochschild, *Strangers in Their Own Land: Anger and Mourning on the American Right* (New Press, 2018).

35. Rory McVeigh, Bill Carbonaro, and Emmanuel Cannady, "It's Not the Message, It's the Messenger: Organizational Identity and White Men's Opposition to Women's and African Americans' Civic Participation," *Social Forces* 192 (2023): 92–115.

36. McAdam, *Political Process and the Development of Black Insurgency*.

37. Doug McAdam and Karina Kloos, *Deeply Divided: Racial Politics and Social Movements in Post-War America* (Oxford University Press, 2014).

38. Rory McVeigh, David Cunningham, and Justin Farrell, "Political Polarization as a Social Movement Outcome: 1960s Klan Activism and Its Enduring Impact on Political Realignment in Southern Counties, 1960 to 2000," *American Sociological Review* 79 (2014): 1144–71.

39. McVeigh, *The Rise of the Ku Klux Klan*; Cecilia L. Ridgeway, *Status: Why Is It Everywhere? Why Does it Matter?* (Russell Sage Foundation, 2019); Gaventa, *Power and Powerlessness*; Steven Lukes, *Power: A Radical View* (Macmillan, 1974).

40. McVeigh, *The Rise of the Ku Klux Klan*.

41. Beth Allison Barr, *The Making of Biblical Womanhood: How the Subjugation of Women Became Gospel Truth* (Brazos, 2021).

42. Eliza Griswold, "The Unmaking of Biblical Womanhood: How a Nascent Movement Against Complementarianism Is Confronting Christian Patriarchy from Within," *New Yorker*, July 25, 2021, https://www.newyorker.com/news/on-religion/the-unmaking-of-biblical-womanhood.

43. J. P. Robinson, "Protecting Our Sons: Navigating a Radical Feminist Culture," Focus on the Family, https://www.focusonthefamily.com/parenting/protecting-our-sons-navigating-a-radical-feminist-culture/, accessed on April 2, 2025.

44. Nancy MacLean, *Behind the Mask of Chivalry: The Making of the Second Ku Klux Klan* (Oxford University Press, 1994).

45. William G. Domhoff, *Who Rules America?* (Prentice-Hall, 1967); C. Wright Mills, *The Power Elite* (Oxford University Press, 1956).

46. Elisabeth Clemens, *The People's Lobby: Organizational Innovation and the Rise of Interest Group Politics in the United States, 1890–1925* (University of Chicago Press, 1997).

47. Theda Skocpol, *Protecting Soldiers and Mothers: The Political Origins of Social Policy in the United States* (Harvard University Press, 1992); Clemens, *The People's Lobby*.

48. McVeigh, *The Rise of the Ku Klux Klan*; also see Blee, *Women of the Ku Klux Klan.*

49. Quotation taken from the Klan's national publication *The Kourier*, April 1925. Quoted in McVeigh, *The Rise of the Ku Klux Klan*, 109.

50. Center for American Women and Politics, "History of Women in the U.S. Congress," Rutgers–New Brunswick Eagleton Institute of Politics, https://cawp.rutgers.edu/facts/levels-office/congress/history-women-us-congress, accessed on April 2, 2025.

51. Kristin Luker, *Abortion and the Politics of Motherhood* (University of California Press, 1984).

52. David S. Pedulla and Sarah Thébaud, "Can We Finish the Revolution? Gender, Work-Family Ideals, and Institutional Constraint," *American Sociological Review* 80 (2015): 116–39.

53. Paula England, *Comparable Worth: Theories and Evidence* (Aldine-Transaction, 1992).

54. David A. Cotter, Joan M. Hermsen, and Reeve Vanneman, "Women's Work and Working Women: The Demand for Female Labor," *Gender and Society* 15 (2001): 429–52.

55. Ling Zhu and David B. Grusky, "The Intergenerational Sources of the U-Turn in Gender Segregation," *Proceedings of the National Academy of Sciences* 119 (2022).

56. Arlie Hochschild with Anne Machung, *The Second Shift: Working Families and the Revolution at Home*, rev. ed. (Penguin, 2012).

57. Jackman, *The Velvet Glove.*

58. Paige L. Sweet, "The Sociology of Gaslighting," *American Sociological Review* 84 (2019): 851–75.

59. McVeigh and Estep, *The Politics of Losing.*

60. The Feed, "Women Increasingly Outnumber Men at U.S. Colleges—But Why? Georgetown University, September 10, 2021, https://feed.georgetown.edu/access-affordability/women-increasingly-outnumber-men-at-u-s-colleges-but-why/.

61. We do this by including an interaction term to examine how the effects of party identity depend on the treatment group of the respondent.

62. See the methodological appendix for full results of the regression analyses.

63. Mancur Olson, *The Logic of Collective Action* (Harvard University Press, 1965).

64. Pamela Oliver, "'If You Don't Do It, Nobody Else Will': Active and Token Contributors to Local Collective Action," *American Sociological Review* 49 (1984): 601–10.

65. John D. McCarthy and Mayer N. Zald, "Resource Mobilization and Social Movements: A Partial Theory," *American Journal of Sociology* 82 (1977): 1212–41; Anthony Oberschall, *Social Conflict and Social Movements* (Prentice-Hall, 1973).

66. Carroll Doherty and Jocelyn Kiley, "In Changing U.S. Electorate, Race and Education Remain Stark Dividing Lines," Pew Research Center, June 2, 2020, https://www.pewresearch.org/politics/2020/06/02/in-changing-u-s-electorate-race-and-education-remain-stark-dividing-lines/.

5. LGBTQ, IMMIGRATION, RELIGION, AND STATUS PRESERVATION

1. History.com Editors, "Stonewall Riots," May 31, 2017, https://www.history.com/topics/gay-rights/the-stonewall-riots.

2. Quote taken from David Carter, *Stonewall: The Riots That Sparked the Gay Revolution* (St. Martin's Griffin, 2004), 266.

3. Jeni Loftus, "America's Liberalization in Attitudes Toward Homosexuality, 1973 to 1998," *American Sociological Review* 66 (2001): 762–82; Rory McVeigh and Maria-Elena Diaz, "Voting to Ban Same-Sex Marriage: Interests, Values, and Communities," *American Sociological Review* 74 (2009): 891–915; Michael J. Rosenfeld, *The Rainbow After the Storm: Marriage Equality and Social Change in the US* (Oxford University Press, 2021); Brian Powell, Catherine Blozendahl, Claudia Geist, and Lala Carr Steelman, "Counted Out: Same-Sex Relations and Americans' Definitions of Family," (Russell Sage Foundation, 2010).

4. Jacob Poushter and Nicholas Kent, "The Global Divide on Homosexuality Persists," Pew Research Center, June 25, 2020, https://www.pewresearch.org/global/2020/06/25/global-divide-on-homosexuality-persists/.

5. Justin McCarthy, "Record-High 70 Percent in U.S. Support Same-Sex Marriage," Gallup, June 8, 2021, https://news.gallup.com/poll/350486/record-high-support-same-sex-marriage.aspx.

6. Human Rights Campaign Foundation, Jay Brown and Tori Cooper, eds., "An Epidemic of Violence 2021: Fatal Violence Against Transgender and

Gender Non-Conforming People in the United States in 1921," Human Rights Campaign Foundation, https://reports.hrc.org/an-epidemic-of -violence-fatal-violence-against-transgender-and-gender-non-confirming -people-in-the-united-states-in-2021, accessed December 1, 2023.

7. Federal Bureau of Investigation, "Crime Data Explorer," https://cde .ucr.cjis.gov/LATEST/webapp/#/pages/explorer/crime/hate-crime, accessed December 5, 2023.

8. Rory McVeigh, Michael R. Welch, and Thoroddur Bjarnason, "Hate Crime Reporting as a Successful Social Movement Outcome," *American Sociological Review* 68 (2003): 843–67.

9. American Civil Liberties Union, "Update on the Status of Sodomy Laws," August 22, 2001, https://www.aclu.org/documents/update-status -sodomy-laws#:~:text=Sodomy%20laws%20generally%20prohibit%20 oral,separating%20parents%20from%20their%20children.

10. Antonin Scalia, Dissenting opinion in *John Geddes Lawrence and Tyron Garner v. Texas*, United States Supreme Court, June 26, 2003, https:// www.law.cornell.edu/supct/html/02-102.ZD.html.

11. James Madison, Federalist Papers no. 10, Bill of Rights Institute, 1787, https://billofrightsinstitute.org/primary-sources/federalist-no-10.

12. Tina Fetner, *How the Religions Right Shaped Lesbian and Gay Activism* (University of Minnesota Press, 2008).

13. Rory McVeigh and David Sikkink, "God, Politics, and Protest: Religious Beliefs and the Legitimation of Contentious Tactics," *Social Forces* 79 (2001): 1425–58.

14. C. J. Pascoe, *Dude, You're a Fag: Masculinity and Sexuality in High School* (University of California Press, 2011).

15. Pascoe, *Dude, You're a Fag.*

16. Kathryn M. Nowotny, Rachel L. Peterson, Jason D. Boardman, "Gendered Contexts: Variation in Suicidal Ideation by Female and Male Youth Across U.S. States," *Journal of Health and Social Behavior* 56 (2015): 114–30.

17. Nicola Beisel, *Imperiled Innocents: Anthony Comstock and Family Reproduction in Victorian America* (Princeton University Press 1996).

18. Anthony Comstock quoted in "Anthony Comstock Seeks to Imprison Inverts (1900)," in Chuck Stewart, ed. *Documents of the LGBT Movement: Eyewitness to History* (ABC-CLIO 2018), 23–24.

19. Brooke Migdon, "Governor DeSantis Spokesperson Says 'Don't Say Gay' Opponents Are 'Groomers,'" The Hill, March 7, 2022, https://thehill .com/changing-america/respect/equality/597215-gov-desantis-spokesperson -says-dont-say-gay-opponents-are/.

20. Elizabeth A. Armstrong and Mary Bernstein, "Culture, Power, and Institutions: A Multi-Institutional Politics Approach to Social Movements," Sociological Theory 26 (2008): 74–99.

21. Jessica Fields, "Normal Queers: Straight Parents Respond to Their Children's 'Coming Out,'" Symbolic Interaction 24 (2001): 165–87; Joseph J. Wardenski, "A Minor Exception? The Impact of Lawrence v. Texas on LGBT Youth," Journal of Criminal Law and Criminology 95 (2005): 1363–1410.

22. Rory McVeigh and Kevin Estep, The Politics of Losing: Trump, the Klan, and the Mainstreaming of Resentment (Columbia University Press, 2019).

23. Nathan Layne, "Trump Repeats 'Poisoning the Blood' Anti-Immigrant Remark," Reuters, December 16, 2023, https://www.reuters.com/world/us /trump-repeats-poisoning-blood-anti-immigrant-remark-2023-12-16/.

24. Evelyn Nakano Glenn, Unequal Freedom: How Race and Gender Shaped American Citizenship and Labor (Harvard University Press, 2002).

25. Kevin Escudero, Organizing While Undocumented: Immigrant Youth's Political Activism Under the Law (New York University Press, 2020).

26. Catherine Lee, "Family Reunification and the Limits of Immigration Reform: Impact and Legacy of the 1965 Immigration Act," Sociological Forum 30 (2015): 528–48.

27. Edna Bonacich, "A Theory of Ethnic Antagonism: The Split Labor Market," American Sociological Review 37 (1972): 547–59.

28. Rory McVeigh, "Structural Influences on Popular Support for Social Movement Activity," Research in Social Movements, Conflict and Change 19 (1996): 247–71; Marshall Ganz, Why David Sometimes Wins: Leadership, Organization, and Strategy in the California Farm Worker Movement (Oxford University Press, 2009).

29. Bonacich, "A Theory of Ethnic Antagonism, 547–59; Susan Olzak, The Dynamics of Ethnic Competition and Conflict (Stanford University Press, 1992); William Julius Wilson, The Declining Significance of Race: Blacks and Changing American Institutions (University of Chicago Press, 1978).

30. Gøsta Esping-Andersen," Power and Distributional Regimes," Politics & Society 14 (1985): 223–56.

31. Lane Kenworthy, "Do Social-Welfare Policies Reduce Poverty? A Cross-National Assessment," *Social Forces* 77 (1999): 1119–39.

32. Marnie Hunter, "The World's Happiest Countries for 2023," CNN, March 20, 2023, https://www.cnn.com/travel/article/world-happiest -countries-2023-wellness/index.html.

33. Wayne A. Santoro, "Conventional Politics Takes Center Stage: The Latino Struggle Against English-Only Laws," *Social Forces* 77 (1999): 887–909.

34. Kenneth T. Andrews and Charles Seguin, "Group Threat and Policy Change: The Spatial Dynamics of Prohibition Politics, 1890–1919," *American Journal of Sociology* 121 (2015): 475–510; Rory McVeigh, *The Rise of the Ku Klux Klan: Right-Wing Movements and National Politics* (University of Minnesota Press, 2009).

35. Geoff Bennett, "Hundreds of Migrant Children Remain Separated from Families Despite Push to Reunite Them," PBS News Hour, February 6, 2023, https://www.pbs.org/newshour/show/hundreds-of-migrant -children-remain-separated-from-families-despite-push-to-reunite-them

36. McVeigh, *The Rise of the Ku Klux Klan.*

37. Stef W. Kight, "The Evolution of Trump's Muslim Ban," Axios, February 20, 2020, https://www.axios.com/2020/02/10/trump-muslim-travel-ban -immigration.

38. Rick Braziel, Frank Straub, George Watson, and Rod Hoops, "Bringing Calm to Chaos: A Critical Incident Review of the San Bernardino Public Safety Response to the December 2, 2015 Terrorist Shooting Incident at the Inland Regional Center," Community Oriented Policing Services, US Department of Justice, September 2016, https://portal.cops .usdoj.gov/resourcecenter/Home.aspx?page=detail&id=COPS-W0808.

39. Kight, "The Evolution of Trump's Muslim Ban."

40. Ilir Disha, James C. Cavendish, and Ryan D. King, "Historical Events and Spaces of Hate: Hate Crimes Against Arabs and Muslims in Post-9/11 America," *Social Problems* 58 (2011): 21–46; Christopher A. Bail, "The Fringe Effect: Civil Society Organizations and the Evolution of Media Discourse About Islam Since the September 11th Attacks," *American Sociological Review* 77 (2012): 855–79.

41. Gregory A. Smith, Michael Rotolo, and Patricia Tevington, "45 Percent of Americans Say U.S. Should be a Christian Nation," Pew Research Center, October 27, 2022, https://www.pewresearch

.org/religion/2022/10/27/45-of-americans-say-u-s-should-be-a
-christian-nation/.

42. Philip S. Gorski and Samuel L. Perry, *The Flag and the Cross: White Christian Nationalism and the Threat to American Democracy* (Oxford University Press, 2022).

43. Monika Hübscher and Sabine von Mering, eds., *Antisemitism on Social Media* (Routledge, 2022).

44. Nicole Chavez, Emanuella Grinberg, and Eliott C. McLaughlin, "Pittsburgh Synagogue Gunman Said He Wanted All Jews to Die, Criminal Complaint Says," CNN, October 31, 2018, https://www.cnn .com/2018/10/28/us/pittsburgh-synagogue-shooting/index.html.

45. Lauren Leatherby, "Gaza Civilians, Under Israeli Barrage, Are Being Killed at Historic Pace," *New York Times*, November 20, 2023, https:// www.nytimes.com/2023/11/25/world/middleeast/israel-gaza-death-toll .html; Masood Farivar, "Why the Gaza War Has Sparked a Wave of Anti-Semitism and Islamophobia in the US," Voice of America, November 17, 2023, https://www.voanews.com/a/why-the-gaza-war-has-sparked-a -wave-of-antisemitism-and-islamophobia-in-the-us-/7358885.html.

46. Mark D. Regnerus, David Sikkink, and Christian Smith, "Voting with the Christian Right: Contextual and Individual Patterns of Electoral Influence," *Social Forces* 77 (1999): 1375–1401.

47. Andrew Whitehead and Samuel L. Perry, *Taking America Back for God: Christian Nationalism in the United States* (Oxford University Press, 2020).

48. Public Religion Research Institute (staff), "Religion and Congregations in a Time of Social Upheaval," May 16, 2023, https://www.prri.org /research/religion-and-congregations-in-a-time-of-social-and-political -upheaval/.

49. McVeigh and Estep, *The Politics of Losing*.

6. STATUS CONTESTATION AND POLITICAL POLARIZATION

1. Rory McVeigh, Bill Carbonaro, and Emmanuel Cannady, "It's Not the Message, It's the Messenger: Organizational Identity and White Men's Opposition to Women's and African Americans' Civic Participation," *Social Forces* 102 (2023): 92–115.

2. Delia Baldassarri and Andrew Gelman, "Partisans Without Constraint: Political Polarization and Trends in American Public Opinion," *American Journal of Sociology* 114 (2008): 408–46.

3. Madeline Berg, "President Obama Is the Real Ratings Machine," Forbes, January 19, 2017, https://www.forbes.com/sites/maddieberg/2017/01/19/president-obama-is-the-real-ratings-machine/?sh=7fa1865652fe.

4. Barack Obama, "Transcript of Barack Obama's Victory Speech," National Public Radio, November 5, 2008, https://www.npr.org/2008/11/05/96624326/transcript-of-barack-obamas-victory-speech.

5. John McCain, "Transcript of John McCain's Concession Speech," National Public Radio, November 5, 2008, https://www.npr.org/2008/11/05/96631784/transcript-of-john-mccains-concession-speech.

6. John Weinberg, "The Great Recession and Its Aftermath," Federal Reserve History, November 22, 2013, https://www.federalreservehistory.org/essays/great-recession-and-its-aftermath.

7. Theda Skocpol and Venessa Williamson, *The Tea Party and the Remaking of Republican Conservatism* (Oxford University Press, 2012).

8. Rory McVeigh, Kraig Beyerlein, Burrel Vann, and Priyamvada Trivedi, "Educational Segregation, Tea Party Organizations, and Battles Over Distributive Justice," *American Sociological Review* 79 (2014): 630–52.

9. Patrick Rafail and John D. McCarthy, *The Rise, Fall, and Influence of the Tea Party Insurgency* (Cambridge University Press, 2024).

10. Preeti Vankar, "Percentage of Public with Favorable or Unfavorable of the Affordable Care Act (ACA) from April 2010 to March 2023," Statista, April 20, 2023, https://www.statista.com/statistics/246901/opinion-on-the-health-reform-law-in-the-united-states/.

11. Hannah Fingerhut, "For the First Time, More Americans Say 2010 Health Care Law Has Had a Positive [Rather] Than Negative Impact on the U.S," Pew Research Center, December 11, 2017, https://www.pewresearch.org/fact-tank/2017/12/11/for-the-first-time-more-americans-say-2010-health-care-law-has-had-a-positive-than-negative-impact-on-u-s/.

12. Christopher S. Parker and Matt A. Barreto, *Change They Can't Believe In: The Tea Party and Reactionary Politics in America* (Princeton University Press, 2013).

13. 2010 election results as reported in the *New York Times*, https://www.nytimes.com/elections/2010/results/house.html, accessed September 5, 2024.

14. David Daley, *Rat F**ked: The True Story Behind the Secret Plan to Steal America's Democracy* (Liveright, 2016).

15. House Freedom Caucus, "House Freedom Caucus Urges Senate to Oppose the Respect for Marriage Act, July 22, 2022, Twitter, https://twitter.com/freedomcaucus/status/1550529116063125504/photo/1.

16. Becky Budds, "Conservative Lawmakers Sue Lexington One Over Critical Race Theory Claims," News19, November 16, 2022, https://www.wltx.com/article/news/education/conservative-sc-lawmakers-sue-lexington-1-crt-claims-south-carolina-education/101-66e39120-17d3-4f05-9c70-7f9896d4a3f6.

17. Talia Richman, "Conservative Texas Lawmakers Call Transgender Guidance to School Boards 'Dangerous,'" The Dallas Morning News, January 18, 2023, https://www.dallasnews.com/news/education/2023/01/18/texas-freedom-caucus-asks-ag-paxton-to-review-tasb-guidance-on-transgender-students/.

18. Domenico Montanaro, "Americans Have Increasingly Negative Views of Those in the Other Political Party," National Public Radio, August 13, 2022, https://www.npr.org/2022/08/13/1117232857/americans-have-increasingly-negative-views-of-those-in-the-other-political-party.

19. Angus Campbell, Philip E. Converse, Warren E. Miller, and Donald E. Stokes, *The American Voter* (University of Chicago Press, 1960).

20. Campbell, Converse, Miller, and Stokes, *The American Voter*.

21. Donald Green, Bradley Palmquist, and Eric Schickler, *Partisan Hearts and Minds: Political Parties and the Social Identity of Voters* (Yale University Press, 2002); Douglas J. Ahler and Gaurav Sood, "The Parties in Our Heads: Misperceptions About Party Composition and Their Consequences," *Journal of Politics* 80 (2018): 964–81; Jordan Brensinger and Ramina Sotoudeh, "Party, Race, and Neutrality: Investigating the Interdependence of Attitudes Toward Social Groups," *American Sociological Review* 87 (2022): 1049–93.

22. Daniel DellaPosta, "Pluralistic Collapse: The 'Oil Spill' Model of Mass Opinion Polarization," *American Sociological Review* 85 (2020): 507–36; Delia Baldassarri and Andrew Gelman, "Partisans Without Constraint: Political Polarization and Trends in American Public Opinion," *American Journal of Sociology* 114 (2008): 408–46.

23. Doug McAdam and Karina Kloos, *Deeply Divided: Racial Politics and Social Movements in Post-War America* (Oxford University Press, 2014);

Sidney Tarrow, *Movements and Parties: Critical Connections in American Political Development* (Cambridge University Press, 2021).

24. Baldassarri and Gelman. "Partisans Without Constraint," 408–46; Paul DiMaggio, John Evans, and Bethany Bryson, "Have American's Social Attitudes Become More Polarized?" *American Journal of Sociology* 102 (1996): 690–755.

25. Jeni Loftus, "America's Liberalization in Attitudes Toward Homosexuality, 1973 to 1998," *American Sociological Review* 66 (2001): 762–82; Michael J. Rosenfeld, *The Rainbow After the Storm: Marriage Equality and Social Change in the US* (Oxford University Press, 2021); Brian Powell, Catherine Blozendahl, Claudia Geist, and Lala Carr Steelman, *Counted Out: Same-Sex Relations and Americans' Definitions of Family* (Russell Sage Foundation, 2010).

26. Rory McVeigh and Maria-Elena Diaz, "Voting to Ban Same-Sex Marriage: Interests, Values, and Communities," *American Sociological Review* 74 (2009): 891–915.

27. Anthony Downs, *An Economic Theory of Democracy* (Harper and Row, 1957).

7. HEATED STATUS BOUNDARIES

1. Eduardo Bonilla-Silva, *Racism Without Racists: Color-Blind Racism and the Persistence of Racial Inequality in America* (Rowman and Littlefield, 2009).

2. Respondent R249.

3. Respondent R323.

4. Respondent R295.

5. Respondent R306.

6. Respondent R308.

7. Respondent R307.

8. Respondent R298.

9. Respondent R252.

10. Respondent R283.

11. Respondent R263.

12. Respondent R260.

13. Respondent D31.

14. Respondent D59.

15. Respondent D1.
16. Respondent D27.
17. Respondent D6.
18. Respondent D67.
19. Respondent D93.
20. Respondent D98.
21. Respondent D90.
22. Respondent D124.
23. Respondent I171.
24. For example, respondents I134, I135, I160, I180.
25. Respondent I145.
26. Respondent I217.
27. Respondent I211.
28. Bonilla-Silva, *Racism Without Racists*.
29. Respondent R247.
30. Respondent R251.
31. Respondent R317.
32. Respondent R318.
33. Respondent R314.
34. Respondent R251.
35. Respondent D43.
36. Respondent D105.
37. Respondent D109.
38. Respondent D96.
39. Respondent D114.
40. Respondent D118.
41. Respondent D91.
42. Respondent D116.
43. Respondent I148.
44. Respondent I54.
45. Respondent I169.
46. Respondent I189.
47. Respondent R255.
48. Respondent R262.
49. Respondent R304.
50. Respondent R242.
51. Respondent R250.

52. Respondent R246.
53. Paige L. Sweet, "The Sociology of Gaslighting," *American Sociological Review* 84 (2019): 851–75.
54. Respondent D8.
55. Respondent D30.
56. Respondent D26.
57. Respondent D45.
58. Respondent D87.
59. Respondent D92.
60. Respondent D23.
61. Respondent D48.
62. Respondent D123.
63. Respondent I172.
64. Respondent I195.
65. Respondent I156
66. Respondent I225.
67. Respondent I132.
68. Respondent I130.
69. Respondent I192.
70. Respondent I147.
71. Respondent I157.
72. Respondent R272.
73. Respondent R276.
74. Respondent R279.
75. Respondent R313.
76. Respondent R319.
77. Respondent D2.
78. Respondent D16.
79. Respondent D77.
80. Respondent D18.
81. Respondent D49.
82. Respondent D79.
83. Respondent D75.
84. Respondent D82.
85. Respondent D34.
86. Respondent D125.
87. Respondent D61.
88. Respondent D112.

89. Respondent I146.

90. Respondent I179.

91. Jeffrey M. Jones, "LGBT Identification in the U.S. Ticks Up to 7.1 Percent," Gallup, February 17, 2022, https://news.gallup.com/poll/389792/lgbt-identification-ticks-up.aspx.

92. Respondent I235.

93. Respondent I237.

94. Respondent I200.

95. Respondent I221.

96. Respondent I231.

97. Evelyn Nakano Glenn, *Unequal Freedom: How Race and Gender Shaped American Citizenship and Labor* (Harvard University Press, 2002).

98. Rory McVeigh, *The Rise of the Ku Klux Klan: Right-Wing Movements and National Politics* (University of Minnesota Press, 2009).

99. Edna Bonacich, "A Theory of Ethnic Antagonism: The Split Labor Market," *American Sociological Review* 37 (1972): 547–59; Jennifer A. Jones, *The Browning of the New South* (University of Chicago Press, 2019); Christopher Zepeda-Millan, *Latino Mass Mobilization: Immigration, Racialization, and Activism* (Cambridge University Press, 2017).

100. Respondent R282.

101. Respondent R294.

102. Respondent R299.

103. Respondent R305.

104. Respondent R240.

105. Respondent D32.

106. Respondent D33.

107. Respondent D104.

108. Respondent D103.

109. Respondent D14.

110. Respondent D21.

111. Respondent I131.

112. Respondent I166.

113. Respondent I149.

114. Respondent I153.

115. Tomás R. Jiménez, *Replenished Ethnicity: Mexican Americans, Immigration, and Identity* (University of California Press, 2009).

116. Respondent I174.

117. Respondent I207.

118. Respondent I227.
119. Respondent I212.
120. Respondent R245.
121. Respondent R258.
122. Southern Poverty Law Center (staff), "Radical Traditional Catholicism, https://www.splcenter.org/fighting-hate/extremist-files/ideology/radical -traditional-catholicism, accessed on July 20, 2023.
123. Respondent D58.
124. Respondent D53.
125. Respondent D7.
126. Respondent D95.
127. Respondent I152.
128. Respondent I173.
129. Respondent I168.
130. Respondent I191.
131. Respondent I167.

8. LOOKING TO THE FUTURE: CRISIS OR NEW COALITION?

1. Board of Governors of the Federal Reserve System, "Distribution of Household Wealth in the U.S. Since 1989," https://www.federalreserve .gov/releases/z1/dataviz/dfa/distribute/table/#quarter:135;series:Net%20 worth;demographic:networth;population:all;units:shares, accessed on November 11, 2023.
2. Joseph R. Gusfield, *Symbolic Crusade: Status Politics and the American Temperance Movement* (University of Illinois Press, 1963); Nicola Beisel, *Imperiled Innocents: Anthony Comstock and Family Reproduction in Victorian America* (Princeton University Press, 1996).
3. Eduardo Bonilla-Silva, "Rethinking Racism: Toward a Structural Interpretation," *American Sociological Review* 62 (1997): 465–80; Victor Ray, "A Theory of Racialized Organizations," *American Sociological Review* 84 (2019): 26–53; Cecilia L. Ridgeway, *Status: Why Is It Everywhere? Why Does It Matter?* (Russell Sage Foundation, 2019).
4. Mary R. Jackman and Michael J. Muha, "Education and Intergroup Attitudes: Moral Enlightenment, Superficial Democratic Commitment,

or Ideological Refinement?" *American Sociological Review* 49 (1984): 751–69.

5. Eduardo Bonilla-Silva, *Racism Without Racists: Color-Blind Racism and the Persistence of Racial Inequality in America* (Rowman and Littlefield, 2009).

6. Hajar Yazdiha, *The Struggle for the People's King: How Politics Transforms the Memory of the Civil Rights Movement* (Princeton University Press, 2023).

7. Rory McVeigh and Kevin Estep, *The Politics of Losing: Trump, the Klan, and the Mainstreaming of Resentment* (Columbia University Press, 2019).

8. Sidney Tarrow, *Power in Movement: Social Movements and Contentious Politics*, 2nd ed. (Cambridge University Press, 2012); Doug McAdam, *Political Process and the Development of Black Insurgency, 1930–1970* (University of Chicago Press, 1982); Charles Tilly, *From Mobilization to Revolution* (Addison-Wesley, 1978).

9. McAdam, *Political Process and the Development of Black Insurgency*.

10. Jeffrey M. Jones and Camille Lloyd, "Larger Majority Says Racism Against Black People Widespread," Gallup, July 23, 2021, https://news.gallup.com/poll/352544/larger-majority-says-racism-against-black-people-widespread.aspx.

11. Andrea Malek Ash, "Majorities Support Racial Education in Schools," Gallup, July 7, 2023, https://news.gallup.com/poll/508172/majorities-support-racial-education-schools.aspx.

12. Lydia Saad, "Concerns About Sexual Harassment Higher Than in 1998," Gallup, November 3, 2017, https://news.gallup.com/poll/221216/concerns-sexual-harassment-higher-1998.aspx.

13. Jeffrey M. Jones, "U.S. LGBT Identity Steady at 7.2 Percent," Gallup, February 22, 2023, https://news.gallup.com/poll/470708/lgbt-identification-steady.aspx.

14. Jeffrey M. Jones, "Fewer in U.S. Say Same-Sex Relations Morally Acceptable," Gallup, June 16, 2023, https://news.gallup.com/poll/507230/fewer-say-sex-relations-morally-acceptable.aspx.

15. Gallup (staff), "Immigration," https://news.gallup.com/poll/1660/immigration.aspx, accessed on May 4, 2024.

16. Jeffrey M. Jones, "How Religious Are Americans?" Gallup, March 29, 2024, https://news.gallup.com/poll/358364/religious-americans.aspx.

INDEX

Page numbers in *italics* indicate figures or tables.

Abbott, Gregg, 96
*Abortion and the Politics of
    Motherhood* (Luker), 68
acts: Affordable Care, 114, 180; Civil
    Rights, 64; Immigration and
    Nationality, 92; Parental Rights
    in Education, 87–88; Respect for
    Marriage, 117; Voting Rights, 64
advantages, 10, 192; of Democratic
    Party, 116; dis-, 13, 22; economic,
    36; educational, 45; males
    securing, 70; of policy agendas,
    37; race and, 30, 58–59, 193; of
    religion, 182; status, 9, 11, 21–22,
    54, 71, 193–94
affective polarization, 37–38, 119
affiliations, with political parties, 50,
    72, 122, *123*, *124*, 206
Affordable Care Act. *See*
    Obamacare
American Civil Liberties Union, 97
American Communities Project, 2

American Dream, the, 56, 183
American exceptionalism, 40
Americanism, 89–90, 91
American National Election
    Study, 122
American Protective Association
    (APA), 56
American Voter, The (Campbell), 119
anti-Catholics, 56
anti-immigrant, 57, 60, 92, *95*
anti-Muslim, 62, 96–98
antiracism, *199*
antisemitism, 90–91, 100–101
antisodomy laws, 84–85
antivice movement, 27, 86–87
APA. *See* American Protective
    Association
Asian Americans, *61*, 61–62

Baldassarri, Delia, 36
Bearman, Peter, 36
Beck, Glenn, 55

Beisel, Nicola, 27, 86–87

beneficiaries: status hierarchies, 7, 22, 89, 189, 192, 193–94; status privilege, 63, 64, 109, 201

Bible, the, 65, 143

Biden, Joe, 95, 98, 195

Biggs, Joe, 5

bigotry, 62, 84, 88, 192; expressions of, 9, 120, 139, 193; religious, 20, 22, 102

Black alliance, 37

Black Americans, 63, 71, 141, 145–46; first president representing, 112, 114, 195; immigrants and, 29–30; Jim Crow laws and, 6, 59–60; McAdam on, 197; middle-class neighborhoods of, 30–31; Park on, 58; privilege and, 31, 59; slavery, 29–30, 31, 59, 92; status hierarchies and, 6; transgender, 83; treatment of, 31, 153, 199; voters, 35, 64; workers inclusion and, 30. *See also* racism

Bonacich, Edna, 92

Bonilla-Silva, Eduardo, 8–9, 139, 192–93

Bowers, Robert, 101

Bracero Program, 92–93

Burgess, Ernest, 58

Bush, George W., 35, 98

campaign contributions, 13, 35, 145, 223

Campbell, Angus, 119

Cannady, Emmanuel, 37

capitalism, 2, 3, 12, 145–46, 149, 186; defense of, 150, 172–73, 179; free market, 50–51, 147

capitalist economy, 93

Carbonaro, William, 37

Carlson, Tucker, 90, 91

Carrol, E. Jean, 71

Carville, James, 1

Catholics, 98–99, 154–55, 164, 170–71, *205, 210, 214*; anti-, 56; Protestant or, 73; traditional, 179–80; voters as, 66

CBS Evening News (TV show), 55

chance variation, 206

Christian faith, 90–91, 143, 162; conservatives in, 65–66; gender hierarchies in, 65–66; non-Christians, 18, 179–81; One America for Working People and, 179–80; privileges of, 98, 179; religion status goals and, 103–9; Republican Party linked to, 102; status hierarchies in, 98–103, 200

Christian nationalism, 102–3

cisgender people, 85, 88, 189

cisnormativity, 84, 88, 163–71

citizenship: religion and, 10, 17, 32, 80, 81; status hierarchies and, 89–90, 91, 94. *See also* immigrants

Citizens United v. Federal Election Commission, 35

Civil Rights Act (1964), 64

civil rights movement, 64, 65, 197, 198

Civil War, 29, 31

class-conscious coalitions, 42

class consciousness, 40–42, 45, 52–53

class inequality, 53, 142, 152, 170, 178–79

class struggle, 4, 79

Clinton, Bill, 1, 89

coalitions: class-conscious, 42; diverse, 15, 53; progressive, 7, 17, 26, 36, 80, 110, 130, 139, 187, 189; reduction of inequality through, 1, 2, 7, 24

college graduates, 70, 143, 144; political parties and, 45, 79–80; racial inequality and, 150

"color-blind," 9, 150, 192, 193

communism, 142, 164, 179

Communist Manifesto, The (Engels and Marx), 2

complementarianism, 65

Comstock, Anthony, 27, 87

conservatives, 53, 193, 194, 199, 201; American exceptionalism and, 40; broadcasters, 55; in Christian faith, 65–66; Focus on the Family organization, 65; on One America for Working People, 141–42; policies of, 25, 39, 130; progressives and, 120; Republican Party and, 34–35; Tea Party movement and, 114, 116, 117; views on economy by, 147; voters as, 34–35

Constitution, United States, 33–34, 55, 59, 66, 83

corporate greed, 143, 145–46

COVID-19 pandemic, 36–37, 61–62, 96

critical race theory, 117–18, *155*

Cronbach's alpha, 223

Cronkite, Walter, 55

cross-pressures, 4

cues, for voters, 37, 111–12

cultural schema theory, 7, 8

dangers, to Democratic Party, 192–96

Declining Significance of Race, The (Wilson), 29

decommodification, 93

defense, of capitalism, 150, 172–73, 179

Democratic Party: advantages of, 116; affective polarization and, 38; dangers to, 192–96; economic inequality and, 81, 138; experimental treatment groups for, 73–76; Latina people for, 159, 166, 175; policy issues and, 122–26, *123*, *124*; power of, 112–13; on race, 151–54; on racial inequality, 151–52, 153, 193; response to One America for Working People, 144–47; status equality and, 76; white supremacy in, 64

demographic transitions, 6–7

Denton, Nancy, 30

deportation, 91, 97

DeSantis, Ron, 87–88, 96, 167–68, 198

differential treatment, 29, 32, 38–39, 137, 189; of immigrants, 91, 93; racism and, 63–64

disadvantages, 13, 22

discrimination, 192; employment, 193; gender, 157, 158, 159, 161; immigrants experiences of, 171, 177; of LGBTQ people, 164–65, 166–67, 170–71, 179, 183; racial, 15, 17–18, 62, 64, 83; racial equality and, 151; religious beliefs and, 98–99, 180–82, 184; violence and, 103, 105, 109, 137, 164–65, 179, 180, 181

discursive strategy, 46
disparities, wealth, 143, 178
diverse coalitions, 15, 53
division, among workers, 3, 15–17, 18, 142–43, 145, 169
Dobbs v. Jackson Women's Health Organization, 68, 71
Don't Say Gay campaign, 168
Downs, Anthony, 128
drag shows, 82, *84*, 88
Du Bois, W. E. B., 58–59

earnings gap, 13
economic advantages, 36
economic elite, 12, 15, 18, 41, 45, 105, 190
economic equality, 13, 15, 76, 105, 111, 188; Independent Party and, 81; One America for Working People and, 133–34, 190; racial equality and, 151–52; status equality and, 23, 130, 132, 133, 137, 189, 201; status goals paired with, 130, 132; for workers, 153
economic inequality, 1–2, 11, 36, 47, *104*, 108; Democratic Party and, 81, 138; Federal Reserve Bank on, 3; in One America for Working People, 13–15; political mobilization to remedy, 138; racial inequality and, 35, 109, 154; status inequality and, 132, 165
Economic Theory of Democracy, An (Downs), 128
economy, 50–51, 114, 146, 149, 150, 172–73; capitalist, 93; conservative

views on, 147; gender identity and, 162; global, 3, 41, 42, 70–71, 135, 156, 158; during Great Depression, 113; high-tech, 30; immigrants affecting the, 175; industrial, 29; manufacturing jobs and, 3, 30, 156; strength of, 1; voters and downturn of, 1
educational advantages, 45
Education and Intergroup Attitudes (Jackman and Muha), 192
elections, 37, 244n13
Electoral College, 35
elite, 11, 47, 101, 114, 144, 172; economic, 12, 15, 18, 41, 45, 105, 190; political, 18, 41, 45, 190; power of, 41
employment discrimination, 193
Engels, Friedrich, 2
esteem, 7, 64, 94; denial of, 6; for Muslims, 99; privileges and, 10, 59, 179; social, 6, 10, 27, 38, 91, 171; societal, 86; status hierarchies and, 39
Estep, Kevin, 17
evangelical Protestants, 25, 103
experimental manipulations, 15, 20, 42, *104*, 137, 190
experimental research designs, 12–13, 42, 103, 138–39
experimental treatment groups, 73–76, 229n47
expression, of bigotry, 9, 120, 139, 193

factions, 33–34
fairness doctrine, 54–55

Falwell, Jerry, 102
favored treatment, 27, 109, 189
FBI, 83, 180
Federal Communications
    Commission (FCC), 55
Federalist Papers, The (Hamilton,
    Madison, and Jay), 33–34
Federal Reserve Bank, 3
feminism, 65
Fields, James, Jr., 101
"Fighting for a Better Future" (web
    page for fictitious organization),
    13–14, 16–18, 215; experimental
    manipulations for, 15, 20, 42, *104*,
    137, 190; experimental treatment
    groups for, 73–76, 229n47;
    outcome variables for, 211, 220;
    Republican Party for, 141–44;
    support of, 19, *74*, *106*
First Amendment, of Constitution, 55
Focus on the Family (conservative
    advocacy organization), 65
Fowler, Mark, 55
Fox News (TV show), 55
frame extension, 15, 137, 167
Freedom Caucus, 116–18
free market capitalism, 50–51, 147
Fuentes, Nick, 101

Gallup polling, 1–2, 199–200
gap: between Democrats and
    Republicans, 75–76, 78,
    106–7, 111; earnings, 13; between
    Independents and Republicans,
    106; between rich and poor, 2
gaslighting, 70

Gaventa, John, 41
Gay Activist Alliance, 82–83
gender, 199–200; discrimination,
    157, 158, 159, 161; equality, 18, 71,
    73, *74*, 75–79, 81, 161–62; One
    America for Working People
    and, 71–76, 157–60; privilege
    and, 80; segregation, 69; social
    construction of, 68; status
    hierarchies and, 64–71, 89;
    treatment groups, 75–76, 79;
    violence and, 18
gender hierarchies, 22, 71–72, 80, 81;
    in Christian faith, 65–66; race
    and, 110
gender identity, 70, 73, 120; economy
    and, 162; roles in, 158; sexual
    orientation and, 10, 17, 32, 80, 81,
    84–87, 89, 104–5, 170, 200
gender reassignment classes, 164
Generation Z, 170, 199
gerrymander, 35, 112, 116–17, 136
global economy, 3, 41, 42, 70–71, 135,
    156, 158
God, 40, 62, 64–65, 96–98, 100
Gosar, Paul, 100–101
Grant Park celebration, for Obama,
    112–13
Great Depression, 113
Greene, Marjorie Taylor, 100–101
Grusky, David, 69
Gusfield, Joseph, 26–27, 191

Hamas, 62, 101–2
Hamilton, Alexander, 33
Harris, Kamala, 5, 96

hate crimes, 63, *123*, 125, 181, *221*; against Asian Americans, 61–62; directed to Muslims, 62, 98, 101–2; towards Jews, 62, 101–2; sexual orientation and, 83

hate groups, 180; Nazis, 101; Proud Boys, *5*, 70–71, *84*, 88

hatred, 99, 102, 145, 167–68, 177, 195

health care, 122, *123*, 181, *221*; Medicare, 36; Obamacare, 114–16, *115*, 180

heteronormativity, 84, 87, 88, 163–71, 193

heterosexuality, 85, 88, 189, 195

high-tech economy, 30

Hitler, Adolf, 91, 100, 101

Hochschild, Arlie, 70

Holocaust, 100

homophobia, 20, 22, 166, 199

House of Representatives, 67, 116–17, 118

HRCF. *See* Human Rights Campaign Foundation

human rights, 40, 166, 174

Human Rights Campaign Foundation (HRCF), 83

identity, of political parties, 3, 20, 33, 37, 119, 238n61

"I Have a Dream" (King), 193

immigrants, *104*; anti-, 57, 60, 92, *95*; Black people and, 29–30; Bracero Program and, 92–93; deportation of, 91, 97; differential treatment of, 91, 93; discrimination of, 171, 177; economy affected by, 175; equality for, 18, 72, 105–7, 171–78, 186; Ku Klux Klan targeted, 56–58; labor of, 93–94, 172–73; language barriers for, 94, 173; legal status of, 171, 177; One America for Working People version for, 106–7, 171–78; protesting against, *95*; racism and, 91, 94; status and, 89–96, 200; Trump on, 90, 94–95; undocumented, 91, 174, 200; workers, 174, 176–77

Immigration and Nationality Act (1965), 92

inclusion, 30, 46, 53, 139, 163, 177

Independent Party, 50, 53; economic equality and, 81; experimental treatment groups for, 73–76; policy issues and, 122–26; voters, 81, 154, 163, 170, 177–78, 183–84

industrial economy, 29

inequality, 23; class, 53, 142, 152, 170, 178–79; coalitions for reduction of, 1, 2, 7, 24; for LGBTQ people, 82–89, *84*; of power, 7, 70, 151, 152–53; wealth, 1–2, 11, 22, 50, 93–94, 190; workers and, 29–30, 47, 105. *See also* economic inequality; racial inequality; status inequality

intergroup conflict, 6, 34, 63, 192, 193

Ipsos Inc., 2, 19, 229n47

Islamic faith, 98, 99

Israel, 62, 101–2

"It's the economy, stupid," 1

Jackman, Mary, 70, 192
January 6th, debacle, 4–5, *5*, 101
Jay, John, 33
Jews, 57, 62, 90–91, 100–102, 180, 182, 195. *See also* antisemitism
Jim Crow, 6, 59, 64

Kaiser Foundation, 115
Kennedy, John F., 98, 197
King, Martin Luther, Jr., 193
Klansmen, 56–57, *57*, 89
Kloos, Karina, 119
Know Nothing Party, 56
Korpi, Walter, 4
Ku Klux Klan, 56–58, *57*, 65, 66–67, 89–91, 238n49

labor: immigrant, 93–94, 172–73; market for, 8, 29, 31, 93, 94; power, 93; shortages in, 30, 92–93, 96; unions, 3, 41, 60
labor force, 69–70, 93, 162
language barriers, 94, 173
Latina people, 161, 177, 185; for Democratic Party, 159, 166, 175; for Republican Party, 143, 153, 156, 173
Lawrence v. Texas, 85
Lee, Bill, 82
legal status, of immigrants, 171, 177
legislators, for Republican Party, 89, 96, 118
LGBTQ people, 18, 33, 73, *104*, 200; discrimination of, 164–65, 166–67, 170–71, 179, 183; Don't Say Gay campaign, 168; drag

shows, 82, *84*, 88; equality for, 83, 88–89, 105–7, 163–71; homophobia effects on, 20, 22, 166, 199; inequality for, 82–89, *84*; polarization and, 119–20; privilege and, 27, 85–86; racial equality and, 169; status hierarchies and, 165
liberals, 23, 45, 47, 50, 51–52, 112; position of, 125–30, 132, 134; voters, 118
Limbaugh, Rush, 55
Lipset, Seymour Martin, 4, 25, 186
Luker, Kristin, 68
lynchings, 60

Madison, James, 33–34
"make America great," 150, 157
male privilege, 22, 68, 70, 156
Manford, Morty, 82–83
manufacturing economy, 3
marginalization, 167, 178
market, for labor, 8, 29, 31, 93, 94
Marx, Karl, 2–4, 12, 34, 169, 172
Marxist organizations, 172
Massey, Douglas, 30
McAdam, Doug, 119
McCain, John, 113, 114
means and proportions for independent variables by treatment category, *204, 205*
Medicare, 36
models: ordinal logistic regression, 211, *212, 216, 217, 218, 219*; ordinary least squares regression, 207–11, *208, 209, 210, 220*

moderate voters, 118, 168, 196
moral reform movements, 27
Morris, Aldon, 58
movements: antivice, 27, 86–87; civil
    rights, 64, 65, 197, 198; moral
    reform, 27; QAnon, 101; social,
    1, 24, 33, 76–77; Tea Party, 114,
    116, 117; temperance, 26–27, 191;
    women's suffrage, 66–68, 67, 193
Muha, Michael, 192
multidimensional privilege
    hierarchies, 17
Muslims, 62, 96–98, 99, 101–2

nations, wealth of, 3, 40–41, 188
Native American Party, 56
Nazis, 101
neo-Nazis, 101
Newman, Lainey, 41
New York, 67, 82–83
non-Christian groups, 18, 102,
    179–81, 194, 200

Obama, Barack, 89, 94, 112–17, 195
Obamacare, 114–16, 115, 180
Ocasio-Cortez, Alexandria, 53
occupational segregation, 69
Occupy Wall Street, 2
OECD. See Organization for
    Economic Co-operation and
    Development
OLS. See ordinary least squares
OLS Regressions Model, 208, 209,
    210; results of, 207–20, 238n62
One America for Working
    People (web page for fictitious

organization), 16–19, 21, 23, 81,
    229n47; attributes of participants,
    42–45; Christian faith and,
    179–80; conservatives on, 141–42;
    descriptive statistics for study
    participants, 43, 44; economic
    equality and, 133–34, 190;
    economic inequality in, 13–15;
    economics only version of, 72,
    75, 79, 105, 111, 132–34, 141–50,
    153–54, 190–91; endorsement for,
    156–57; experimental research
    designs for, 12–13, 42, 103, 138–39;
    gender and, 71–76, 157–60;
    immigrant equality version of,
    106–7, 171–78; LGBTQ equality
    in, 163–71; mission statement
    for, 13, 22, 38, 42, 45–51, 46, 48,
    49, 51, 52; mobilization for,
    76–80; policy index distribution
    for, 126, 128, 129, 129–36, 131,
    133; policy preferences and,
    111–12; progressive agenda
    for, 50; Qualtrics Experience
    Management surveys for, 140–41;
    race and, 71–76, 149–55; religion
    and, 182–87; status hierarchies
    and, 109–10, 138–39; status
    preservation and, 42; treatment
    groups, 20, 73; unity and, 169;
    willingness to support, 77, 78,
    107, 108, 207, 218, 219. See also
    "Fighting for a Better Future"
Opponents of Obamacare, 115
ordinal logistic regression models,
    211, 212, 216, 217, 218, 219

ordinary least squares (OLS) regression models, 207–11, *208*, *209*, *210*, 220

Organization for Economic Co-operation and Development (OECD), 52–53

outcome variables, 211, 220

PAC. *See* political action committees

Palin, Sarah, 114

pandemic, COVID-19, 36–37, 61–62, 96

Parental Rights in Education Act (2022), 87–88

Park, Robert, 58

Pascoe, C. J., 86

paternalistic domination, 70

Patillo, Mary, 30

Pew Foundation, 55, 62, 79, 83, 100, 116

Pledge of Allegiance, 99–100

polarization, 32, 129; affective, 37–38, 119; driven by status hierarchies, 38; LGBTQ people and, 119–20; of policy preferences, 111–12; in progressive coalitions, 130. *See also* political polarization

policy agendas, 37

policy index distribution, for One America for Working People, *126, 128, 129,* 129–36, *131, 133*

policy issues, 17, 21, 125–27; Democratic Party and, 122–26, *123, 124*; Independent Party and, 122–26, *123, 124*; range of, 19, 112, 122, 129, 134, 191; Republican Party and, 122–26, *123, 124*; voters interpretation of, 119

policy preferences, 23, 89, 121, *123, 124*, 220; consolidation of, 32–36; index of, *126,* 126–29, *128, 129,* 191; for One America for Working People, 111–12; polarization of, 111–12; scale and contributions to scale reliability, *221, 222*

policy proposals, 120, 189

political action committees (PAC), 145

political alliances, 23, 28, 39, 111, 129

political behavior, 9–10, 11–12, 25–26; fairness doctrine and, 54–55; status contestation politics theory and, 38–39; status goals driven by, 137; status motivating, 28, 188–89

political corruption, 13, 66, 186

political elite, 18, 41, 45, 190

political mobilization, 34, 110, 138

political news, 55–56

political parties, 21, *51*; affiliation with, 50, 72, 122, *123, 124,* 206; college graduates and, 45, 79–80; identity of, 3, 20, 33, 37, 119, 238n61; political polarization influenced by, 119–20; representatives of, 34; status threatened by, *208, 209, 210*; unaffiliated respondents of, 103, 147–48, 154, 160, 161, 163; voters shaped by, 118–19. *See also* Democratic Party; Independent Party; Republican Party political polarization, 21, 23, *28*, 32, 36–39, 50; narratives about, 47, 110; policy preferences and, 111–12; political parties influence on, 119–20; status contestation and, 121–34; status goals and, 121–22

political power, 13, 67, 68, 90, 196–97

political process, 2, 6, 32–33, 39, 47

political stability, 4, 128–29

political team, 111–12

politics. *See specific topics*

populism, 2, 3, 46, 114

positions, of privilege, 27, 59–60

poverty, 150–51; OECD on, 52–53; social security and, 36. *See also* economic inequality

power, 10, 75, 89, 91, 160, 195; of Democratic Party, 112–13; of elites, 41; inequality of, 7, 70, 151, 152–53; labor, 93; over workers, 66; political, 13, 67, 68, 90, 196–97; of Republican Party, 118–19; status and, 6, 7; of status positioning, 29; structures of, 45–46; Trump schemes to stay in, 4–5; union, 146; of white people, 58–59

preferential treatment, 26–29, 31, 99, 120, 193

prejudices, 12, 98, 168, 182

preservation, of wealth, 36, 79

privileges, 32, 56, 91, 139, 141, 165; Black people and, 31, 59; of Christian faith, 98, 179; denial of, 29, 31; esteem and, 10, 59, 179; gender, 80; hierarchies of, 171; LGBTQ people and, 27, 85–86; male, 22, 68, 70, 156; multidimensional privilege hierarchies, 17; positions of, 27, 59–60; racial hierarchies and, 31; societal, 10, 60; status, 6, 11–12, 63–64, 108–9, 188–89, 198–99, 201; treatment groups and, 29, 70; white, 22, 31, 60, 64, 71

progressive agenda, 48–51, 53

progressive alliances, *28*–32, 54, 81, 108–9, 111

progressive coalitions, 7, 17, 26, 36, 80, 110, 187; formation of, 139; polarization in, 130; status hierarchies opposed to, 189

progressives, 40, 120, 147

property owners, 2, 34

property-owning white men, 65–66

Protestants, 98, *205*, *210*, *214*; Catholics or, 73; evangelical, 25, 103

protesting, 153; anti-immigrant, *95*; antiracism, *199*; critical race theory, *155*; Obamacare, *115*; Proud Boys, *84*; Tea Party movement, 114

Proud Boys, *5*, 70–71, *84*, 88

Pushaw, Christina, 88

QAnon (conspiracy theories movement), 101

Qualtrics Experience Management, 140–41

race: advantages and, 30, 58–59, 193; critical race theory, 117–18, *155*; *The Declining Significance of Race*, 29; Democratic Party on, 151–54; gender hierarchies and, 110; One America for Working People and, 71–76, 149–55; social class and, 8; status hierarchies and, 17, 56–64, 71–72

racial discrimination, 15, 17–18, 62, 64, 83

racial divide, 48–50, *49*, 53, 79–80

racial equality, 15–17, *16*, 186; discrimination and, 151; economic equality and, 151–52; gender equality and, 18, 73, 75–79, 81; King and, 193; LGBTQ people and, 169; negative responses to, 149–50; for workers, 153

racial hierarchies, 31, 59

racial identities, 8, 9, 17

racial inequality, 8, 29–30, 58–59, 118, 146–47, 215; college graduates and, 150; Democratic Party on, 151–52, 153, 193; Du Bois on, 58–59; economic inequality and, 35, 109, 154; policy agendas and, 37; racism and, 153–54, 169; Republican Party and, 149–50, 156

racism, 8, 58, 151, 167; "color-blind," 9, 150, 192, 193; combatting, 15–17, 20; Democratic Party and, 192; differential treatment and, 63–64; gender hierarchies and, 22, 71–72, 80, 81, 110; immigrants and, 91, 94; impacts of, 199; lynchings and, 60; power and, 9; protesting of anti-, *199*; racial inequality and, 153–54, 169; segregation, 30, 59, 69; sexism and, 20, 31, 86, 103; slavery and, 29–30, 31, 59, 92; structural, 9, 63, 191; systemic, 31

Racism Without Racists (Bonilla-Silva), 192–93

radical feminism, 65

random assignment to treatment categories, 203–7, 229n48

Ray, Victor, 9

Reagan, Ronald, 55, 102

recessions, 1, 113–14

redistribution, of wealth, 114

Rehnquist, William H., 85

religion: advantages of, 182; Christian faith, 18, 65–66, 90–91, 98–109, 143, 162, 179–81, 200; citizenship and, 10, 17, 32, 80, 81; class inequality within, 178–79; discrimination in, 98–99, 180–82, 184; God, 40, 62, 64–65, 96–98, 100; One America for Working People and, 182–87; sexual orientation and biases of, 86; status goals and, 103–9; status hierarchies and, 178–87

religious bigotry, 20, 22, 102

religious equality, 18, 72

replacement theory, 90–91, 195

reproduction, 87

Republican National Convention, *99*, 121

Republican Party: affective polarization and, 38; Christianity linked to, 102; civil rights movement and, 198; conservative policies of, 34–35; economic inequality supported by, 81; "Fighting for a Better Future" and, 141–44; House of Representatives for, 116–17; Latina people for, 143, 153, 156, 173; legislators for, 89, 96, 118; on male privilege, 156; objections to Obamacare by, 114–16; policy issues and, 122–26; power of, 118–19; on race, 149–51; racial inequality and, 149–50, 156
Respect for Marriage Act (2022), 117
Ridgeway, Cecilia, 6, 7, 8
Robertson, Pat, 102
Roe v. Wade, 68–69, 71

Sanders, Bernie, 2, 53
scale reliability, 220, *221*, 223
Scalia, Antonin, 85–86
segregation, 30, 59, 69
Senate, 35, 67, 115, 116, 117
September 11th, 2001, 97, 98
sexism, 18, 156–62; racism and, 20, 31, 86, 103; structural, 191
sexual harassment, *124*, 125, 199, *222*
sexual orientation: discrimination based on, 193; gender identity and, 10, 17, 32, 80, 81, 84–87, 89, 104–5, 170, 200; hate crimes and, 83; policies related to, 110; religious biases regarding, 86;

transgender people, 82, 83, 118, 158, 168, 181. *See also* LGBTQ people
shortages, in labor, 30, 92–93, 96
Skocpol, Theda, 41
slavery, 29–30, 31, 59, 92
Snow, David, 15
social bases of politics, 25, 186
social class, 25, 29–30, *44*, 159; race and, 8; voters influencing, 4
social constructions, 58, 68
social desirability bias, 12
social esteem, 6, 10, 27, 38, 91, 171
socialist communist nation, 164
social movements, 1, 24, 33, 76–77
social scientists, 6, 24, 25, 109
social security, 36, 93
societal esteem, 86
societal privileges, 10, 60
status, of immigrants, 89–96, 200
status advantages, 9, 11, 21–22, 54, 71, 193–94
status boundaries, 54, 88; historical construction of, 56; maintaining, 60, 86–87; racial, 59
status contestation and politics theory, 21–22, 26, *28*, 189; political behavior and, 38–39; political polarization and, 121–34; progressive alliances and, 29–32, 54, 81, 111
status equality, 9, 111, 139, 186, 187; Democratic Party interested in, 76; economic equality and, 23, 130, 132, 133, 137, 189, 201
status goals, 32–33, 53, 136, 163, 185; economic equality paired

with, 130, 132; political behavior driving, 137; political polarization and, 121–22; religion, 103–9

status hierarchies, 20–21, 54, 201; beneficiaries of, 7, 22, 89, 189, 192, 193–94; Black people and, 6; in Christian faith, 98–103, 200; citizenship and, 89–90, 91, 94; differential treatment and, 29, 32, 38–39, 63; esteem and, 39; gender and, 64–71, 89; LGBTQ people and, 165; One America for Working People and, 109–10, 138–39; overturning, 38, 120, 121, 195; polarization driving, 38; politics and, 6–10, 11, *28*; progressive coalitions opposed by, 189; race and, 17, 56–64, 71–72; religion as, 178–87; sexual orientation and, 89; status privileges and, 188–89; wealth and, 186

status inequality, 64, 69, 134, 138, 164, 190; economic inequality and, 132, 165; forms of, 81, 105, 122, 200

status interests, 23, 26, 33, 36, 81, 189

status positioning, 29

status preservation, 27, 33, 64, 196, 234–39; goals, 11, 21, 53, 71–72, 136, 189–90; One America For Working People and, 42

status privileges, 6, 11–12, 195, 198–99; beneficiaries of, 63, 64, 109, 201; progressive alliances and, 108–9; status hierarchies and, 188–89

Stonewall Riots, New York, 82–83

structural racism, 9, 63, 191

structural sexism, 191

Supreme Court, US, 98–99, 117, 145, 158, 179; *Citizens United v. Federal Election Commission*, 35; *Dobbs v. Jackson Women's Health Organization*, 69, 71; *Lawrence v. Texas*, 85; *Roe v. Wade*, 68–69, 71; Trump ban implemented by, 97–98

Sweet, Paige, 70

swing states, 48–49

Symbolic Crusade (Gusfield), 26–27

symbolic victories, in temperance movement, 26, 27

systemic racism, 31

Tea Party movement, 114, 116, 117

temperance movement, 26–27, 191

terrorists, 60, 97, 98, 102, 181

Thomas, Clarence, 85

traditional Catholics, 179–80

transgender people, 82, 83, 118, 158, 168, 181

treatment groups, 238n61; Black people, 31, 153, 199; differential treatment of, 32, 38–39, 63–64, 93, 137, 189; experimental, 73–76, 229n47; favored treatment, 27, 109, 189; gender equality, 75, 79; One America for Working People, 20, 73; preferential, 26–29, 31, 99, 120, 193; privilege and, 29, 70; unequal status treatment and, 86, 165

Trump, Donald, 2–3, 70, 118, 150; anti-Muslim sentiments of, 96–98; ban implemented by Supreme Court, 97–98; Carlson and, 91; DeSantis on, 168; on immigrants, 90, 94–95; January 6th debacle and, 4–5, 101; multidimensional privilege hierarchies and, 17; neo-Nazis and, 101; political rally of, 95; popularity of, 194; power schemes of, 4–5; sexual abuse allegations, 71; supporter of, 99; voters reelecting, 5, 17

Trumpism, 17, 146

unaffiliated respondents, 103, 147–48, 154, 160, 161, 163

undocumented immigrants, 91, 174, 200

unequal status treatment, 86, 165

Uniform Crime Report, FBI, 83

unions, 30, 93; American Civil Liberties Union, 97; labor, 3, 41, 60; power of, 146

United States: Constitution of, 33–34, 55, 59, 66, 83; House of Representatives in, 67, 116, 118. See also Supreme Court; specific topics

unity, 13, 112, 113; calling for, 143, 161, 166, 169, 172; inclusion and, 177; in One American for Working People, 169; of voters, 120–21; worker, 2, 38, 40–41, 92–93, 172

variation, 9, 90, 127–28, 135, 206

violence: discrimination and, 103, 105, 109, 137, 164–65, 179, 180, 181; gender equality and, 18; hatred and, 99, 102, 145, 167–68, 177, 195; of Proud Boys, 70–71, 84, 88; racial discrimination and, 15, 17–18, 62, 64, 83

voters: Black people, 35, 64; Brown people, 35; Catholic, 66; conservative, 34–35; cues for, 37, 111–12; economy downturn and, 1; Independent Party, 81, 154, 163, 170, 177–78, 183–84; liberal, 118; moderate, 118, 168, 196; policy issues interpreted by, 119; political party shaping, 118–19; political team of, 111–12; social class influencing, 4; Trump reelected by, 5, 17; unity of, 120–21; wealthy, 135; women's suffrage movement influencing, 66–68

Voting Rights Act (1965), 64

Warren, Elizabeth, 53

wars: Civil War, 29, 31; between Israel and Hamas, 62, 101–2; World War II, 30, 61, 61, 92–93

wealth, 157, 172, 175; campaign contributions from, 13, 35, 145, 223; disparities in, 143, 178; favored treatment due to, 189; of Federal Reserve Bank, 3;

inequality of, 1–2, 11, 22, 50, 93–94, 190; of nations, 3, 40–41, 188; political corruption and, 13; political process and role of, 47; preservation of, 36, 79; redistribution of, 114; slavery and, 31; status hierarchies and, 186; voters that are, 135

Weber, Max, 6, 27

welfare, 94, 151, 173

West, Kanye, 101

"What Do We Do?," 46

white people, 30, 31, 42, 48–49, 62–63, 103; demographic transitions and, 6–7; manufacturing economy and, 3; power of, 58–59

white privilege, 22, 31, 60, 64, 71

white supremacy, 56–57, 59, 62, 64, 90–91, 100–101

willingness, 24, 26, 140, 194; to support "Fighting for a Better Future," 19; to support One America for Working People, 77, 78, 107, 108, 207, 218, 219

Wilson, William Julius, 29–30

wokeness, 121, 142, 173

women's suffrage movement, 66–68, 67, 193

workers, 70, 94, 100, 148; benefits for, 12, 144; division among, 3, 15–17, 18, 142–43, 145, 169; earnings gap of, 13; economic and racial equality for, 153; immigrant, 174, 176–77; inclusion of black people, 30; inequality and, 29–30, 47, 105; plight of, 146; power over, 66; status interests of, 36; unity among, 2, 38, 40–41, 92–93, 172, 232–34

World Trade Center, 97, 98

World War II, 30, 61, 61, 92–93

Yazdiha, Hajar, 193

Zhu, Ling, 69

GPSR Authorized Representative: Easy Access System Europe, Mustamäe tee 50, 10621 Tallinn, Estonia, gpsr.requests@easproject.com